PUBLIC POLICY AND THE RURAL POOR IN INDIA

CESS Research Studies

1. Public Policy and the Rural Poor in India
2. Public Policies for Rural Development in Andhra Pradesh : A Review of Research Trends
3. Distance in Levels of Living : Temporal and Spatial

CESS RESEARCH STUDIES 1

PUBLIC POLICY AND THE RURAL POOR IN INDIA

A Study of SFDA in Andhra Pradesh

G. RAM REDDY
G. HARAGOPAL

Foreword by
A. M. KHUSRO

Centre for Economic and Social Studies, Hyderabad
and
CONCEPT PUBLISHING COMPANY, NEW DELHI

First Published 1985

Published by
Naurang Rai
Concept Publishing Company
H-13, Bali Nagar
NEW DELHI-110015 (India)

Printed in India by
Chauhan Composing Agency
at Kiran Mudran Kendra, Mayapuri
NEW DELHI 110064

Dedicated

to

Mrs. G. PRAMILA
and
Mrs. G. VANAMALA

Foreword

SINCE the early 50s the pace and direction of social and economic change in India has been consciously influenced by an elaborate process of planning. In the course of years, the context of change itself has become extensive and more dynamic. From time to time new assumptions and concepts have been added to the planners' perception of issues and new policies and instruments for change have been devised. It is nobody's case that the outcome of planned development efforts in the country has been entirely satisfactory. Taking a long run view of the process it is quite apparent that while some problems have been solved, others still loom large.

Planned development is a long drawn out process. In a vast and complex democratic set-up it is also a difficult process because of such factors as incomplete initial information, institutional inertia, resource constraint, and daunting scale of problems and others. But these cannot be either arguments for minimum interventions or alibis for their unsatisfactory results. Indeed, as should be obvious, conscious and far-reaching policy interventions become necessary precisely because of the existence of these disabilities and problems. Therefore, what is required is not less of policy but a better appreciation of the underlying structures and processes to improve articulation of the problems and their solutions.

While planners know more now than before about the economy and society both at the aggregate and local levels, it seems, nevertheless, that more needs to be known about the new dimensions which are being discovered from time to time. The questions that are now being asked in development planning are different both in depth and range from those that appeared to be sufficient for plan formulation a decade ago. This shows the extent to which our understanding of the processes and issues involved in initiating and managing social and economic change has improved. And in creating a better understanding the social sciences and other development-related disciplines have made invaluable contributions. This useful role of social science research is now ungrudgingly recognised on all hands.

The Centre for Economic and Social Studies has been established with the objective of undertaking mutually supportive and inter-related research, training, and documentation activities in the area of economic and social development. The broad dimensions of the Centre's research programme are defined by the basic consideration that a critical examination of structural and behavioural aspects is continuously required to improve the planning and implementation process. The Centre proposes to undertake a series of studies on various facets of development in Andhra Pradesh. This is the report of the Centre's first research project in the area of public policy. It focuses on the small-farmers' development programme which is one of the first beneficiary-oriented programmes of its kind to be implemented in the country.

In this study a critical evaluation of the programme has been attempted, including its assumptions, concepts and the modalities of its implementation. Issues such as adequacy of the policy framework, suitability of administrative structures for implementation of the programme, viability of the schemes, and institutional and private responses have been examined to understand the reasons for the feeble impact of the policy. Thus, the approach of the study is more comprehensive than is usual for evaluation studies.

In the findings of this study the inadequacies of bureaucracy at the grass-root level and lack of effective linkages with higher levels in the administrative hierarchy feature prominently as important constraints to proper implementation of the programme; the institution of the middleman comes out as a rampant phenomenon of dubious utility; and pronounced individualistic bias which characterises the behaviour of the target group is seen as a formidable impediment to promoting participative culture. Also, the narrow range of schemes by means of which the production base of the target group families is sought to be improved turns out to be a serious limitation of the programme. As the study shows, some of the schemes have been counterproductive because of their unsuitability for the target group families.

The study does indeed bring out new aspects which will be found useful in formulating beneficiary-oriented policies and programmes in the future.

August 1984

A. M. KHUSRO
Chairman
Centre for Economic
& Social Studies

Acknowledgements

In the preparation of this report we have taken the help and assistance of several institutions and individuals. The Government of Andhra Pradesh in particular the Departments of Finance and Planning, Forest and Rural Development and Bureau of Economics and Statistics extended their co-operation. The Osmania and Kakatiya Universities to which we belong gave us permission to take up this work. We availed of the excellent library facilities that exist at the National Institute of Rural Development and Administrative Staff College of India. The staff of the Computer Centre of Osmania University helped us in processing the data collected by us. We are beholden to all these institutions.

We have received continuous encouragement and academic support from Dr. Radhakrishna of the Department of Economics, University of Hyderabad. Sri B.P.R. Vithal, who was Chairman of the Centre for Economic and Social Studies when this study was taken up, was a source of great inspiration to us. Prof. A.M. Khusro, who is now the Chairman, evinced keen interest in the Study. We have benefitted a great deal from our discussions with Sri T. L. Shanker, Sri K.M. Ahmed, Dr. Y. Venugopal Reddy, Sri U. B. Raghavendra Rao of the Government of Andhra Pradesh. Dr. Waheeduddin Khan, Director of the Centre, guided us throughout the period of this study. We express our deep sense of gratitude to all of them.

Our thanks are due to our colleagues Messrs R. Nageswara Rao, A. Samrat Ashok Kumar and J. Kumara Swamy, who have done the field work in the two districts. Doing field work in our villages is the most difficult, hazardous and at times a thankless task. But they have done the work with a deep sense of commitment and involvement. The credit for the present work, in a large measure should go to these young, enthusiastic and highly motivated members of our research team.

We also wish to thank the faculty and the staff of the Centre for Economic and Social Studies. Prof. Afzal Mohammed Sri P.T. Venugopal, Sri S.N. Mathur, Mrs. Neela Jagannathan, Mrs. Lucy Vaz, helped us in various ways. We also received support from Messrs P. Praveen Kumar, P. Padmanabha Rao, K.S. Prasad and Miss Ruquia Begum.

A study of this type which depends heavily on the data collected from the field cannot be successfully conducted without the cooperation of officials and non-officials at the district, block and village levels. Innumerable people generously gave us their time and discussed with us problems connected with rural development. It is not possible for us to mention all the names but a few whose support was crucial to our work are being mentioned here. They are : Sri A.K. Goel, District Collector, East Godavari, Ms. Gayatri Ramachandram District Collector, Medak, Sri Balagurunathan, Project Director, D.R.D.A., Medak, Sri K. Krishna Murthy, P.A. to the Collector, East Godavari. We are grateful to all these officials and several others at the district and block level who shared their experiences with us.

We place on record our appreciation of the help given by Dr. V. Sivalinga Prasad, Reader in Public Administration, Andhra Pradesh Open University, Sri P. Satyanarayana, Deputy Director, ICSSR Southern Regional Centre, Hyderabad. Dr. Ch. Balaramulu, Shri G. Sudarshan, Lecturers and K. Venkataiah, P. Sambaiah, Research Scholars, Department of Public Administration, Kakatiya University, at various stages of this work. Sri D. Vijaya Kumar, Sri K. Laxman and Sri Shaik Khader Basha did the typing work of the earlier drafts. We thank them specially for doing the work efficiently and cheerfully. Sri S.K.N. Sastry, the Stenographer, deserves a special mention for his devotion to work in typing the report cheerfully and with a sense of involvement.

We gratefully acknowledge the considerateness shown by the members of our families in not making such demands on our time as would have come in the way of completing this work in time.

G. Ram Reddy
and
G. Haragopal

Contents

List of Tables

1

Introduction

PUBLIC policy has come to assume vital importance in modern times. The state, through a number of public policies, seeks to intervene positively in the developmental process by stimulating production and ensuring distributive justice. The entire thrust appears to be on improving the quality of life of all the citizens. The policies are broadly of two types: one, the policies which might be called comprehensive and lead to structural transformation; and two, incremental policies which are of a reformative type. Policies like land reforms, ceilings on property and wealth belong to the former category as they touch the ownership of the means of production, and policies like reservations, public distribution system, subsidised anti poverty schemes fall in the latter category. The incremental policies are intended to provide some relief to the poorer sections without affecting the basic socio-economic structure of the society. The modern state pursues both types of policies and covers a wide range of socio-economic processes touching the life of the community at various points. The state invests huge resources in these developmental policies and attempts to implement them through its complex organisational network. The administrative structures intended to formulate and implement the public policies are so pervasive and penetrating that the modern state has come to be described as the 'administrative state'. It is these policy processes and structures that deserve utmost attention.

In the recent past the major stated objective of public policies, particularly in the developing countries, has been removal of poverty. The state is expected to protect the disadvantaged groups. In fact the qualitative difference between a police state and a welfare state lies in its methods and approach to the people: while the former believes in managing the society through its coercive arm, the latter considers improvement in the living conditions of the poor masses as a justification and source of legitimation for its existence. "The state's responsibility in the production and distribution process may lead one to describe the system as characterised by a socialistic pattern".[1] "In the dynamic process of change that will thus develop the task of the state, which will itself be a rapidly changing institution, will be to plan the use of all its resources in the name of community, to secure the fullest rights to workers in every type of economic organisation, and above all, to seek to create in our own time a society, free from poverty and injustice, in which the supreme principle of social action and the test of all public policies will be the interest and welfare of the masses".[2]

It is aptly stated that "policy might be viewed as a means of creating a new future, and the absence of policy is an acceptance of the status quo".[3] It is a conscious intervention to alter the existing conditions in the society. Here the economic assumption is that "the volume of effective demand and investment and the utilisation of resources should no longer be the resultant of a parallelogram of economic forces with a self controlling and self propelling autonomous machinery but should be subjected more and more to the interplay of conscious human policy within the national economy".[4]

The general problem of the abolition of poverty has increasingly merged with, and has often become the foundation of the social and political policy of government.[5] "It also presupposes an ability to overcome the elements of moral aggression against the poor who seems to be clinging to an outmoded way of life. This aggression may have one of its sources in the fact that the existence of these groups challenges the very ideological foundation on which the welfare state is built".[6] This assumes importance in view of the appalling poverty which, instead of declining, has been spreading. Most of the studies conducted in Africa, Asia and Latin America highlighted the ubiquitous and ever deepening poverty.[7] India being one of the largest countries, increase in its poverty ridden millions has not only explosive national implications but far reaching global consequences. Therefore, poverty in India calls for serious and concerted action.

A detailed discussion on the magnitude of poverty in India would suggest the sensitive area to be covered by public policy. The study by Dandekar and Rath in the early seventies estimated that in 1960-61 about one third of the rural people and half of the urban population lived on a diet inadequate even in respect of calories.[8] On the basis of trends emerging they forecast that by 1980-81 the poverty will have grown in absolute size.[9] Colin Clark indicated that "approximately one fourth of India's population are living in hunger, even on the minimum estimates of the amount of physical work done".[10] In another study, Bardhan pointed out that Rs. 250 per capita, per annum the percentage of poor constituted 46 per cent in 1960-61, 56.2 per cent in 1964-65 and 63.1 per cent in 1967-68.[11]

Several studies indicate that poverty in India has been increasing and concentrated in the rural area. Raj Krishna pointed out that "landless labourers and farmers with less than five acres of dry land constitute the hard core of the rural poverty and population".[12] Colin Clark observed that "while considerable poverty can be seen in the cities, the greatest amount of real poverty is probably in the rural areas".[13] He added that "a decline in the real rural wage is noticed".[14] Ranjit Sau observed that "minimum wage has no meaning unless at the same time somebody gurantees employment at the prescribed minimum wage".[15] For "the Agriculture Minimum Wages Act has been on the statute book for over 20 years and every one acquainted with its operation knows that it has not been enforced".[16] Compared to 1960-61, the nutritional deficiency in the rural areas got widened considerably by 1967-68. Bardhan estimated the percentage of rural poor as 30 per cent in 1960-61, 46 per cent in 1964-65 and 54.0 per cent in 1967-68.[17] According to the estimation of Ojha "as compared to only 52 per cent of the rural population in 1960-61, 70 per cent of the population was found to be below the poverty line".[18] Michael Lypton maintained that Indians below a fixed poverty line almost certainly rose between 1950 and 1970.[19] Thus these studies confirm the gravity and deteriorating situation in India.

After the advent of independence poverty was sought to be removed through public policy. There has been hardly any rural development policy which did not lay emphasis on rural poverty. This approach broadly agreed with the premise that "a process of economic development without a positive and effective policy to ensure an equitable distribution of the gains of development, inevitably benefit the richer classes much more than it does the poor classes".[20] Although quite a few policies were formulated and implemented, that they did not have much impact on rural poverty can hardly be missed. T. N. Srinivasan observed that "although a large number of policies have been adopted for reduction of poverty and inequality, none of these have succeeded in achieving their objective".[21] He further added that "regardless of intentions the economic policies adopted have by and large benefited the upper income groups".[22] Dantwala also remarked "there is no denying that the policy package for reduction of poverty and inequality has not made any significant impact on the problem".[23]

The evolution of public policy for rural development in India passed through different phases. During the fifties and sixties the emphasis was on Community Development, Panchayati Raj, Intensive Area Development, Development of Backward Regions, Modernisation of Agriculture and so on. In the late sixties, it was realised that any indirect policy measuce would not be of much help to the rural poor. It is in the wake of this approach that the policy of Small Farmers Development Agency (SFDA) and Marginal Farmers and Agricultural Labour Development Agency (MFALDA) was adopted.

The Small Farmers Development Agency is expected to cover the three segments of the rural poor, namely, the small farmers, marginal farmers and agricultural labourers. This was largely due to the fact that rural poverty revolved around these categories. Milton Esman observed that "as many as 53 per cent of the landless and near-landless in India are poor".[24] That poverty is concentrated in these segments of the rural poor is also evident from Minhas' observation that "out of 164 million people below the poverty line, 60 million people belong to rural labour households, the remaining 103 to 104 million belong to land operating households who possess small holdings".[25] According to the Agricultural Census of 1970-71, nearly 70 per cent rural households have operational holdings of five acres or less and 51 per cent have 2-5 acres of land or less. The number of such holdings reported by the Census was 70.49 million, this included 49 million small farmers, of which 36 million were marginal farmers and the rest agricultural labourers.[26] As for landless workers their number was estimated in the draft plan 1978-83 as 50.4 millions.[27] Apart from all other considerations, the sheer number presents a formidable problem for rural development policy and planning.

A World Bank staff working paper pointed out that the absolute number of the rural poor has increased in South Asia in the past two decades.[28] They also held that the small and marginal farmers constitute a large chunk of the category. However, they doubted the efficacy of the criteria of five acres and less to categorise the small farmers. For they felt that "a correct transformation should take account of the quality of land, the cropping pattern, irrigation, conditions of tenure and other characteristics".[29] Yet they conceded that a cut-off of five acres of operated area (two hectares) serves as an acceptable proxy. Among the characteristics peculiar to small farmers, according to the paper are: (i) a high proportion of land devoted to the food crops, (ii) a low proportion of output marketed, (iii) a more diverse crop portfolio, (iv) greater aversion to risk, (v) more abundant family labour than other larger farms.[30] The World Bank maintained that "it is a misconception to view small farmers as inefficient, tradition bound, unresponsive to economic opportunities or unwilling to adopt new ideas and technology or to view the small farm sector as unproductive and stagnant".[31] Therefore, they suggested that "building up the necessary infrastructure, economic viability and administrative capacity to instal and exploit complex surface command area and ground water irrigation system and then assure small farmers access to the infrastructure".[32] It is pointed out that this is one of the major challenges Asian agriculture has to tackle. Thus improving the small farm and those dependent on it has come to be one of the major concerns of public policy. As a part of this process there was a need to design the agencies and schemes to help the target groups to cross the poverty line. The SFDA and MFAL originated as a part of this strategy.

In India the SFDA and MFAL agencies were introduced on the recommendations of the Rural Credit Review Committee in 1969 with a view to improving the economic conditions of small and marginal farmers and agricultural labourers. In the case of small and marginal farmers this was sought to be done by developing the capacity of their land through additional capital. For most of them hardly have any surplus income to spare for investment to improve their production.[33] The high incidence of indebtedness among this group confirms this assumption.[34] In the case of agricultural labourers who are paid low wages and have no other avenues of income, the need for assistance is all the greater. Added to it, it is observed, that there is decline in employment for all categories of earners from agricultural labour households.[35] Therefore, SFDA and MFAL agencies were expected to offer schemes which can generate additional income and employment. These agencies were expected to bring the benefits of modern technology to the small and marginal farmers and agricultural labourers and raise their standards of living by improved agriculture, subsidiary occupations and supplementary employment.[36]

These agencies were started in 1969-70 on a pilot basis in 87 project areas throughout the country. These 87 projects include 46 SFDA projects and 41 MFAL projects. However, it did take some time to get the whole scheme implemented. Thus 1971-72 was the first full year of working for most of the projects. "The projects were to continue till 1975-76 to complete five years duration".[37] In the year 1973 the National Commission on Agriculture recommended that "the artificial distinction between SFDA programmes and MFAL programme be given up" and asked for "considerable expansion of these programmes".[38] Accordingly, during the first year of the Fifth Five Year Plan, these programmes were brought under a single agency, namely, SFDA. And the total number of the projects was raised from 87 to 168 which included eight projects of Command Area Development "Authority".[39]

Of late SFDA is merged with the Integrated Rural Development Programme. The organisation of SFDA has been expanded and its nomenclature is changed to District Rural Development Agency.[40] This programme is a synthesis of the strategies tested and found effective from experience gained after implementing special programmes like SFDA, DPAP, CAD Agencies, and so on. The IRD programmes, in addition to medium farmers, aim at enabling the rural poor comprising the target groups of small and marginal farmers, agricultural and non-agricultural labourers, rural artisans and craftsmen, scheduled castes and scheduled tribes in rural areas to cross the poverty line.[41] Thus SFDA transformed itself into a more vital and comprehensive agency in importance and scope. Therefore, its success or failure has far reaching implications to the public policies aimed at the elimination of poverty. This calls for a frank evaluation of their performance so as to gain insights which could be of some help in understanding the phenomenon and formulating the strategy in future.

In the light of the experience gained, doubts are expressed about the capacity of the present state to perform this role. "The question is whether the welfare state can permit itself to assume a posture which is beset with the ambiguities is no easy matter. It costs money and it requires real inventiveness in community development under difficult natural conditions. The fear has been that the state may not be able to help the poor in a normal developmental process in a given socio-economic set-up. It is further pointed out that although the government in recent years devoted a growing share of the nation's resources to policies and programmes for meeting societal needs: dissatisfaction with these programmes has never been more widespread: complaints about inefficiency, ineffectiveness and waste are increasing".[42] It is these factors that call for continuous evaluation of public policy.

Viewed from the scientific perspective, "policy evaluation research is the objective, systematic, empirical examination of the effects, on-going policies and public programmes have on their targets in terms of the goals they are meant to achieve".[43] In this sense "policy evaluation research is goal oriented research focusing on effectiveness rather than on the decision-making processes that lead to the adoption of policies".[44] From the broader perspective policy impact evaluations, Laswell pointed out, "characterize the aggregate flow of decisions, according to policy objectives of the body politic, and identify those who are causally or formally responsible for success or failure".[45] It is observed that analysis of even policy failures is quite beneficial as "more could be gained from it, going beyond the immediate measures through which governments seek relief, institutions of research and learned scholars associated with them could examine causes and manifestations with uncompromising objectivity, tear apart the myths and ignorance which often surround public policy, and seek more fundamental and long-range action for the future".[46]

II

In 1974-75 the Planning Commission conducted a study on the working of SFDAs. They pointed out that the proportion of target population identified was quite low. In nearly 17 per cent of small farmers development agencies, not more than 25 per cent of the target population had been identified and in another 44 per cent of them, the coverage ranged between 26-50 per cent. The percentage of SFDAs where more than 50 per cent, of the target population had been identified was 39. In the case of marginal farmers 50 per cent of the agencies identified between 26 and 50 per cent of the members of the target group, and the rest covered less than 25 per cent of the target group. In so far as agricultural labourers are concerned only about 17 per cent of the agencies had identified more than 25 per cent and the rest less than 25 per cent. The position in regard to identification of agricultural labourers by MFAL was even more unsatisfactory. Of the 13 MFAL projects covered, three had not laid down any criteria for identification of agricultural labourers. In 19 per cent projects not more than 15 per cent of the total agricultural labourers were identified and in another 25 per cent only 11-15 per cent of the agricultural labourers had been identified.[47]

A pathetic aspect which emerges from the study is an almost total neglect of agricultural labourers in the field of credit requirements. Out of total loans of nearly Rs. 80.10 crores advanced during 1973-74 by various credit institutions, in all the project areas covered, the share of agricultural labourers was an insignificant sum of Rs. 79.5 lakhs, that is about 1 per cent.[48] The report also pointed out inadequacy of extension staff and procedural defects which hampered the development schemes. This they pointed out affected even the minor irrigation schemes, selection of beneficiaries and proper utilisation of loans.

Although the agencies were given detailed guidelines for implementing the programmes, the manner in which the programme was executed shows that most of the agencies had failed to grasp the import of the guidelines. Generally, they neither exercised proper care in selection of beneficiary nor in ensuring the facilities which were crucial for the successful working of the programme. For instance, certain schemes were launched ignoring marketing facilities, without which the schemes had no chances of success.

Selection of inexperienced beneficiaries or unsuitable animals for distribution in the case of animal husbandry programme coupled with lack of extension services resulted in animal becoming a liability rather than an asset. The animal husbandry programme, according to the report, did not succeed in generating substantial additional net income to beneficiaries in any of the project areas.[49]

This study holds that the scheme has not been a success even as regards poultry. The main factors responsible for the failure were: improper selection of beneficiaries, lack of experience or training in upkeep of birds among beneficiaries, absence of extension service and inadequate or no arrangement for health cover for birds nor for marketing of the produce. The scheme got into crisis as the feed grew scarce and costly. In the absence of any arrangement for supply of feed at reasonable prices and necessary infrastructure, premature abandonment of the scheme becomes inevitable. As a result of these gaps many participants suffered in the schemes heavily on account of high mortality rate among the birds.

The survey conducted by the Reserve Bank of India of the small farmers development agencies in 1972-73,[50] attempts to present a balance sheet of performance of the agency.

In respect of the land based programmes, the report points out that considerable success was achieved under conditions where: (1) a compact irrigable area was available, (2) the villages were electrified, (3) the procedural delay in sanctioning loans was reduced, and (4) full co-operation existed between agencies like agro-industries corporation, state electricity board, ground water directorate and so on.

The factors that hampered the progress were: (1) inability of tenant farmers to get investment credit; (2) stipulation imposed by land development banks regarding minimum benefiting area as one compact block; (3) fragmentation of holdings as a corollary of item two; (4) procedural delays in sanctioning loans by land development banks; (5) out-of-date land records; (6) indifference of extension officials; (7) unfair practices of dealers in agricultural machinery; (8) insistence of minimum distance between two wells; (9) lack of guidance from ground water directorate; (10) limited availability of cement for agricultural purposes and (11) the frequent incidence of failure of wells.[51] The report further observed that programme-wise minor irrigation schemes occupied the foremost place in all the selected districts and finance provided for these schemes varied from 68 per cent to 100 per cent of the total credit.[52]

About the milch cattle programmes the common difficulties pointed out by the field study were (1) the high cost of cattle feed (2) inadequate attention paid to the cultivation of green fodder (3) lack of cattle breeding arrangement, (4) inadequacy of veterinary facilities, (5) lack of co-ordination with the programmes of the animal husbandry departments of the state governments, and (6) non-participation of the specialised institutions like Dairy Development Corporation, NCDC and Operation Flood in formulating plans and executing them. It further added that in the implementation of dairy schemes it appears imperative to adopt a 'package approach' providing for the simultaneous introduction of: (1) breeding facilities for high-yielding stock. (2) provision for feeds and concentrates. (3) establishment of market links with important consuming centres and (4) institution of cattle mortality funds.[53]

About the poultry schemes in most of the districts the report points out that the poultry enterprise was caught up in a situation of rising input cost not adequately compensated by the rise in output price which belied the expectations of the agencies' optimistic model plans. Most of these problems stemmed from the lack of well organised poultry co-operatives for making bulk purchases, stocking medicines, arranging for sale etc. The veterinary department officials also could have rendered effective assistance to groups of polutry farmers through co-operatives instead of dealing with them on individual basis. The financing agencies too would have come forward more willingly to concentrate poultry credit in a cluster of villages rather than disburse it over wide areas.[54]

With regard to the sheep farming and goat rearing programmes the report observes that these programmes were successful in areas with adequate grazing facilities and inhabitation of particular communities who followed sheep breeding as a traditional occupation. A selective approach, therefore, was essential. Adequate arrangement for marketing and supervision over utilisation of credit are two other essential prerequisites for the success of this scheme.[55]

About the coverage of target groups the report observed that "on the whole identification of small farmers in most of the districts was done on faulty basis. With the result the marginal farmers on the one side and viable farmers on the other came to be included among them. A good proportion of identified farmers derived their bulk of income from non-farm sources". It added that "implementation of the subsidy schemes was hampered by lack of coordination among the concerned state government departments and inadequate marketing facilities".[56]

The role of the credit agencies was not as bold and favourable to small farmers as it could have been. This was largely due to the hesitant attitude on the part of the commercial banks and in the case of co-operatives the socio-economic composition of small farmers turned into a constraint.

In addition to these two major surveys, an attempt is made to review the specific studies conducted on the impact of SFDA in different states to gain a comparative perspective of the working of the agency in the national context. These studies cover the states of Assam,[57] Bihar,[58] Haryana,[59] Himachal Pradesh,[60] Karnataka,[61] Kerala,[62] Madhya Pradesh,[63] Maharashtra,[64] Rajasthan,[65] and Uttar Pradesh.[66]

For purposes of convenience the findings of these studies are broadly categorised into coverage of target groups, viability of the schemes and administrative problems.

About the coverage of the target groups, the studies from Bihar, Kerala, Karnataka, Rajasthan, Madhya Pradesh and Uttar Pradesh point out that it was very low and fell short of the targets awfully. The cases of wrong identification of the beneficiaries have been pointed out. Most of these studies maintain that the benefits did not percolate to the target groups. Ineffectiveness of the agency is traced to lack of awareness about the agency on the part of target groups, reluctance of the target groups to take government loans, misutilisation of the loan amount and cornering of the benefits by richer sections.

With regard to the viability and impact of the schemes the studies point out the uneconomic nature of the holding, ignoring micro problems involved in the schemes, inadequacy of the schemes and lack of their geo-climatic suitability. Further, lack of infrastructure particularly the technological support and marketing linkages are widely reported. All these factors collectively affected the schemes adversely.

The third aspect which received wide attention of these studies has been the administrative structure and its behavioural style. Almost all the studies reported that the bureaucracy lacked commitment to the programme. This is considered to be the reason for indifference, inertia and corruption in bureaucracy. The second major problem has been the problem of coordination. Several issues relating to coordination are highlighted by these studies. For instance, the agency has no control over the field machinery nor do they have staff of their own. Inadequay of staff found a mention in almost all the reports. The third finding of these reports relates to the cumbersome and time consuming procedures. Lastly, the studies drew the attention to non-availability of reliable statistics about the land and economic conditions of the members of the target group. They also pointed out widespread fabrication of the information and distortions in the evaluation and implementation.

The studies from Karnataka, Haryana and Himachal Pradesh reported success of certain schemes. Karnataka study reveals that households under sheep rearing category derived the benefit. The studies from Haryana report that the agency has left a favourable impact on the employment conditions of the beneficiaries since a rise both in the man days of work and wages is noticed. This study reported proper utilisation of the loan and the subsidy. The dairy development programme, it is pointed out, attained marked progress crossing the set targets more than 2½ times.

The reports offered the following suggestions for improving the performance of the agency. Firstly, giving more powers to the people ; secondly, greater decentralisation of decision-making to the district headquarters ; thirdly, organising the target groups ; fourthly, restricting the farm size for efficient land use ; fifthly, co-operative management of technology ; and lastly, improving the administration of the agency emphasising integrated approach, strict supervision and follow-up action. It was also thought that separate department comprising dedicated persons, simplification of the procedures and greater power to project officer to draft the necessary staff would also improve the situation.

While almost all the reports highlighted the unimpressive performance of the agency, a study from Himachal Pradesh came out with a success story. The case is presented in detail.

The study points out that there has been considerable integration of the process. For instance, in the case of dairy programmes, marketing facilities were taken care of. Wherever the milk collection facilities were not available the small and marginal farmers were supplied with the improved Marino sheep units. Availability of pastures facilitated spread of this programme. Similarly, breeding of piggery units was widely accepted by the scheduled caste beneficiaries. The performance of the piggery units encouraged other castes to take up piggery. The poultry programme was tried and abandoned owing to ; (a) non-availability of balanced feed ; (b) lack of marketing arrangement ; (c) high mortality risks and (d) non-availability of adequate health facility.

The success of the agency was traced to its capacity to avoid unnecessary expenditure on the one hand and ability to achieve complete coordination, cohesion, liaison with the concerned departments on the other. All this was possible because of the continuity of the same project officer throughout the six year period. It was also noticed that the concerned departments and institutions perceived the agency's work an their own.[67]

The study pointed out the following factors that accounted for the success of the SFDA of Sirmur district of Himachal Pradesh. One, the project officer who remained in-charge of the project for six years provided continuous leadership. Two, the agency's work covered all the facets of the farmers' economic life with which all government departments and institutions in the field were connected. As such the agency provided a sense of collective leadership among the field officers of the agriculture, animal husbandry and other development departments. Three, the project officer was given the choice in selecting the schemes. Four, frequent discussions, consultations, meetings, seminars and camps were held involving both higher level officials and the functionaries at lower level. This served the purpose of training and education. Five, the agency attached utmost importance for marketing facilities. It co-operated with the various state departments to establish regulated markets. Marketing of cereals and cash crops like fruits, vegetables, ginger and so on, were taken care of. And market facilities for the milk produce of the small and marginal farmers were organised on institutional basis.[68]

III

In Andhra Pradesh also studies on the working of the Small Farmers Development Agency have been conducted in different districts. These studies mainly cover the districts of Adilabad,[69] Hyderabad,[70] Medak,[71] Nalgonda,[72] (case study of a Telangana District)[73], East Godavari,[74] Srikakulam,[75] Visakhapatnam,[76] and a departmental study was undertaken covering Adilabad, Krishna and Srikakulam.[77] The findings of these studies are grouped under three broad categories viz., target group coverage, viability of the schemes and administrative difficulties.

About the target group coverage these studies made the following observations. Firstly, there has been low coverage of the target groups. Secondly, there is low level of awareness of the programmes among the target groups. Thirdly, the identification of beneficiaries has not only been unsatisfactory but defective. Fourthly, the category of agricultural labourers got completely neglected. Lastly, the richer sections cornered off the benefits.

The second aspect deals with the viability of the schemes. Firstly, one study points out that from the target groups covered, economic position of 43% improved, 24% deteriorated and no improvement was registered in the rest of the cases. Secondly, the funds are underutilised. Thirdly, large scale diversion of the loans for unproductive purposes is reported. Fourthly, the schemes are non-viable in nature. Lastly, the inadequacy of infrastructure for the effective implementation of the schemes is also considered as a major administrative bottle-neck.

With regard to the administrative problems a number of bottlenecks have been highlighted. Firstly, the number of offices involved are too many, this includes the offices such as revenue, panchayat samiti, sub-registrar, state ground water directorate, department of agriculture, animal husbandry, electricity and banks and so on. Secondly, the coordination among these departments has been missing. Thirdly, the beneficiaries are made to go to a number of offices. Fourthly, the agency has not received co-operation from the banks which are found to be highly commercial in outlook. Fifthly, the agency lacks adequate staff. Sixthly, delays in processing of applications, corruption and cumbersome procedures are widely reported. Seventhly, the land records are not scientific and up-to-date owing to absence of mutation and unregistered sales. The reluctance of revenue officials to make the records available complicates the issue further. Lastly, the villagers are helplessly dependent on local leaders and others who act as brokers or *pyraveekars* between the target groups and official institutions.

Thus several studies on the impact of SFDA in the districts of both the Telangana and Andhra Regions reveal that there is much to be accomplished. For the agencies could not make the impact that was expected of them. They encountered a number of operational difficulties. However, the need to probe deep into the causes for such a gap between promise and performance is too obvious to need any emphasis.

IV

Most of the studies that are conducted on the working of the SFDA, as is evident from the above analysis, focused their attention on the impact of the agency on the target group and the problems they faced in actual implementation causing a gap between promise and performance. These studies mainly focused their attention on economic issues linked with the policy framework, but organisation linkages and participative dimension remained largely unexamined. Therefore, the present duty proposes to examine:

(a) The adequacy and the suitability of the existing

administrative structures.

(b) The viability of the schemes and their impact on the target groups.

(c) The role of the middle-man[78] in the schemes, and

(d) The participation of the target groups.

Thus the study attempts to cover not only the organisational structure of SFDA but the entire bureaucratic machinery at the grass-root level which is associated with the implementation of the SFDA programmes. For a mere examination of the machinery of the SFDA and the problems it encountered will not be of much help in understanding the phenomenon. Most of the administrative problems stem not only from the internal structure but also from the larger socio-economic structure.

This study also examines the impact of different schemes and their viability. This is considered important to analyse the suitability and effectiveness of a public policy for removal of poverty.

The study also attempts to analyse the role of the institution of the middle-man as it has come to assume importance in the context of subsidy based anti-poverty policies for rural development.

Lastly, participation of the target groups in the implementation of the policies is examined. This is considered vital for the success of a public policy like the SFDA. For this purpose the attitudinal pattern of the beneficiaries is examined on the basis of which the emerging pattern is discerned.

The study, therefore, examines the working of the SFDA in a larger policy perspective and wider socio-economic context. It is hoped that this would provide an insight into the working of the schemes necessary to improve the existing understanding of public policy for target group development.

For the purpose of this study two districts in Andhra Pradesh, namely, East Godavari and Medak are selected. The criterion for selecting these two districts has been the overall performance of the agencies, the SFDA in East Godavari which relatively fared better and SFDA in Medak which could not give a good account of itself were selected. The indicators employed to determine the performance are: (1) the number of beneficiaries covered, (2) the amount of subsidy released and (3) the number of schemes covered under the programme. Consultation with the senior state officials in the secretariat was also done in the selection of the districts.

To get an objective picture of working of the agency, the secondary data about all the SFDA blocks in each selected districts was collected and analysed. For the purpose of this study the blocks which did fairly well and the blocks which lagged far behind were avoided. The SFDA blocks were arranged in order of their performance and the block on the mid-point was chosen. The criteria in assessing the performance of the blocks are the same that are applied in selection of the district.

After the selection of the block, performance of the SFDA in all the villages of the selected block is examined. The criterion in selecting the villages was different. For the purpose of the study three villages were selected. These three villages included one best village where maximum number of beneficiaries were covered, the largest amount of subsidy released and largest number of schemes undertaken. The second is an average village in terms of coverage and performance. The average is picked up almost from the middle range of villages on the performance continuum. The third village is the one where the coverage, the subsidy released and schemes implemented have been unsatisfactory. Thus it is hoped that these three villages will in combination provide scope for an objective assessment of the performance of the agency.

The study employed multi-staged purposive random sampling technique. Since the study proposes to examine the impact of the agency on the beneficiaries, it was attempted to cover almost all the beneficiaries in the three selected villages. This was thought necessary to gain an insight into the problems faced in getting the scheme and its implementation. In the absence of coverage of large number of beneficiaries, it is feared, that the study would not be able to generate adequate information on the aspects that the study seeks to cover. The sample also includes beneficiaries even under related programmes such as IRDP, bonded labour, land distribution, house sites and so on. A sample of non-beneficiaries is also drawn mostly from the neglected villages. The sample details are presented in the following Table.

In the district of Medak, as shown by the table 1.1, out of the 305 respondents drawn for the purpose of the study, 142

TABLE 1.1 : **Sample particulars**

Sl. No.	Name of the village	SFDA Beneficiaries	Beneficiaries of related programmes	Non-beneficiaries	Total
	Medak dist.				
1.	Marpadga	120	42	28	190
2.	Sirsingandla	20	16	29	65
3.	Peddamasanpally	2	12	36	50
	Total	142	70	93	305
	East Godavari dist.				
4.	Shankavaram	120	27	41	188
5.	Vajrakutam	30	10	30	70
6.	Balarampuram	4	14	32	50
	Total	154	51	103	308
	Grand Total	296	121	196	613

SFDA beneficiaries and 70 related schemes beneficiaries, and 93 non-beneficiaries covering all the three categories of the target groups are also included.

In the district of East Godavari, out of 308 respondents 154 are SFDA beneficiaries, 51 are covered under related programmes and 103 are non-beneficiaries covering all the three categories of the target group, namely, small farmers, marginal farmers and agricultural labourers.

In all 613 respondents were interviewed with the help of a questionnaire specially designed for the purpose of collecting the information. The questionnaire was referred to a few experts and persons with field experience. It was pre-tested before it was finally designed and administered.

Survey research of this type has its own limitations. The information generated with the help of these questionnaires is likely to be incomplete as it may not be able to throw sufficient light on certain nuances of the reality. Keeping these limitations in view a few case histories of the beneficiaries and non-beneficiaries in these villages have been prepared. This information is used as a supplementary data to cross-check the data generated by the questionnaire.

In addition to the interview schedule and case histories,

detailed discussions were held with different officers at various levels. Information was also collected by observing two or three district coordinating committee meetings and district and block level review committee meetings. The discussions were also held with bank officials in addition to collecting the factual information from banks. There were also informal discussions with political elite and Pyraveekars at various levels. An interview schedule was administered to the field functionaries which included the village development officers and the extension officers who directly deal with the SFDA programmes in the block.

Participant observation method was also employed and the information so generated is also used for the purpose of analysis.

The factual information was collected from secondary sources.

Thus the study is multi-dimensional and attempts to cover a wider area. It examines the phenomenon basically from a public policy angle and attempts to explain the gap between promise and performance. The study does not entirely depend upon the survey method although that is the major tool used. Other tools like participant observation, case histories, and informal discussions with different categories of people are also employed. Thus the study took all the possible care which would improve its scientific validity on the one hand and reflect the reality on the other.

REFERENCES

1. Yogesh Atal, Role of values and institutions, in A. J. Fonseca (Ed), *Challenge of Poverty in India*, Vikas Publications, New Delhi, 1971, p. 91.
2. Tarlok Singh, *Poverty and Social Change*, Longmans Green & Company Limited, 1945, p. 196.
3. Nicholas Jequier, Science policy in the developing countries: The role of the multinational firms, in Gustove Ranis (Ed), *The Gap Between Rich and Poor Nations*, Macmillan, London, 1972, p. 344.
4. David Horowitz, *The Abolition of Poverty*, Praeger Publishers, New York, 1969, p. 4.
5. E.J. Habsbawm, *Poverty*, *International Encyclopaedia of Social Sciences* The Macmillan Company and The Free Press, London, 1968.

6. Vilhelm Aubdert, Rural poverty and community isolation, in Peter Townsend (Ed), *The Concept of Poverty*, Hienmann, London, 1970, p. 250.
7. Montek S. Ahluwalia, Nicholas G. Carter, and Hollis B. Chenery, Growth and poverty in developing countries, *World Bank Reprint Series*, No. 118, 1979.
8. V.M. Dandekar and Neelakantha Rath, Poverty in India, *Indian School of Political Economy*, Bombay, 1971, pp. 29 - 30.
9. Ibid. p. 46.
10. Colin Clark, Extent of hunger in India, *Economic and Political Weekly*, Vol. VII, No. 40, 1972, pp. 2026.
11. P. K. Bardhan, On the Incidence of poverty in rural India of the sixties, *Economic and Political Weekly*, Vol. 8, No. 4-6, 1973.
12. Raj Krishna, Review of SFDA : Philosophy and performance essential, *Kurukshetra*, Vol. 27, July 16, 1979, p. 4.
13. Colin Clark, *Extent of Hunger in India*, op. cit., p. 2026.
14. Ibid. p. 2026.
15. Ranjit Sau, On rural poverty—A tentative hypothesis, *Economic and Political Weekly*, Vol. 6, No. 2, 1971, p. 108.
16 Ibid. p. 108.
17. P. K. Bardhan, Earlier estimates of rural poor, *Indian Economic Review*, Vol. V, No. 1, 1970.
18. P.D. Ojha, A configuration of Indian poverty—Inequality and levels of living, in A.J. Fonseca, (Ed.), *Challenge of Poverty in India*, op. cit., p. 40.
19. Michael Lypton, *Why Poor People Stay Poor: Urban Bias in World Development*, Temple Smith, London, 1977, p. 31.
20. V.M. Dandekar and Rath, *Poverty of India*, op. cit., p. 46.
21. Quoted by Dantwala, Poverty : Not by Statistics Alone, *Economic and Political Weekly*, Vol. 10, No. 76, 1975, p. 663.
22. Ibid. pp. 662-63.
23. Ibid. p. 663.
24. Milton J. Esman, *Landless and Near-Landless in Developing Countries*, Rural Development Committee, Centre for International Studies, Cornell University, Ithaca, 1978, p. 6.
25. B.S. Minhas, *Planning and the Poor*, S. Chand and Co., Ltd., New Delhi, 1978, pp. 74-5.
26. Government of India, Ministry of Agriculture and Irrigation, Compendium, 1975, p. 1.
27. T.K. Chakravarthy, Development of Small and Marginal Farmers and Agricultural Lobourers: An Overview of Policies and Programmes, National Institute of Rural Development, Hyderabad, 1980, p. 9.
28. Small Farmers and Landless in South Asia, *World Bank Staff Working Paper*, No 320, The World Bank, Washington, February, 1979, p. I.
29. Small Farmers and Landless in South Asia, *World Bank Working Paper*, op. cit., p. 1.
30. Ibid. p. i.

31. Ibid. p. ii.
32. Ibid. p. vi.
33. T.K. Chakravarthy, *Development of Small and Marginal Farmers and Agricultural Labourers*, op. cit., p. 24.
34. Ibid. p. 24.
35. Labour enquiry, Summary Report (1974-75) Labour Bureau, Chandigarh, Ministry of Labour, 1978, p. 15.
36. Compendium of instruction on SFDA/MFAL projects, Government of India, Ministry of Agriculture and Irrigation (Department of Rural Development), September 1975, p. 1.
37. Ibid, p. 1.
38. National Commission on Agriculture, Interim report on reorganisation of programmes of small farmers and marginal farmers and agricultural labourers development agencies, Government of India, New Delhi, 1973, pp. 19-20.
39. Department of Rural Development, Some special programmes of rural development: Statistics, 1977-78, Administrative Intelligence Division, Ministry of Agriculture and Irrigation, Government of India, New Delhi, 1979 (memo), p. 1.
40. Department of Rural Development, D.O. No. 11011/80/80-IRD III, Ministry of Rural Reconstruction, Krishi Bhavan, New Delhi, dated 8th Oct. 1980. The present study is confined to the erstwhile SFDA.
41. Interim Report of reorganisation of programmes of small farmers and marginal farmers and agricultural labourers development agency, Government of India, New Delhi, 1973, pp. 19-20.
42. David Nichimias, *Public Policy Evaluation: Approaches and* Methods, St. Martins Press, New York, 1979, p. 1.
43. Ibid. p. 4.
44. Ibid. p. 4.
45. Harold Laswell, *A Preview of Policy Sciences*, Elsevier, New York, p. 29.
46. Tarlok Singh, *The Planning Process and Public Policy: A Reassessment*, Gokhale Institute of Politics and Economics, Pune, 1979, p. 2.
47. Report on Evaluation Study of Small Farmers, Marginal Farmers and Agricultural labourers projects ; 1974-75, PEO. Planning Commission, Government of India, 1978, p. 26.
48. Ibid. p. 88.
49. Ibid. p. 88.
50. The small farmers development agencies (72-73), The Field Study, Reserve Bank of India, Bombay, 1975, p. 54.
51. Ibid. p. 54.
52. Ibid. p. 153.
53. Ibid. p. 153.
54. Ibid. p. 67.
55. Ibid. p. 74.
56. Ibid. p. 79.
57. M.J. Ali, and G.C. Barthakur, *An Assessment of Small and Marginal*

Farmers' Development Programmes in Assam : A Case study of kharif programme in Kamrup District, Agro-Economic Research Centre for North East India, Assam Agricultural University, Jorhat, 1972. P.C., Dutta, and K., Gogoi, *An Assessment of Small and Marginal Farmers' Development Programmes in Assam : A Case study of kharif programme in Nowgong District*, Assam Agro-Economic Research Centre for North East India, Assam Agricultural University, Jorhat, 1973.

58. Surendra Prasad Sinha, Marginal and Small Farmers : Perspectives, problems and prospects, Manisha, Muzaffarpur 1978, S. Singh, R. P. Singh and Radhey Shyam, Field Workshop of Problems of Small Farmers Development and its Institutional Aspects in North Bihar, Agro-Economic Research Centre, University of Allahabad, (Cyclo), 1976, p. 19, R. P. Singh, and H. G. Goswami, Study of Small Farmers' Development Agency, Purnea (North Bihar), Agro-Economic Research Centre, Motilal Nehru Institute of Research, University of Allahabad, Allahabad, 1974.
59. Govt. of Haryana, Evaluation Report on The Working of SFDA, Ambala, Economic and Statistical Organisation, Planning Department, Haryana, 1978. S.S. Tyagi, Small Farmers Development Programmes in District Ambala, Agricultural Economics Research Centre, University of Delhi, 1975.
60. I.S. Kingra, Performance of the SFDA and Its Programmes, Sirmur District, Himachal Pradesh, in B. M. Desai, *Intervention in Rural Development*, Indian Institute of Management, Ahmedabad, 1979.
61. Mumtaz Ali Khan, Sociological Analysis of Working of SFDA., Indian Institute of Advanced Study, Simla, 1978. A.R. Rajpurohit, Evaluation of SFDA, Mysore District, Karnataka, Gokhale Institute of Politics and Economics, Pune, 1975. The Report on Evaluation of SFDA, Hassan District Karnataka, Consultancy and Applied Research Division, Administrative Staff College of India, Hydrabad, 1978.
62. Government of Kerala, SFDA : Cannanore, Evaluation Division Study, Planning Board, Kerala, 1977.
63. D.K. Maitra : Experiences in organising economic activities, SFDA : Raisen—Sehore, Bhopal, Madhya Pradesh, in B.M. Desai (Ed), *Intervention in Rural Development*, op. cit., Athavale M.C., *Small Farmers Development Agencies in Madhya Pradesh*, Jabalpur, Agro-Economic Research Centre, 1973.
64. D.P. Apte, Identification and organisation of economic programmes for small farmers, in B. M. Desai (Ed.), *Intervention for Rural Development*, op. cit.
65. S. S. Acharya et. al. Problems and Prospects for Small and Marginal Farmers and Agricultural labourers in Rajasthan, Department of Agriculture Economics, University of Udaipur, Jobner, 1978.
66. An Enquiry into the Economics of Small Farmers in the Context of Small Farmers Development Agency Programme in The District Pratap garh (U.P.), Kanpur, the Department of Agriculture and Economics, C.S. Azad, University of Agriculture and Technology, Kanpur, 1978.

67. I.S. Kingra, Performance of the SFDA and its Programmes, Sirmur District, Himachal Pradesh, op. cit., p. 156,
68. I.S. Kingra, Performance of the SFDA and programmes, Sirmur District, Himachal Pradesh, op. cit., pp. 157-9.
69. Evaluation study of Small Farmers Development Agency in Adilabad District of Andhra Pradesh, Technical Cell, Osmania University, 1979.
70. J.E. Neilan, *Planning for Rural Development : Mal development or both? A case study of a SFDA Programme in Hyderabad District, Andhra Pradesh, India*, Free University Press, Amsterdam, 1979.
71. Evaluation study of SFDA in Medak District of Andhra Pradesh Technical Cell, Osmania University, 1979.
72. Study of the SFDA,Nalgonda district, Andhra Pradesh, Agro Economic Research Centre, Andhra University, Waltair, 1973.
73. Ch. Balaramulu, Administration of Anti-Poverty Programmes: A study of SFDA, Kakatiya School of Public Administration, Warangal, 1984,
74. Department of Planning and Statistics, Study of the SFDA, East Godavari District, Kakinada, 1979.
75. S.K. Pachauri, Performance of beneficiaries : selected cases of SFDA, Srikakulam in B.M. Desai, *Intervention for Rural Development*, op cit.
76. N. Desinga Rao, administration of selected schemes of SFDA, Visakhapatnam in B. M. Desai, *Intervention for Rural Development*, op cit.
77. SFDA in three districts of Andhra Pradesh in B.M. Desai, *Intervention for Rural Development*, op. cit.
78. The middleman is widely known as *Pyraveekar* in the Telangana region of Andhra Pradesh.

2

The Universe of the Study

ANY RESEARCH investigation must take into account the general conditions obtaining in a particular area for the purpose of understanding and analysis. There has been a growing feeling that the secondary data is inadequate and does not give a total picture. With this view the particulars relating to the social and economic conditions of the area and the details generated by the primary data about the respondents selected for the purpose of this study along with the secondary data are presented here.

In the districts of Medak and East Godavari, as stated earlier, two samithis, namely, Siddipet and Shankavaram have been selected. These two samithis present certain similarities. Although East Godavari is considered to be a developed district in Andhra Pradesh, this is not true of the samithi selected for our study. All the blocks in East Godavari district are divided into three categories : (1) the delta blocks, (2) upland blocks and (3) the agency blocks which are in the tribal belt. The blocks in the delta area are considered rich because of irrigation facilities. Shankavaram samithi being an upland block the conditions are largely similar to those obtaining in Siddipet block.

The total geographical area of Medak is 9,685 sq. kms. According to the 1971 census the population of the district of Medak was 14,67,944 which rose to 18,27,588 (19.7%) in 1981. Out of this, the males constitute 7,39,066 and females 7,28,878 in 1971 which increased to 9,22,066 and 9,04,756 (19.4%) in 1981. In 1971 rural population was 13,42,958 and 1,23,966 was urban but it increased to 16,11,139 (16.6%) rural population and 2,16,449 (42.7%) urban population in 1981.

The literacy in the district was 16.1 per cent in 1971 which rose to 21.09 per cent in 1981. This includes 25.2 per cent of males and 6.9 per cent of females in 1971 but touched 31.18 per cent males and 10.81 per cent females in 1981.

The percentage of workers in total population was 45.6 per cent in 1971 and 44.9 per cent in 1981. This included 60.7 per cent males and 30.31 per cent females in 1971 and 57.32 per cent males and 32.35 per cent females in 1981. In the total work force 44.3 per cent were cultivators, 32.3 per cent agricultural labourers and 23.4 per cent other workers. In 1981 the cultivators constituts 44.6 per cent agricultural labourers 31.5 per cent and 4.49 per cent are engaged in the household industry and 19.29 per cent are categorised as other workers.

The total geographical area of East Godavari is 10,970 sq. kms. In the district the total population was 30,87,262 in 1971. It rose to 37,01,714 (33.3 per cent) in 1981 and consisted of 18,57,482 males and 18,44,232 females. In 1971 the rural and urban population was 24,93,668 and 5,93,594 respectively. This increased to 28,79,784 (13.4 per cent) rural and 8,21,930 (27.8 per cent) urban population in 1981.

In 1971 the literacy was 30.8 per cent which includes 37.3 per cent males and 24.3 per cent females. In 1981 it is recorded as 34.05 per cent and includes 40.85 per cent males and 28.12 per cent females.

The number of cultivators was 21.1 per cent in 1971 and 21.51 per cent in 1981. The agricultural labourers in 1971 was 45.2 per cent and 42.7 per cent in 1981. The ratio of the male and female in 1971 was 37.2 per cent and 72.1 per cent respectively. In 1981 it stood at 35.16 per cent males and 67.72 per cent females. The other workers constituted 33.7 per cent in 1971 and 30.65 per cent in 1981.

The particulars about the two blocks namely, Siddipet and Shankavaram that are selected for this study are as follows:

Siddipet is a backward block in the district of Medak. There are 74 revenue villages 66 gram panchayats in this block. The total geographical area is 673 sq.kms. The population of the block is 1,05,451. This includes 19,976 scheduled castes and 1,792 scheduled tribes. The total households is 20,224.

There are 23,800 cultivators, 18,051 agricultural labourers, 3,707 marginal farmers and 2,412 small farmers. The total cultivable area is 90,000 acres which includes 21,000 acres of wet land and 69,000 acres of dry land. The irrigation sources are mainly wells. There are 8,924 irrigation wells which cover 13,191 acres and tanks cover 7,809 acres. The number of villages electrified is 49. The block has 2,918 electric motors and 1,017 oil engines.

The agricultural implements in the samithi include two tractors, 16,846 ploughs, 117 sprayers, 11 power sprayers, 50 sugarcane crushers and 4,090 carts.

Shankavaram in East Godavari is also a backward block. It has 125 villages and 58 gram panchayats. The total geographical area is 578 sq. kms. The population of the samithi is 1,33,142 which includes 20,819 scheduled castes and 10,440 scheduled tribes. The backward class population is 83,015 and other castes 19,498. There are 62,750 agricultural labourers, 9,872 marginal farmers and 7,098 small farmers and 2,926 medium or big farmers. The total cultivable area is 48,410 acres which includes 20,170 acres of dry land.

Three villages have been chosen from each selected block for the purpose of a detailed study. As stated earlier, the villages are selected on the basis of the coverage of the SFDA programmes. The criteria applied are : one village which received the largest coverage, one with average coverage, and one village which received least attention under the SFDA schemes. In Siddipet the largest coverage was done in Marpadga, Srisingandla received average coverage and the least coverage was in the village of Peddamasanpally. In Shankavaram samithi, the village which received the largest coverage was Shankavaram village, Vajrakutam falls under average coverage category and the least covered village was Balarampuram. Here is the brief sketch of each village. The particulars are presented in the Tables 2.1, 2.2, 2.3, and 2.4.

Marpadga

The village of Marpadga is located at a distance of 14 kms from Siddipet town. The area of the village is 11.54 sq. miles. This village consists of three hamlets namely, Khammampally, Nagireddypally and Rampally.

TABLE 2.1 : **Area—population**

Sl. No.	Name of the village	Area in Sq. miles	Total population	Males	Females	SCs	STs	Literacy
	Medak Dist.							
1.	Marpadga	11.54	4925	2521	2404	1168		592
	(%)			(51.2)	(48.8)	(23.7)		(12.0)
2.	Sirsingandla	8.19	3373	1711	1662	695		348
	(%)			(50.7)	(49.3)	(20.6)		(10.3)
3.	Peddamasanpally	5.23	990	516	474	118	13	105
	(%)			(52.1)	(47.9)	(11.9)	(1.3)	(10.6)
	East Godavari Dist.							
4.	Shankavaram	3.45	9020	4555	4465	1750		1731
	(%)			(50.5)	(49.5)	(10.4)		(19.2)
5.	Vajrakutam	3.03	565	287	278	149		157
	(%)			(50.8)	(49.2)	(26.4)		(27.8)
6.	Balarampuram	0.83	1348	695	653	149		154
	(%)			(51.6)	(48.4)	(11.1)		(11.4)

Note : Figures in parenthesis indicate percentages.

TABLE 2.2 : **Workforce**

Sl. No.	Name of the village	Total Workers Male	Total Workers Female	S.F.	M.F.	A.L.	Livestock	Household industry	Others
	Medak Dist.								
1.	Marpadga	1374	833	270	502	795	130	122	167
	(%)	(32.5)	(19.7)	(12.2)	(22.7)	(36.0)	(5.9)	(5.5)	(7.6)
2.	Sirsingandla	954	571	218	289	408	124	134	143
	(%)	(33.1)	(19.8)	(14.3)	(19.0)	(26.8)	(8.1)	(8.8)	(9.4)
3.	Peddamasanpally	315	199	60	202	149	27	35	55
	(%)	(33.3)	(21.0)	(11.7)	(39.3)	(29.0)	(5.3)	(6.8)	(10.7)
	East Godavari Dist.								
4.	Shankavaram	2200	735	150	450	1795	63	117	432
	(%)	(30.8)	(10.3)	(5.1)	(15.3)	(61.2)	(2.1)	(4.0)	(14.7)
5.	Vajrakutam	167	44	4	16	186	—	—	5
	(%)	(29.6)	(7.8)	(1.9)	(7.6)	(88.2)			(2.4)
6.	Balarampuram	353	134	12	100	237	17	7	58
	(%)	(30.3)	(11.5)	(2.5)	(20.5)	(48.7)	(3.5)	(1.9)	(11.9)

Note : Figures in parenthesis indicate percentage.

TABLE 2.3 : **Landuse pattern**

Sl. No.	Name of the village	Total Land in Acres	Type of Soil in Acres		Cultivable Land in Acres	Wet Land Irrigated Under in Acres		Dry Land in Acres	Cultivable Waste Land in Acres	Forest Land in Acres
			Red	Black		Tanks	Wells			
	Medak dist:									
1.	Marpadga	6836	2612	870	3482	298	111	3062	511	1449
2.	Sirsingandla	5241	2178	392	2570	150	383	2037	678	1569
3.	Peddamasanpally	3347	1683	30	1713	311	50	1387	511	756
	East Godavari dist:									
4.	Shankavaram	2208	924	550	1474	162	30	1312	150	—
5.	Vajrakutam	1939			532	52	—	480	200	—
6.	Balarampuram	729	253	183	436	173	5	263	93	—

TABLE 2.4 : **Infrastructure**

Sl. No.	Name of the village	Drinking water	Medical	Veterinary Hospital	Education	Communication	Post & Telegraphs	Electricity
	Medak Dist.							
1.	Marpadga	PWS	FPC	—	4 P.S. 1 H.S.	KR	SPO TP	EC
2.	Sirsingandla	—	—	—	1 M.S.	KR	PO	EC
3.	Peddamasanpally	—	—	—	1 P.S.	KR	—	EC
	East Godavari Dist.							
4.	Shankavaram	PWS	PHC	LSU	2 P.S. 1 H.S.	PR	BPO	EC
5.	Vajrakutam	—	—	—	1 P.S.	KR	—	EC
6.	Balarampuram	—	—	—	1 P.H.	PR	—	EC

N. B. :

PWS — Protected Water Supply
FPC — Family Planning Centre
PHC — Primary Health Centre
PS — Primary School
MS — Middle School
HS — High School
LSU — Live Stock Unit
PR — Pucca Road
KR — Kutcha Road
SPO — Sub-Post Office
BPO — Branch Post Office
TP — Telephone
EC — Electricity

The population is 4,925 and the total number of households is 809. The females account for 48.8 per cent in the total population of the village. The scheduled caste population constitutes 23.7 per cent. The literacy percentage is 12.

There are 2,207 workers in the village and non-workers number 2,070. The female workers outnumber male workers in non-working group. In the work force 993 are cultivators and 795 are agricultural labourers, and 122 persons have household industries. The wage rate in the village is Rs. 2.50 per day for the female and Rs. 5 for the male labourers.

The total land in the village is 6,836 acres out of which 3,482 acres is the cultivable area. The cultivable land represents 51 per cent of the total acreage. The irrigated land is 6.1 per cent of the total land and 12.1 per cent of the cultivable land. The forest land and cultivable waste land constitute 17.2 per cent and 7.8 per cent of the total land respectively. The soil types indicate that 75 per cent is red soil and rest is black soil.

The land holding pattern shows certain important trends ; those who possess below 2½ acres of land comprising 36.5 per cent belong to the scheduled castes, 54.8 per cent backward castes, 0.4 per cent scheduled tribes and 8.7 per cent forward castes ; in the category of the small farmers possessing between 2½ to 5 acres land, backward castes constitute 63.3 per cent, the scheduled castes 15.9 per cent and forward castes 20.7 per cent ; in the category of 5.1 to 12.5 acres, 16.4 per cent are the scheduled castes, 51.8 per cent are backward castes and 31.8 per cent are forward castes ; in the 12.6 to 25 acres land holding group the scheduled castes constitute 3.7 per cent, backward castes 23.6 per cent and forward castes 72.7 per cent ; and in the category of 25 acres and above the scheduled castes constitute 4.3 per cent and forward castes 95.7 per cent. There is none from the backward castes in this category.

The major sources of irrigation are tanks and wells. There are five big tanks, four small tanks and 300 wells. The village has 225 electric motors and ten oil engines.

The cropping pattern of the village indicates that commercial crops like sugarcane and groundnut are cultivated in certain fertile irrigated pockets. In all 14 types of crops are raised in the village. Usually they cultivate the food crops twice a year depending upon the availability of water. Though maize is the principal crop in the area, jowar and wheat are also cultivated.

The village of Marpadga has four primary schools and one higher secondary school. The village is provided with modern facilities such as protected water supply, telephone exchange and a branch post-office. However, there is no hospital for the sick people and veterinary facilities for sick animals. This village is connected with its block headquarters by a kutcha road and a private bus.

Sirsingandla

Sirsingandla is a revenue village in Siddipet taluk and it has one hamlet, Giraipally. It is located at a distance of about 18 kms. from the block headquarters. The geographical area of the village is 8.19 sq. miles.

The total population in the village is 3,373, of this 50.7 per cent are males and 49.3 per cent females. The caste-wise break-up of the population indicates that the scheduled castes constitute 20.6 per cent, backward castes 70.4 per cent and other castes 9 per cent. The population of Mudiraj community is quite large. The other castes such as Kapu, Padmasali, Chakali, Golla have a population ranging between 200 to 300. The literacy rate indicates that there are 285 (7%) male, 63 (1.8%) female literates in the village. In all the literacy percentage is 10.3.

The number of workers in the village is 1,525 which constitutes 52.9 per cent. Out of this, the male work force constitute 33.1 per cent and female 19.8 per cent. There are nearly 507 small and marginal farmers. The small farmers represent 14.3 per cent and marginal farmers 19 per cent in the total work force. The wage rate in the village is Rs. 2 for female and Rs. 4 for male labourers.

The total land in the village is 5,241 acres. This consists of 533 acres of wet, 2,037 acres of dry and 678 acres of waste land. Forest area is spread over 1,569 acres.

The number of small farmers in the village is 218 which includes 16.9 per cent scheduled castes, 0.9 per cent scheduled tribes, 62.5 per cent backward castes and 19.7 per cent forward castes. There are 289 marginal farmers : 24.5 per cent are scheduled castes, 1.3 per cent scheduled tribes, 69.4 per cent backward castes and 4.8 per cent other castes. The total number of agricultural labourers is 408 which includes 164 male and 244 female labourers. There are no scheduled caste and scheduled tribe farmers in the $12\frac{1}{2}$ to 25 acre land owning category. The farmers in this category include 81 per cent forward castes and 19 per cent backward castes. The distribution of the land among the forward castes reveals that 5 per cent of the forward castes have control over 70 per cent of the land. Although scheduled castes constitute $\frac{1}{3}$ of the population they own very negligible percentage (17%) of the land.

The cropping pattern consists of mainly paddy, maize, jowar, castor seeds, pulses and so on. However, the major crops are paddy and maize.

The major source of irrigation is wells. There are in all 350 wells in the village. The land covered under the well irrigation is about 383 acres. There are also three big and two small tanks which irrigate about 150 acres of land. The unirrigated area is about 2,037 acres. The cultivable waste land is 678 acres and non-cultivable area 2,037 acres. There are 86 electric motors and 19 oil engines in the village.

Educational facilities are very meagre ; there is only one upper primary school. After the completion of upper primary education the children have to trek long distances to have access to higher education. Although the village has modern facilities such as electricity, post office and telephone exchange, it does not have any medical facilities nor is it provided with protected water. The village is connected with block headquarters by a kutcha road and a private bus.

Peddamasanpally

This village is located at a distance of 14 kms. from the taluka headquarters. The area of the village is 5.23 sq. miles.

The total population in the village is 990. The village did not register any growth in population as 50 families migrated to different places during the last decade owing to severe drought in 1972. Ratio of male and female members is 52.1 per cent and 47.9 per cent respectively. The scheduled castes constitute 11.9 per cent of the total population and scheduled tribes 1.3 per cent. The Reddys constitute 22.7 per cent and the rest of them belong to backward castes. The literacy rate in the village is 10.6 per cent which includes 3.2 per cent female literacy.

The total work force is 54.3 per cent of the total population. 48.2 per cent are cultivators and 29 per cent are agricultural labourers. The wage rate is Rs. 5 for male and Rs. 1.50 to Rs. 2 for female.

The pattern of the soil indicates that a very large proportion of land is red sandy soil and there are a few pockets of land falling under the category of black cotton soil.

The total land in the village is 3,347 acres of which the land available for cultivation is 51.2 per cent. Within the cultivable land the irrigated land constitutes 19.1 per cent and unirrigated 80.9 per cent. The cultivable waste is 15.3 per cent and non-cultivable land is 11 per cent of the total land. The irrigated land is about 9.7 per cent. There are one big tank and five small tanks which together irrigate 311 acres of land. Out of 1,713 acres of cultivable land only 35.9 per cent of the land is cultivated while 64.1 per cent lie fallow.

The land holding particulars indicates that in the category of small farmers, forward castes constitute 66.7 per cent and the backward castes 33.3 per cent. There is one from the scheduled castes. In the category of marginal farmers 88.1 per cent are from backward castes and the rest belong to the scheduled castes. Those who have 5 acres and above are all from the forward castes.

Three crops that are raised in this area are paddy, jowar and maize. Owing to scarcity of water there has not been much scope for raising double crop. The availability of underground water is also very limited.

The village has twelve electric pump sets and 20 oil engines for agricultural purposes. Except for one primary school the village does not have any modern facilities such as telephone exchange, electricity, protected water, primary health centre and veterinary hospital. They are dependent on the town located at 14 kms. distance for some of these facilities. The village is connected by a kutcha road to the main road but there is no bus service.

Shankavaram

Shankavaram happens to be a village which received maximum

coverage in terms of beneficiaries, subsidy released and the programmes taken up. Shankavaram is also the headquarters of the samithi. The present and the past presidents of the samithi hail from this village. In Siddipet block of Medak Marpadga which received maximum coverage under SFDA, is the village that the previous samithi president come from.

Shankavaram is at a distance of 32 kms. from Pithapuram and 50 kms, from the district headquarters. The samithi being not a very advanced one, the villages of the samithi, including Shankavaram, broadly reflect the backward conditions.

The total population of the villages is 9,020 which includes 4,555 male and 4,465 female members. This works out to 50.5 per cent male and 49.5 per cent female members. The total number of literates in the village is 19.2 per cent which includes 11.5 per cent male and 7.7 per cent female literates.

The total work force of the village is 41.1 per cent. The work force comprises of 61.2 per cent (1795) agricultural labourers, 15.3 per cent (450) marginal farmers, 5.1 per cent (150) small farmers and 14.7 per cent (432) were engaged in other occupations.

The soil pattern shows that 62.7 per cent is red sandy and 37.3 per cent black cotton soil. The total land available in Shankavaram is 2,208 acres which includes 66.7 per cent dry land. There are no fallow lands in this village. However, 6.8 per cent of land can be brought under cultivation.

The land holding pattern of the village presents the following trends. All the medium and big farmers are from forward castes. In the category of small farmer it is again the forward castes who comprise 86.7 per cent and backward castes 13.3 per cent. It denotes absence of the scheduled castes in the land owning categories. Among the marginal farmers, the scheduled castes represent 4.4 per cent, backward castes 28.9 per cent and the forward castes 66.7 per cent.

The irrigation facilities are scanty and inadequate. There are two tanks and 25 wells for cultivation purpose in the village. There are eight electric motors, six oil engines, and two tractors.

Important crops grown in the village are paddy and commercial crops such as sugarcane and chillies. The conditions are not suitable for growing a second crop.

The wage rate in the village of Shankavaram is : male gets

Rs. 5 per day and female Rs. 3 to 4.

In the village there is a branch of the State Bank of India and also a telephone exchange. In addition a primary health centre, a veterinary hospital, protected water supply, a primary school and high school are located in the village. There is also a single teacher school exclusively meant for Harijans. The village is connected by a pucca road and the buses of the Road Transport Corporation ply on this route. Even private taxies are available for transport.

Vajrakutam

Vajrakutam is selected as an average village in terms of SFDA coverage. It is a small revenue village. The total area of the village is 3.03 sq. miles and has a population of 565. This includes 50.8 per cent male and 49.2 per cent female population. The scheduled castes comprise 26.4 per cent of the total population. The Kapus constitute 66 per cent and other castes are around 20 per cent in the village. The total number of households is 104. The village, being a part of an upland area, reflects the general backwardness of the area.

The occupational particulars of the village show that a majority of the villagers are engaged in agriculture. However, it is noticed that even from those who have land more than half of them depend on their physical labour. The total number of workers is 211-167 male and 44 female. Among the agricultural labourers 76.3 per cent are male and 23.7 per cent female labourers. The low participation of female labour is on account of the cultural traditions of Kapu caste which does not send their women for work even under economic stress. The literacy rate in the village is 27.8 per cent.

The wage rate in this village is slightly higher than in most of the other areas. A male member is paid per day Rs. 8 and female Rs. 6 This is generally raised to Rs. 12 and Rs. 8 for male and female respectively during the harvest season.

Total land available in the village is 1,939 acres. This includes 2.6 per cent, irrigated and 24.7 per cent unirrigated land. The cultivable waste is 10.3 per cent. Most of the land is black cotton soil. The land not available for cultivation is 62.25 per cent ; this is on account of hillocks surrounding the village.

The land ownership pattern ranges from 0.2 cents to 25 acres. There is not much of concentration of land in a few hands in the village. 27.8 per cent of the scheduled castes, 18.9 per cent backward castes and 53.3 per cent other castes own less than 2½ acres of land. In the 2½ to 5 acres category, scheduled castes constitute 4.1 per cent, backward castes 29.1 per cent and other castes 66.6 per cent. In the 5 to 12½ acres category there is none from the scheduled castes, a negligible 7 per cent are from backward castes. The rest are from the forward castes. In the category of 12½ to 25 acres there is none from either the backward castes or the scheduled castes.

The village is dependent on rain fall for its irrigation. There is only one tank in the village which irrigates 52 acres of land. There are in all 12 wells and new wells cannot be dug because of rocky nature of the area. There are five electric motors and one oil engine.

The village is provided with very few facilities. There is neither a primary health centre nor a veterinary hospital. There are no post and telegraphic facilities. It is not connected with any highway. There is not even a fair weather road. However, a primary school, protected water supply and electricity are the facilities that presently exist in the village.

Balarampuram

Balarampuram is backward and is also a neglected village under the SFDA scheme. The village perhaps is the most neglected of all the six villages covered by this study.

Balarampuram is located at a distance of 35 kms. from Pithapuram town. It is surrounded by medium size hillocks and dense forest. The area of this village is 0.83 sq. miles and the population is 1,348. It includes 51.6 per cent of male, 48.4 per cent female population. The scheduled castes population constitute 11.1 per cent, the backward castes 55.4 per cent and forward castes 37 per cent. In all, 11.4 per cent of the villagers are literates of which 2.7 per cent are female and 8.7 per cent male members.

The total number of workers in the village is 41.8 per cent; the non-workers constitute 58.2 per cent of the total population. 34.5 per cent of the work force is engaged in cultivation and 48.7 per cent are agricultural labourers.

The wage rate in the village is Rs. 6 per day for male and Rs. 3 for female labourer.

The total land in the village is 729 acres. 59.8 per cent of the total land is available for cultivation and 23.7 per cent is under irrigated crops. In the total land, 12.8 per cent is cultivable waste and 27.4 per cent cannot be used for agricultural purpose. However, most of the land is black cotton soil.

The land distribution pattern indicates that 5 per cent scheduled castes, 25 per cent forward castes and 70 per cent backward castes belong to the category of marginal farmers, that is, those who have less than 2½ acres of land. 16.7 per cent of scheduled castes, 83.3 per cent of forward castes fall under small farmers category. In 5 to 12½ acres category 40 per cent belong to the backward castes and 60 per cent forward castes. In the category of more than 12½ acres, all the cultivators are from the forward castes. The scheduled castes are not found owning more than five acres of land. The major source of irrigation is tanks. In all there are two big and two small tanks.

Food crops are the principal crops in the village. They constitute around 59 per cent while the rest of the area is covered by commercial crops such as groundnut, cotton and vegetables and so on.

The village is deprived of many of the modern facilities. Except a primary school, no other facility such as post office, primary health centre, protected water supply, telephone exchange exists. However, the village is connected by a road which leads to Visakhapatnam and the Road Transport Corporation buses ply on it.

II

The particulars of the respondents are presented in this part of the study. This would throw light on various socio-economic facets of the sample and provide an insight into their nature and living conditions. A study on public policy of this kind needs to be analysed and understood against this background.

The age particulars (in Appendix-II.1) show that in the case of Siddipet block 52.8 per cent are in the age group of 20-40 years, 30.8 per cent are middle age that is, 41-55 years and 16.4

TABLE 2.5: **Caste particulars of respondents**

Sl. No.	Name of the village	CASTE		
		O.C.	B.C.	S.C.
	Medak Dist.			
1.	Marpadga	16	93	81
	(%)	(8.5)	(48.9)	(42.6)
2.	Sirsingandla	9	26	30
	(%)	(13.8)	(40.0)	(46.2)
3.	Peddamasanpally	2	33	15
	(%)	(4.0)	(66.0)	(30.0)
	Total	27	152	126
		(8.9)	(49.8)	(41.3)
	East Godavari Dist.			
4.	Shankavaram	103	26	59
	(%)	(54.8)	(13.8)	(31.4)
5.	Vajrakutam	42	14	14
	(%)	(60.0)	(20.0)	(20.0)
6.	Balarampuram	19	20	11
	(%)	(38.0)	(40.0)	(22.0)
	Total	164	60	84
		(53.2)	(19.5)	(27.3)
	Grand Total	191	212	210
		(31.2)	(34.6)	(34.2)

Note : Figures in parenthesis indicate percentages.

per cent are in the old aged group. In the case of Shankavaram block 57.6 per cent are young, 27.6 per cent middle aged and 14.8 per cent are in the old age group.

The caste particulars of the respondents in Siddipet block (Table 2.5) reveals that 8.9 per cent are from the forward castes, 49.8 per cent and 41.3 per cent are from the backward and scheduled castes respectively. In Shankavaram block 53.2 per cent, 19.5 per cent and 27.3 per cent are from forward, backward and scheduled castes respectively. A comparison indicates that there has been a wider coverage of the forward castes in Shankavaram block than in Siddipet block.

The educational background of the respondents in Siddipet samithi reveals (Appendix-II.2) that there are 72.8 per cent illiterates, 20.7 per cent near literates (less than primary) 4.6 per cent passed secondary and higher secondary and 1.9 per cent are college graduates. Thus the total number of literate is 27.5 per cent which includes 6.5 per cent educated. In Shankavaram block there are 60.1 per cent illiterates, 31.8 per cent near literates. Among the educated category 7.5 per cent passed secondary and higher secondary and about 0.6 per cent are college graduates.

In each block the data of the three villages selected for the study shows that villages which received more attention have more number of literates than the villages which received lesser attention. For instance the villages of Marpadga and Sirsingandla have 31.6 per cent and 21.5 per cent literates while Peddamasanpally which received lesser attention has 20 per cent literates. In the case of Shankavarm block the villages of Shankavaram and Vajrakutam which received relatively more attention have 29.2 per cent and 38.6 per cent literacy level while Balarampuram which received lesser attention has only 14 per cent of literacy. Compared to the overall literacy in the village, the literacy level of the respondents is higher.

In Siddipet block occupational groups (Appendix-II.3) comprise 70.5 per cent cultivators, 16.1 per cent agricultural labourers and 13 per cent others. In Shankavaram block they comprise 51.3 per cent cultivators, 35.4 per cent agricultural labourers and 13 per cent members of other occupations. This shows that more number of agricultural labourers are covered in Shankavaram block than in the Siddipet block. However, the secondary occupational details of the respondents from Siddipet block reveal that 32.5 per cent small and marginal farmers depend on labour as secondary occupation and there are 22.3 per cent small and marginal farmers who stated agricultural labour as primary occupation. This indicates the uneconomic nature of their holdings and poor quality of land. In the case of Shankavaram block while 17.9 per cent small and marginal farmers depend on labour as secondary occupation 14.6 per cent stated labour as their primary occupation and 7.8 per cent are engaged in other occupations.

From the point of view of coverage of the programmes the data indicates that in the Siddipet block the villages of Marpadga and Sirsingandla—which received wider coverage—have 75.3 per cent and 66.2 per cent of the respondents having agriculture as the primary occupation, while in the village Peddamasanpally—which received lesser coverage—their number is 58 per cent. More number of agricultural labourers are covered in Peddamasanpally than the villages of Marpadga and Sirsingandla. The pattern is slightly different in the case of Shankavaram block. The village of Shankavaram has lesser number of respondents from cultivators than Balarampuram. However, in the village of Shankavaram there are 18.1 per cent of the respondents who are engaged in other occupations. Vajrakutam—which received average coverage—has 72.9 per cent respondents having agriculture as their occupation. The pattern of agricultural labourers is similar to that of Siddipet. The villages of Shankavaram and Vajrakutam have lesser number of agricultural labourers among our respondents than Balarampuram—the neglected village—where 50 per cent of the respondents are agricultural labourers.

An analysis of the type of families of the respondents indicate (Appendix-II.4) that 39 per cent of the respondents in Siddipet continue to be in the joint family system whereas 61 per cent belong to the nuclear type of family. In Shankavaram 20.0 per cent are in the joint family while about 80 per cent belong to the nuclear family. The joint family system appears to be on the decline. However, the system appears to be relatively more widespread in Siddipet block compared with Shankavaram block. With regard to the size of the family the dominant trend appears to be 1 to 5 member family followed by 6 to 10. The families having more than 11 members are negligible in the sample.

The land particulars of the respondents indicate that the landless labourers constitute 18.8 per cent, the marginal farmers 41.8 per cent, small farmers 33.6 per cent. The sample also includes 6 per cent of the medium farmers having more than five acres of land.

When we look at the income levels of the respondents (Table 2.6) the data reveals that 23 families in Siddipet and 26 families in Shankavaram get less than half a rupee per capita income per day. Those who are getting around one rupee or less constitute 23.6 per cent in Siddipet and 21.1 per cent in Shankavaram blocks. In Siddipet 39.7 per cent get between one to two rupees per day, while 33.1 per cent belong to this category in Shankavaram. Twenty per cent get between two to three rupees per day in Siddipet block and their number is 22.4 per cent in Shankavaram. Those who get more than three rupees per day belong to groups above the poverty line. They constitute 16.7 per cent in Siddipet block and 23.4 per cent in Shankavaram block. There are families which get more than five rupees in both the blocks ; in Siddipet their percentage is 4.6 and in Shankavaram it is 9.1 per cent. However, the data reveals that 83.1 per cent in Siddipet and 76.6 per cent in Shankavaram are below the poverty line according to the existing norm of poverty line.

A village-wise examination of income groups reveals that those who get less than one rupee constitute 21.5 per cent, 35.5 per cent and 18 per cent in Marpadga, Sirsingandla and Peddamasanpally respectively. 33.6 per cent from Marpadga, 24.6 per cent from Sirsingandla and 46 per cent from Peddamasanpally belong to one to two rupees income group. Two to three rupees are earned by 15.1 per cent in Marpadga, 18.3 per cent in Sirsingandla and 12 per cent in Peddamasanpally. In the category of those who earn more than three rupees, 15 per cent are from Marpadga, 7 per cent from Sirsingandla and 6 per cent are from Peddamasanpally.

In the case of Shankavaram block 19 per cent from Shankavaram, 56 per cent from Balarampuram earn less than one rupee. Those who get between rupees two to three constitute 43.1 per cent in Shankavaram village, 52.3 per cent in Vajrakutam and 12 per cent in Balarampuram. And 22.1 per cent in

TABLE 2.6 : **Percapita income particulars of respondents**

Sl. No. Name of the village	0-300	301-600	601-900	901-1200	1201 & above	Total
Medak dist.						
1. Marpadga	40	77	37	22	14	190
(%)	(21.0)	(40.5)	(19.5)	(11.6)	(7.4)	(100)
2. Sirsingandla	23	19	14	3	6	56
(%)	(35.5)	(29.2)	(21.5)	(4.6)	(9.2)	(100)
3. Peddamasanpally	9	25	10	3	3	50
(%)	(18.0)	(50.0)	(20.0)	(6.0)	(6.0)	(100)
Total	72	121	61	28	23	305
	(23.6)	(39.7)	(20.0)	(9.2)	(7.5)	(100)
East Godavari dist.						
4. Shankavaram	37	69	39	15	28	188
(%)	(19.7)	(36.7)	(20.7)	(8.0)	(14.9)	(100)
5. Vajrakutam	—	15	26	11	18	70
(%)		(21.4)	(37.1)	(15.7)	(25.8)	(100)
6. Balarampuram	28	18	4	—	—	50
(%)	(56.0)	(36.0)	(8.0)			(100)
Total	65	102	69	26	46	308
	(21.1)	(33.1)	(22.4)	(8.4)	(15.0)	(100)
Grand Total	137	223	130	54	69	613
	(22.3)	(36.4)	(21.2)	(8.8)	(11.3)	(100)

Note: Figures in parenthesis indicate percentages.

Shankavaram, 38.2 per cent in Vajrakutam get more than three rupees, but none from Balarampuram is in this income group.

The Appendix-II.5 presents the nature of the labour in the sample. This indicates that 15.7 per cent depend on their own cultivation ; the rest of them depend on various other forms of labour. Those who depend solely on their labour constitute 22.2 per cent. A further division of the labour indicates that 3.5 per cent are attached labourers, 1.7 per cent are contract labourers and 17.0 per cent are daily wage earners. This means that among the forms of labour, the wage labour is predominantly in vogue. There are 11.4 per cent who depend on various other occupations other than agriculture and labour. The striking trend that the table indicates is that more than ⅓rd of the labourers depend on their own cultivation coupled with daily wage labour. This in turn indicates the uneconomic nature of the holdings which compel them to go for daily wage labour for their livelihood. About 12 per cent are found to be dependent on the combination of own agriculture and other petty business or own cultivation and other forms of labour (Appendix-II.6). The data regarding the combination of attached labour and cultivation with other sources of income further indicates the low income and employment that small holdings generate.

A discussion on other possessions of the respondents in these villages would throw more light on their economic conditions. Next to land, it is the livestock (Appendix-II.7) which occupies a prominent place in the rural areas. Therefore, the details about the animals possessed by the respondents are presented here.

The data reveals that 15.3 per cent households in Siddipet block and 33.4 per cent in Shankavaram do not possess any animal. The number in Shankavaram is double that of Siddipet. In Shankavaram while 9.1 per cent possess poultry units, in Medak it is only 0.9 per cent. 4.9 per cent households in Siddipet and 3.6 per cent in Shankavaram possess goat and sheep units. The number of respondents possessing milch cattle and bullocks and so on, is 64.3 per cent in Siddipet and 49.7 per cent in Shankavaram. The respondents having animals of all types constitute 14.3 per cent in Siddipet and 3.6 per cent in Shankavaram.

Villagewise analysis reveals that in the villages of Sirsingandla and Marpadga—relatively better covered villages—those who do not possess animals is lesser than Peddamasanpally where the number is as high as 24 per cent. However, an overwhelming majority (97.2 per cent) of the respondents in Vajrakutam possess animals.* In the villages of Shankavaram and Balarampuram 42.5 per cent in each of the villages do not possess any animal.

In the case of poultry units Marpadga—a better covered village—has three poultry units while the other two do not have even a single unit. In the case of Shankavaram block, Shankavaram and Vajrakutam villages possess 17 and 13 poultry units respectively. With regard to sheep and goat units, 4.2 per cent in Marpadga, 4.6 per cent in Sirsingandla and 8 per cent in Peddamasanpally possess them. In Shankavaram block 4.2 per cent in Shankavaram village, 4.6 per cent in Vajrakutam possess sheep and goat while there is none in Balarampuram.

In the villages of Marpadga and Sirsingandla 63.2 per cent and 70.8 per cent households respectively possess milch cattle. And in Peddamasanpally 60 per cent households have milch cattle. Similarly, in Shankavaram block 43.6 per cent in Shankavaram village, 62.6 per cent in Vajrakutam possess milch cattle. This number is 54 per cent in Balarampuram—the neglected village.

Those who possess all types of animals in the villages of Marpadga and Sirsingandla constitute 15.2 per cent and 16.9 per cent respectively while it is 8 per cent in Peddamasanpally. In Shankavaram block, in the villages of Shankavaram, Vajrakutam and Balarampuram, 0.53 per cent, 11.5 per cent and 4.0 per cent respectively possess all types of animals.

The details about the agricultural implements (Appendix-II.8) indicates not only the economic conditions of the respondents; but their overall equipment for cultivation. In Siddipet block 22.3 per cent of the households do not possess any agricultural implements while this number is as high as 56.8 per cent in Shankavaram block. With regard to the ploughs 6.9 per cent in Siddipet possess one plough while it is 22.8 per cent in Shan-

* The possible explanation for this phenomenon could be that this village is surrounded by hillocks and forest. This provides fodder facility for the animals which might work as a stimulus to maintain animals.

kavaram block. In respect of other agricultural implements, 46.9 per cent in Siddipet block possess two or more than two items of agricultural implements while only 6.8 per cent in Shankavaram have anything like agricultural implements.

The village-wise analysis reveals that from among those who do not have agricultural implements, the largest number in Siddipet block is from Peddamasanpally—the neglected village. In Shankavaram block this category is high both in Shankavaram and Balarampuram villages. In the case of respondents owing one plough, the number in Peddamasanpally and Balarampram is slightly larger. Peddamasanpally has 26 per cent households having two or more items. In Shankavaram block in the village of Shankavaram and Balarampuram the number is quite small. In Vajrakutam 20 per cent households have more than two implements. With regard to all types of implements possessed by the respondents, the data reveals that 26.3 per cent in Marpadga, 20 per cent in Sirsingandla and 20 per cent in Peddamasanpally possess all implements. In Shankavaram block, while in Vajrakutam village 55.7 per cent households possess all items, in Shankavaram and Balarampuram villages it is less than 2 per cent.

The data with regard to the possession of cart and bi-cycle, (Appendix-II. 9) has thrown up certain striking trends; 77.8 per cent in Siddipet, 66.5 in Shankavaram do not own any vehicle, in Siddipet and Shankavaram 14.0 per cent and 14.6 per cent respectively possess a cart, 4.6 per cent in Siddipet and 14.3 per cent in Shankavaram own a bi-cycle and 3.5 per cent in Medak and 4.5 per cent in Shankavaram own both a cart and bi-cycle. Villagewise analysis indicates that 80 per cent in Marpadga, 78.5 per cent in Sirsingandla and 68.0 per cent in Peddamasanpally do not own any vehicle. In Shankavaram block 69.7 per cent in Shankavaram village and 44.3 per cent in Vajrakutam do not have any vehicle. In Balarampuram—the neglected village—this number is as high as 86 per cent. In Peddamasanpally there are 20 per cent who possess carts. This situation is better when compared to Marpadga and Sirsingandla where it is 13.7 per cent and 10.8 per cent respectively. In Balarampuram—the neglected village—6 per cent own a bi-cycle and another 6 per cent a cart. The condition of the respondents in other two villages of the block seem to be better.

TABLE 2.7 : **Clothing particulars of respondents**

Sl. No.	Name of the village	Number of Clothes possessed by respondents: One pair	Two pairs	Three and more than three	Total
	Medak Dist.				
1.	Marpadga	143	43	4	190
	(%)	(75.3)	(22.6)	(2.1)	(100)
2.	Sirsingandla	24	35	6	65
	(%)	(36.9)	(53.8)	(9.3)	(100)
3.	Peddamasanpally	30	19	1	50
	(%)	(60.0)	(38.0)	(2.0)	(100)
	Total	197	97	11	305
		(64.6)	(31.8)	(3.6)	(100)
	East Godavari Dist.				
4.	Shankavaram	46	92	50	188
	(%)	(24.5)	(48.9)	(26.6)	(100)
5.	Vajrakutam	17	33	20	70
	(%)	(24.3)	(47.1)	(28.6)	(100)
6.	Balarampuram	30	17	3	50
	(%)	(60.0)	(34.0)	(6.0)	(100)
	Total	93	142	73	308
		(30.2)	(46.1)	(23.7)	(100)
	Grand Total	290	239	84	613
		(47.3)	(38.9)	(13.8)	(100)

Note: Figures in parenthesis indicate percentages.

The clothing—one of the basic necessities—possessed by the respondents reflects their living conditions (Table 2.7). For this purpose the data about clothing is collected from the respondents. This data indicates that in Siddipet 64.6 per cent and in Shankavaram 30.2 per cent possess only one pair of clothes to wear. Those who possess two pair of clothes constitute 31.8 per cent in Siddipet and 46.1 per cent in Shankavaram. Similarly, those who possess three pairs and above constitute 23.7 per cent in Shankavaram and 3.6 per cent in Siddipet block. In this regard the respondents in Shankavaram block are found to be in a better condition than their counterparts in Siddipet.

The village details indicate that 75.3 per cent in Marpadga, 60 per cent in Peddamasanpally and 36.9 per cent in Sirsingandla possess one pair of clothes. 24.7 per cent in Marpadga, 40 per cent in Peddamasanpally and 63.1 per cent in Sirsingandla possess two pairs or more than two pairs. 24.5 per cent in the village of Shankavaram another 24.5 per cent in Vajrakutam and 60 per cent in Balarampuram possess only one pair of clothes, This is similar to the situation obtained in Peddamassanpally. 75.5 per cent in Vajrakutam and 40 per cent in Balrampuram possess two or more than two pairs.

Analysis of the housing conditions—another basic necessity—of the respondents (Table 2.8) in the six villages has thrown up certain significant trends. 1.3 per cent in Siddipet and 1.6 per cent of respondents in Shankavaram have pucca houses. It means that in all around 97.1 per cent do not have pucca houses. The data further reveals that 83.6 per cent in Siddipet and 43.2 per cent in Shankavaram have houses with thatched roof. 14.1 per cent in Siddipet and 38.3 per cent in Shankavaram have huts. Further 1 per cent from Siddipet and 16.9 per cent from Shankavaram reported that they have no shelter. Housing seems to be a common problem of the respondents irrespective of the land ownership, development in the village and other economic conditions.

III

The universe of the study broadly reflects the overall backwardness of the rural areas selected for this study. At the level of district, although variations are striking between

TABLE 2.8 : **Housing particulars of respondents**

Sl. No.	Name of the village	Pucca house	Semi-Pucca house	Kutcha house	Others	Total
		Type of the House				
	Medak Dist.					
1.	Marpadga	4	156	28	2	190
	(%)	(2.1)	(82.1)	(14.7)	(1.1)	(100)
2.	Sirsingandla	—	57	7	1	65
	(%)		(87.7)	(10.8)	(1.5)	(100)
3.	Peddamasanpally	—	42	8	—	50
	(%)		(84.0)	(16.0)		(100)
	Total	4	255	43	3	305
		(1.3)	(83.6)	(14.1)	(1.0)	(100)
	East Godavari dist.					
4.	Shankavaram	5	100	45	38	188
	(%)	(2.7)	(53.2)	(23.9)	(20.2)	(100)
5.	Vajrakutam	—	21	39	10	70
	(%)		(30.0)	(55.7)	(14.3)	(100)
6.	Balarampuram	—	12	34	4	50
	(%)		(24.0)	(68.0)	(8.0)	(100)
	Total	5	133	118	52	308
		(1.6)	(43.2)	(38.3)	(16.9)	(100)
	Grand Total	9	388	161	55	613
		(1.5)	(63.3)	(26.3)	(8.9)	(100)

Note : Figures in Brackets indicate percentages.

East Godavari and Medak, at the block level the differences do not appear to be that striking. The Shankavaram block is situated in the backward upland belt of East Godavari district. In the two blocks, while numerical strength of the target groups is sizeable, the strength of these groups in Shankavaram has been three times more than in Siddipet. However, the scheduled caste population is almost equal in both the blocks. Population-wise land man ratio is three times more in Shankavaram comparred to Siddipet. The quality of land indicates that irrigated land constitute one third of the total land; in Shankavaram it is double that of Siddipet. These two blocks put together are representatives of the backward areas in the state.

As we have seen for a detailed study three sample villages from each district are selected. The criterion adopted in the selection of the villages was the extent of coverage of the target groups, subsidy released and schemes covered. Out of the three villages chosen one is from the largest coverage category, the second from average coverage category and the third belongs to the neglected category. The details relating to small and marginal farmers and agricultural labourers categories, scheduled caste population, land particulars, occupational pattern, male and female ratio in the population; cropping pattern, facilities presently existing at the village level and so on, are discussed to portray the overall rural conditions.

The general condition in almost all the six villages is dismal. The villagers do not have most of the basic necessities. The facilities that exist are not evenly distributed. It is interesting to note that some of the villages have facility of telephone exchange but not drinking water. The wage rate is not only very low but is discriminative between male and female workers. Further, in Siddipet block the daily wage ranges from Rs. 1.50 to Rs. 5 and in the case of Shankavaram block, it is between Rs. 3 to Rs 12. This indicates that the maximum in Shankavaram touches Rs. 12 and minimum Rs. 3 whereas in Siddipet it does not exceed Rs. 5 and goes as low as Rs. 1.50.

The land-holding position in the six villages shows that in the medium and rich peasant category there is virtually monopoly of the forward castes. In almost all the six villages the dominance of forward castes in the land ownership is noticed. The backward and the scheduled castes are found in the category of small and marginal farmers but not among the medium and big farmers. The data indicates skewed distribution of land among various caste groups. While the forward castes in Siddipet own big chunks of land, they are in sizeable number even among small and marginal farmers in Shankavaram.

The scheduled caste population ranges between 24 to 11.9 per cent in these six villages. The percentage of agricultural labourers is considerable in all the six villages. The irrigated land constitutes one tenth of the land in three villages, one fifth in two villages and about two fifths in one village. The current fallows range between 7 per cent to 15 per cent. And a major portion of the land in all the six villages is red soil; it ranges between 98 per cent to 58 per cent.

The six villages present a wide landscape covering various facets of rural socio-economic situation. Thus it is this wide spectrum that would make the study comprehensive and representative in character. Therefore, the conclusions emerging from the study may have wider relevance and help in understanding the development phenomenon in a larger perspective.

A comparison of the coverage of the target groups in the six villages with their socio-economic conditions, reveals that the SFDA benefits were extended to those villages which were endowed with better resources and facilities than the villages which were backward and handicapped by paucity of resources.

For a better understanding and greater insight, the detailed socio-economic conditions of the respondents are presented. Although such an analysis suffers from certain pit-falls owing to the purposive nature of the sampling, they do reflect the conditions of the target groups—both beneficiaries and non-beneficiaries

In respect of age most of the respondents are young or middle aged. The caste particulars indicate that the sample is drawn from all the three major caste groups, namely, scheduled castes, backward castes and forward castes. However, in the case of Shankavaram the representation of forward castes is quite high as the coverage of this group under SFDA scheme was larger. While the percentage of literacy among the respondents is quite low, it is slightly higher when compared to the overall literacy in their respective villages. Occupational details reveal that not only a large chunk of the respondents depend on their labour for livelihood, but even from the category of small and marginal farmers more than half of them in Siddipet and one third in Shankavaram treat agriculture labour either as a primary or secondary source of income. This reflects the non-viability of their farm size and poor quality of the land. Family particulars indicate that nuclear family is the dominant phenomenon. However, the joint family systems is more widespread among the Siddipet respondents than Shankavaram respondents.

The details of economic conditions present widespread poverty in the area. The income levels of the respondents reveal that 83.1 per cent in Siddipet and 76.6 per cent in Shankavaram are below the poverty line. The magnitude of poverty is further confirmed by the data that a large number of respondents including the small and marginal farmers depend on daily wage labour. The particulars of livestock—poultry, sheep and goat units, milch cattle—indicate that it has become an important source of livelihood in the rural areas although a sizeable number do not possess them. With regard to agricultural implements, 2/5th of the respondents do not possess any type of implement. Further 2/3rd of the respondents in Shankavaram and ¾ths in Siddipet neither possess a cart nor a bicycle. In matters of clothing and housing the conditions are equally dismal. About half of the respondents have only one pair of clothes and 4/5th of them have about two pairs of clothes. In respect of housing only a negligible 1.3 per cent in Siddipet and 1.6 per cent in Shankavaram have pucca houses and rest of them take shelter under thatched roof or hut.

The details of socio-economic conditions in the six villages of two blocks and the conditions of 613 respondents drawn from the two regions of Andhra Pradesh present an appalling picture of poverty. It also indicates that poverty is present among all the caste groups although its severity is higher among the scheduled and backward castes. This only indicates that the post independent development strategies—including anti-poverty policies like SFDA—have not made any significant dent on the living conditions of the rural poor. It is this phenomenon that calls for deeper analysis of the development phenomenon,

3

The SFDA : The Impact on Target Groups

The Small Farmers Development Agency, as stated earlier, was expected to cover over 50,000 households of the target groups during the plan period. It was also expected to enable the households to cross the poverty line through its developmental schemes. These target groups included, as pointed out earlier, small farmers, marginal farmers and agricultural labourers. The agency offered as subsidy 25 per cent to small farmers and 33.3 per cent to marginal farmers and agricultural labourers. The subsidy amount was intended to provide relief and stimulate investment by the cooperative and commercial banks in agriculture in the case of small and marginal farmers and in livestock or subsidiary occupations in the case of agricultural labourers. As the agency had completed the plan period and as the whole scheme has been converted into DRDA, it is time to evaluate its performance and examine its overall impact on the target groups.

It is widely known that the coverage of the three target groups has not been upto the mark. Even in the case of households covered by the agency the schemes could not make the intended impact. Research reports indicate that most of the schemes sponsored by the agency ran into difficulties, leaving the target groups in a stagnant situation, if not causing further deterioration in their living conditions. It is observed that in the total coverage the agricultural labourers were the most neglected. Here the impact of the agency on all the three target groups and the problems and processes involved therein are examined.

For the purpose of this study, the analysis is attempted at two levels, macro and micro. The macro analysis includes an examination of the performance of SFDA in the sixteen districts of Andhra Pradesh. This is done with the help of secondary data. Although it suffers from all the limitations that are associated with the secondary data, it throws up certain broad trends. For the micro level analysis the primary data from the two districts of Medak and East Godavari is used. An attempt is made to use both factual data and opinions of respondents mainly to assess the impact of the agency in respect of generation of additional employment and income to the target groups.

All the 16 small farmers' development agencies in Andhra Pradesh during their 10 years' existence ought to have helped ten lakh households to cross the poverty line. Of the sixteen agencies, four—in the districts of Srikakulam, Visakhapatnam, Nalgonda and Cuddapah—were started in the year 1970-71 and have completed two plan periods. In the districts of Adilabad, Khammam, Medak, Hyderabad, East Godavari and Nellore the agencies were established in 1974-75. These agencies ought to have covered 50,000 each, and entered the second phase with fresh targets. Again four agencies were set up in the districts of Karimnagar, Nizamabad, Warangal and Prakasam in 1975-76, which should have been on the verge of achievi the target of 50,000 each.

In a target of ten lakh households the total number of members covered accounted for 4.81 lakhs (Appendix-III. 1). This works out to 48 per cent. Of the households covered the small farmers constitute 1.67 lakhs, the marginal farmers 2.32 lakhs, and agricultural labourers 81.5 thousands. Among the farmers covered the largest number is that of marginal farmers followed by small farmers. The table shows that the coverage includes 17 per cent agricultural labourers and 28 per cent of scheduled castes. Out of the total of 56 lakh small and marginal farmers in Andhra Pradesh the target covered works out to seven per cent. From the 83 lakh agricultural labourers the target covered is less than one per cent.

The year wise coverage shows wide fluctuations. While in the year 1975-76, 1.26 lakh households were covered, in 1974-75 it was only 31.5 thousands. In the year 1977-78 86.6 thousands were covered which in the following years declined to

TABLE 3.1 : **The Achievement of targets upto 1979-1980**

Sl. No.	Name of the village	Year of inception	No. of Participants identified	No. of Participants covered	Average coverage per year
1.	Srikakulam	1970-71	1,35,787	94,182	9,418
2.	Vishakhapatnam	1970-71	1,31,384	65,531	6,553
3.	Nalgonda	1970-71	83,103	82,359	8,235
4.	Cuddapah	1970-71	51,225	24,735	2,473
5.	Adilabad	1974-75	36,828	10,508	1,751
6.	Khammam	1974-75	64,908	23,993	3,998
7.	Medak	1974-75	18,710	11,996	1,999
8.	Hyderabad	1974-75	49,056	23,479	3,913
9.	East Godavari	1974-75	81,705	39,439	6,573
10.	Nellore	1974-75	85,032	27,770	4,628
11.	Karimnagar	1975-76	31,319	18,088	3,617
12.	Nizamabad	1975-76	40,097	13,136	2,627
13.	Warangal	1975-76	29,173	10,406	2,081
14.	Prakasam	1975-76	38,843	20,204	4,040
15.	Krishna	1976-77	26,850	7,216	1,804
16.	Guntur	1976-77	40,723	7,857	1,964
	Total		9,44,473	4,81,415	65,679

52.4 thousands. Thus there has not been any yearwise consistency in the coverage of the targets under SFDA programmes.

A comparison between the total number of households identified and the number of beneficiaries actually covered reveals the following trends (Table 3.1). It is in Srikakulam that the largest number, that is, 1.35 lakh households were identified of which 94.18 thousands were covered. In Vishakhapatnam 1.31 lakhs were identified and 65.53 thousands were covered. In the districts of Adilabad, Warangal and Medak 36.8 thousands, 29.1 thousands and 18.7 thousands were identified of which 20. 81, 19.99 and 17.51 thousands were covered respectively. In all 9.44 lakh households had been identified but only 4.81 lakhs were covered. This shows that the agencies could not even identify households necessary for coverege, not to speak of achieving the actual target set for coverage.

From the point of view of each target group* (Appendix-III.2) in Srikakulam 26,365 small farmers, 47,104 marginal farmers and 14,262 agricultural labourers were covered. In the case of marginal farmers the highest coverage was in

Srikakulam followed by Nalgonda. In Vishakhapatnam while the number of agricultural labourers, that is, 26,438 covered was the highest, that of small farmers covered was the lowest, that is, 3,464. In the districts of Hyderabad and Warangal the coverage of small farmers was the lowest being 3,778 and 3,424 respectively. In the districts of Medak, Khammam and Adilabad, the marginal farmers covered numbered 4,689, 4,348 and 3,063 respectively. The largest number of agricultural labourers were covered in the districts of Srikakulam and East Godavari. The coverage of agricultural labourers has been very poor in the districts of Adilabad, Nellore, Nizamabad, Medak and Karimnagar — in particular the districts of Medak and Karimnagar, where it touched the lowest point.

The amount released (Appendix-III. 3) by the Central and State Governments to SFDAs which were started in 1970-71 shows that in the Fourth Plan period Srikakulam received

TABLE 3.2 : **Districtwise performance of SFDAs**

Sl. No.	Name of the agencies	Total No. of years	Average No. of beneficiaries covered	Average amount spent	Total No. of Programmes
				Rs. in Lakhs	
1.	Srikakulam	10	9,418	47.26	15
2.	Vishakhapatnam	10	6,553	21.19	12
3.	Nalgonda	10	8,235	40.25	11
4.	Cuddaph	10	2,473	16.57	8
5.	Adilabad	6	1,751	18.76	11
6.	Khammam	6	3,998	36.51	18
7.	Medak	6	1,999	20.32	12
8.	Hyderabad	6	3,913	29.78	17
9.	East Godavari	6	6,573	32.17	17
10.	Nellore	6	4,628	31.89	15
11.	Karimnagar	5	3,617	21.55	12
12.	Nizamabad	5	2,627	27.62	13
13.	Warangal	5	2,081	21.91	12
14.	Prakasam	5	4,040	23.59	20
15.	Krishna	4	1,804	17.39	12
16.	Guntur	4	1,964	14.00	8

* The data was available up to 1978-79. Therefore, the interpretation is valid up to that period.

Rs. 109.72 lakhs while Cuddapah got only Rs. 45 lakhs. During the period, 1974-1980, the total amount released to Srikakulam district was Rs. 470 lakhs whereas Cuddapah's share was only Rs. 165.78 lakhs. This is partly on account of the scale of utilisation of funds in the respective districts.

The SFDAs started in 1974-75 also had a similar experience in respect of grants. For instance, the SFDAs of Khammam and East Godavari got Rs. 219.09 lakhs and Rs. 213.06 lakhs respectively, while that of Adilabad got Rs. 122.16 lakhs. For the SFDAs started in the year 1975-76 Nizamabad got Rs. 138.12 lakhs and Karimnagar got only Rs. 107.79 lakhs. Although in principle the targets fixed and the subsidies given are uniform, the data conclusively proves that in the actual allotment the principle has not been adhered to.

It is evident from the data furnished above that under the SFDA programmes Srikakulam and Nalgonda received the highest amounts followed by Khammam and East Godavari districts. The districts that of Krishna and Guntur received the lowest amounts as they were only brought under SFDAs. The SFDAs in the districts of Warangal, Karimnagar, Adilabad and Medak, when compared to their counterparts in the other districts received lesser amounts in that order.

About the utilisation of the amounts (Appendix-III.4 and 5) the data reveals that in the Fourth Plan period four SFDAs, namely Srikakulam, Vishakhapatnam, Nalgonda and Cuddapah together had received Rs. 301 lakhs of which they spent only Rs. 184 lakhs. It means 117 lakhs (about 40 per cent) went unspent during this period. Except in the years 1974-75 and 1979-80 the amount utilised was far lesser than the actual amount released under the SFDA. Of the total amount of 2,869.29 lakhs, leaving an unspent balance of Rs. 449 lakhs. This subsidy of Rs. 449 lakhs would have generated a loan amount to the tune of Rs. 2,000 lakhs.

For the purpose of assessment a comparative analysis of the average coverage of the beneficiaries per year (Table 3.2) has been worked out. This indicates that the districts of Srikakulam, Nalgonda and East Godavari on an average covered 9,418, 8,235 and 6,573 beneficiaries per year respectively. The beneficiaries in Adilabad, Warangal and Medak covered by the SFDA number 1,751, 2,081 and 1,999 per year respectively. The average amount spent by these agencies in 16 districts of Andhra Pradesh also reflects their performance. In the districts of Srikakulam, Nalgonda, Khammam and East Godavari the average amount of subsidy released has been Rs. 47.26, Rs. 40.25, Rs. 36.51 and Rs. 32.17 lakhs respectively. In the districts of Karimnagar, Warangal and Medak the subsidy released has been Rs. 21.55, Rs. 21,91 and Rs. 20.32 lakhs respectively. In the districts of Adilabad and Cuddapah it has been Rs. 18.76 and Rs. 16.57 lakhs respectively. This indicates wide variations in coverage of the target groups and subsidy released to the sixteen agencies in the State.

More than 16 types of programmes were taken up in the districts of Prakasam, Khammam, Hyderabad and East Godavari. Twelve types of programmes were undertaken in the districts of Medak, Warangal, Karimnagar, Krishna and Vishakhapatnam. The other districts took up less than 11 types of programmes. Although the policy guidelines include around 28 schemes, the choice to take up the programmes appears to be restricted.

The SFDAs started during the Fourth Plan period disbursed a total amount of Rs. 400 lakhs up to 1975. The total loan amount sanctioned in 1975-76 by the commercial banks and co-operative institutions stood at Rs. 673 lakhs and Rs. 360 lakhs respectively. While the cooperative banks gave short term and long term loans, the commercial banks sanctioned medium term loans. In 1976-77 the cooperative institutions gave the maximum amount towards long term loans, while the commercial banks gave loans for medium term requirement. In 1977-78 the share of Khammam alone accounted for Rs. 1,197.25 lakhs.* In 1978-79 the cooperative institutions gave loans to the tune of Rs. 815 lakhs with greater emphasis on long term loans while the commercial banks released Rs 667.01 lakhs of which the medium term loans constituted Rs. 535.29 lakhs. In 1979-80 the cooperative institutions released Rs. 358 lakhs of which long term loans claimed a major share while commercial banks gave loans to the tune of Rs. 528.10 lakhs in which the share of medium term loans was as high as Rs. 506.30

---

* During this period the Chief Minister of Andhra Pradesh was from Khammam who is reported to have evinced keen interest in development of Khammam.

lakhs (Appendix-III.5, III.6, III.7).

In the year 1975-76 the highest amount, namely Rs. 577.59 lakhs from both the cooperative and commercial banks was received by Nalgonda and the lowest, namely Rs. 1.75 lakhs and Rs. 3.37 lakhs by Adilabad and Medak respectively. The difference between the highest and lowest amounts is about 300 times. In 1976-77 East Godavari got the highest amount, namely Rs. 140.30 lakhs from both the cooperative and commercial banks followed by Srikakulam, Cuddapah, Vishakhapatnam, Adilabad and Medak which received Rs. 7.83 Rs. 22.65, Rs. 24.71 and Rs. 36.63 lakhs respectively (Appendix-III.8). Karimnagar could get only Rs. 4.46 lakhs. The difference between the highest and the lowest amounts is about 45 times. In the year 1977-78 Khammam got Rs. 1,231 lakhs which accounted for more than 55 per cent of the total loan amount released that year for the whole of the State. East Godavari got Rs. 147.64 lakhs and the districts of Cuddaph, Adilabad and Medak got Rs. 10.62, Rs. 36.19 and Rs. 45.61 lakhs respectively during 1977-78. The difference between the lowest and the highest amount is 123 times. In 1978-79 East Godavari got Rs. 252.63 lakhs followed by Khammam. And the districts of Cuddaph, Nellore, Warangal and Medak got Rs. 9.54, Rs. 41.73, Rs. 20.61 and 60.75 lakhs respectively. In the year 1979-80 Srikakulam and Nalgonda each received about Rs. 200 lakhs as loans followed by East Godavari which got Rs 157.26 lakhs. The districts of Nellore, Karimnagar and Medak got Rs. 22.44, Rs. 38.71 and Rs. 16.53 lakhs respectively.

The enrolment of members of the target groups as members of cooperatives under SFDA since its inception is presented here. Cooperatives are considered to be effective devices for promoting participation and development. During the entire period they enrolled 2,03,856 as members of co-operatives. Yearwise enrolment indicates that in the year 1976-77 the maximum number was enrolled. Districtwise data shows that the districts of Visakhapatnam, Srikakulam, Nellore and Nalgonda enrolled the maximum number of members in that order. The enrolment of the small farmers in the districts of Warangal, Khammam, Adilabad and Medak has been unimpressive as the total number of small farmers enrolled was only

77,452. The largest number of small farmers were enrolled in the districts of Srikakulam, Nalgonda, Hyderabad and East Godavari and the smallest in the districts of Guntur, Krishna, Warangal, Medak, Khammam and Karimnagar in that order (Appendix-III.9) Of the marginal farmers the largest number was enrolled in Nellore followed by Vishakhapatnam, Srikakulam, Nalgonda and Prakasam and the smallest in Guntur, Warangal, Khammam, Adilabad, Nizamabad and Karimnagar. The total number of marginal farmers enrolled was 98,834. Thus immense variations among the sixteen SFDAs in Andhra Pradesh even in the enrolment of the members of cooperatives are noticeable (Appendix-III.10).

The agricultural labourers are the most neglected of the three target groups. One of the ways of helping the agricultural labourers is through co-operative institutions. Therefore, the enrolment of agricultural labourers as members of co-operatives is important to national reconstruction. An analysis of their enrolment reveals that in the districts of Srikakulam, Vishakhapatnam and East Godavari it was 8,599, 7,716 and 1,678 respectively (Appendix-III.11 & III.12). In the districts of Adilabad, Khammam, Karimnagar, Nellore, Nizamabad and Warangal it was negligible. During the entire period in the district of Medak only 37 agricultural labourers were enrolled as members of co-operatives. In all the 16 SFDA districts enrolled 25,611 agricultural labourers during the past 10 years (Appendix-III.13, III.14 & III.15).

The macro analysis of all the 16 SFDAs in the State indicates wide fluctuations in not only the release of amounts from year to year but also from district to district. Wide variations are noticed in the coverage of the target groups from year to year and from district to district. The wide gap in the performance of the 16 SFDAs need to be investigated in order to obtain clues for greater understanding of the phenomenon. On the whole, the achievement is far below the targets set both in terms of coverage and of utilisation of the subsidy amounts. The coverage of the targets is less than half of what was expected. Huge subsidy amounts which could have generated a loan amount of Rs. 2,000 lakhs remained unspent. This shows big gap between promise and performance in an anti-poverty oriented public policy which was launched with high expectations. It is obvious that it could not be implemented with full vigour.

II

In the two districts selected for the purpose of this study, the blockwise performance of the agency is discussed. In the district of Medak during 1975-81 period in all the seven blocks adopted by the agency the total number of persons identified (Table 3.3) has been 24,442 of which 10,697 were benefited. This achievement judged against the target of 50,000 households to be covered during this period works out to only 20 per cent.

TABLE 3.3 : **Blockwise performance of SFDA in Medak district from 1975-81**

Sl. No.	Name of the block	Total outlay from 1975-81	Total No. of persons identified from 1975-81	Total No. of persons benefitted from 75-81
1.	Ramayanpet	83,84,983	6,728	2,275
2.	Medak	82,58,265	5,895	3,283
3.	Dubbak	41,11,581	3,974	1,916
4.	Siddipet	25,44,643	3,220	1,711
5.	Jogipet	18,70,996	3,513	1,126
6.	Narsapur	5,36,589	643	175
7.	Gajwel	4,01,105	469	211
		2,61,08,162	24,442	10,697

The SFDA in the district of Medak during the five years of its existence (Table 3.4) identified 11,106 small farmers which included 2,555 scheduled castes and 499 scheduled tribes. It identified 10,078 marginal farmers of which scheduled castes numbered 3,644 and scheduled tribes 231. Of the 818 agricultural labourers identified 349 were scheduled castes and 43 were scheduled tribes. Yearwise coverage indicates that in the year 1975-76, 606 households were identified which in 1976-77 rose upto 6,260 and in 1977-78 to 6,800. It started declining from 1978-79 when it touched 5,044 and further declined in 1979-80 to 3,292 (Appendix III-14.)

The blockwise identification shows that in Medak block 5895 persons were identified of which 3,283 were covered

TABLE 3.4 : **Number of farmers identified since inception of the agency under SFDA programme in Medak dist**

(*Caste-wise*)

Sl.		Small Farmers					Marginal Farmers					Agricultural Labourers					TOTAL				
No.	Year	S.C	S.T	B.C	O.C	Total	S.C	S.T	B.C	O.C	Total	S.C	S.T	B.C	O.C	Total	S.C	S.T	B.C	O.C	Total
1	1975-76	57	—	145	51	253	148	—	155	28	331	6	—	12	4	22	211	—	312	83	606
2	1976-77	879	14	2,203	285	3,381	1,205	3	1,425	159	2,792	70	—	15	2	87	2,154	17	3,643	446	6260
3	1977-78	818	139	2,252	381	3,590	1,119	39	1,622	175	2,955	172	3	77	3	255	2,109	181	3,951	559	6800
4	1978-79	557	193	1,539	269	2,558	780	96	1,248	153	2,277	54	3	147	5	209	1,391	292	2,934	427	5044
5	1979-80	244	153	790	137	1,324	392	93	1,100	138	1,723	47	37	129	32	245	683	283	2,019	307	3292
	TOTAL	2,555	499	6,929	1,123	11,106	3,644	231	5,550	653	10,078	349	43	380	46	818	6,548	773	12,859	1,822	22,002

while in Ramayanpet block the total number identified was 6,728 of which 2,275 were covered. In Gajwel and Narsapur blocks the number of persons identified was 469 and 643 respectively of which those actually covered numbered only 211 and 175 respectively. A comparison of the highest with the lowest coverage in the seven blocks indicates a twenty times difference. With regard to the total outlay while Ramayanpet and Medak block had an outlay of Rs. 83.85 and Rs. 82.58 lakhs respectively, the blocks of Gajwel and Narsapur had an outlay of only Rs. 4.01 and Rs. 5.36 lakhs respectively. In terms of coverage and outlay the Siddipet block was found to be at mid-point. It had an outlay of Rs. 25.44 lakhs and identified 3,220 households of which those actually covered were 1,711. Therefore, the Siddipet block was selected for our study.

In East Godavari of the seven blocks covered by the SFDA in all 81,705 were identified*. The actual number covered by the end of 1980 has been 19,606, of which 3,681 were from Pithapuram 3,105 from Shankavaram and 3,075 from Rajanagaram. In Korukonda, Rangampet and Tuni blocks, the coverage was 1566, 2,488 and 2,766 respectively. Thus the coverage among the blocks in East Godavari also has not been even (Table 3.5).

The subsidy released indicates that the Tuni, Pithapuram and Peddapuram blocks got highest share—17.08, 15.74 and 14.54 lakhs respectively. The Rajanagaram, Rangampet and Korukonda blocks received only 5.84, 5.79 and 4.38 lakhs respectively. The Shankavaram block which got 14.38 lakhs stands exactly at the midpoint among all the seven blocks covered by the SFDA in the district of East Godavari in terms of subsidy though not of coverage; since the subsidy is considered a criterion for the purpose of assessing the impact.

Of the 19.600 beneficiaries, 3,892 were small farmers, 7,825 were marginal farmers and 7,035 were agricultural labourers. This works out to 26 per cent small farmers, 41 per cent marginal farmers and 31 per cent agricultural labourers. The overall achievement in relation to the 50,000 target set stands at 40 per cent. The coverage of agricultural labourers in this

---

* In East Godavari the identification of the target groups has been far higher than the actual expected number.

TABLE 3.5 : **Statement showing blockwise subsidy released and farmers covered in East Godavari district SFDA 1975-80**

Sl. No.	Name of the Block	Minor irrigation lakhs	Animal husbandry lakhs	Agriculture lakhs	Fisheries lakhs	Other schemes lakhs	Total subsidy lakhs	S.F. coverage	M.F. coverage	A.L. coverage	Total coverage of beneficiaries
1.	Tuni	4.52	5.60	1.96	5.00	—	17.08	598	144	702	2,766
2.	Pithapuram	2.37	7.98	2.70	1.48	1.21	15.74	802	969	1,644	3,681
3.	Peddapuram	3.36	8.71	2.40	—	0.07	14.54	385	940	1,281	2,925
4.	Shankavaram	3.30	7.58	2.91	—	0.59	14.38	874	1,263	914	3,105
5.	Rajanagaram	2.22	2.21	1.03	0.20	0.18	5.84	398	1,249	1,353	3,075
6.	Rangampeta	1.04	1.63	2.75	0.06	0.31	5.79	524	1,111	736	2,488
7.	Korukonda	0.28	2.72	1.38	—	—	4.38	311	850	405	1,566
	Grand Total	17.09	36.43	15.13	6.74	2.36	77.75	3,892	7,825	7,035	19,606

TABLE 3.6 : **Awareness of the Programmes**

Sl. No.	District Respondents	One programme			Two and three programmes			Four and above programmes			Total
		SF	MF	AL	SF	MF	AL	SF	MF	AL	
	Medak										
1.	Beneficiaries	5	2		35	34	2	71	59	4	212
	(%)	(2.5)	(0.9)		(16.5)	(16.0)	(0.9)	(33.5)	(27.8)	(1.9)	(100)
2.	Non-beneficiaries	4	3	3	13	15	8	18	19	10	93
	(%)	(4.3)	(3.2)	(3.2)	(14.0)	(16.1)	(8.6)	(19.4)	(20.4)	(18.8)	(100)
	Total	9	5	3	48	49	10	89	78	14	305
		(3.0)	(1.6)	(1.0)	(15.7)	(16.1)	(3.3)	(29.2)	(25.6)	(4.6)	(100)
	East Godavari										
3.	Beneficiaries	3	6	9	18	46	49	33	28	13	105
	(%)	(1.5)	(2.9)	(4.4)	(8.8)	(22.4)	(23.9)	(16.1)	(13.7)	(6.3)	(100)
4.	Non-beneficiaries	1	3	11	14	15	16	18	16	9	103
	(%)	(1.0)	(2.9)	(10.7)	(13.6)	(14.6)	(15.5)	(17.5)	(15.5)	(8.7)	(100)
	Total	4	9	20	32	61	65	51	44	24	308
		(1.3)	(2.9)	(6.5)	(10.4)	(19.1)	(21.1)	(16.6)	(14.3)	(7.8)	(100)
	Grand total										
5.	Beneficiaries	8	8	9	53	80	51	104	87	14	417
	(%)	(1.9)	(1.9)	(2.2)	(12.7)	(19.2)	(12.2)	(24.9)	(20.9)	(4.1)	(100)
6.	Non-beneficiaries	5	6	14	27	30	24	36	35	19	196
	(%)	(2.6)	(3.1)	(7.1)	(13.8)	(15.3)	(12.2)	(18.4)	(17.9)	(9.7)	(100)
	Total	13	14	23	80	110	75	140	122	26	613
		(2.1)	(2.3)	(3.8)	(13.1)	(17.9)	(12.2)	(22.8)	(19.9)	(4.2)	(100)

Note : Figures in brackets indicate percentages

district has been relatively far better than in Medak.

III

To know the micro level position an analysis of the impact of the agency on target groups is done. The respondents were asked adout the schemes that the government had undertaken for the benefit of the rural poor. All the beneficiaries stated (Table 3.6) that they were aware of the programmes. They were asked to list the programmes they were aware of. In response to that they listed minor irrigation schemes such as the digging of a new well, the repairing of old well, electric motor and oil engine; livestock schemes such as milch cattle, sheep and goat,

TABLE 3.7: **Awareness of SFDA**

Sl. No.	District	Heard SF	Heard MF	Heard AL	Not Heard SF	Not Heard MF	Not Heard AL	Total
1.	Medak Dist.							
	Beneficiaries	77	62	3	34	33	4	212
	(%)	(36.3)	(29.3)	(0.9)	(16.0)	(15.6)	(1.9)	(100)
	Non-beneficiaries	16	23	10	19	14	11	93
	(%)	(17.2)	(24.7)	(10.8)	(20.4)	(15.1)	(11.8)	(100)
	Total	93	85	12	53	47	15	305
		(30.4)	(27.8)	(3.9)	(17.3)	(15.4)	(4.9)	(100)
2.	East Godavari Dist.							
	Beneficiaries	39	54	37	15	26	34	205
	(%)	(19.1)	(26.3)	(18.0)	(7.3)	(12.7)	(16.6)	(100)
	Non-beneficiaries	18	20	19	15	14	17	103
	(%)	(17.5)	(19.4)	(18.4)	(14.5)	(13.6)	(16.5)	(100)
	Total	57	74	56	30	40	51	308
		(18.6)	(24.0)	(18.1)	(9.8)	(12.9)	(16.6)	(100)
	Two Districts Total							
	Beneficiaries	116	116	39	49	59	38	417
	(%)	(27.8)	(27.8)	(9.4)	(11.8)	(14.1)	(9.1)	(100)
	Non-beneficiaries	34	43	29	34	28	28	196
	(%)	(17.3)	(21.9)	(14.4)	(17.3)	(14.2)	(14.2)	(100)
	Total	150	159	68	83	87	66	613
		(24.4)	(25.9)	(11.4)	(13.5)	(14.1)	(10.7)	(100)

Note : Figures in brackets indicate percentages.

and poultry units, and so on, and other schemes like those involving house sites and land distribution. The data shows that the number of persons who mentioned only one programme was negligible being 5.6 per cent in Medak and 8.8 per cent in East Godavari. 35.1 per cent in Medak and 50.6 per cent in East Godavari could mention two to three programmes. 59.9 per cent from Medak and 49.7 per cent from East Godavari mentioned more than four programmes. If the number of programmes enumerated by the respondents is any indication of the awareness, their awareness is higher in Medak than in East Godavari.

About the awareness of the general developmental programmes sponsored by the government, the data indicates that all the non-beneficiaries were also in the know of the programmes. In Medak 10.7 per cent were aware of one programme, 14 per cent of two, 24.8 per cent of three, 31.2 per cent of four and 19.3 per cent of five or more programmes. In East Godavari 14.5 per cent were aware of one programme, 17.5 per cent of two, 26.6 per cent of three, 25.2 per cent of four, and 16.2 of five or more programmes. The data further shows that the awareness of the developmental programmes is slightly higher among the small and marginal farmers than among the agricultural labourers (Table 3.7).

To a question whether the respondents had known of the SFDA, 65.6 per cent from Medak and 63.1 per cent from East Godavari answered that they knew of the existence of the agency, but 34.4 per cent in Medak, 36.9 per cent in East Godavari had not heard about the agency at all. This ignorance of the target groups can be traced partly to the institution of the middle-man, since most of the respondents sought the schemes through the middle-man. It is no wonder that they do not know the exact agency which gives them the schemes.

Among the non-beneficiaries only 52.7 per cent in Medak and 55.3 per cent in East Godavari had heard of the SFDA. On the whole only 53.6 per cent knew of the agency and the level of awareness is almost equitably distributed among all the categories of respondents.

The respondents who had heard of the SFDA were asked about the objectives of the agency. An overwhelming number of them regarded the provision of subsidy to the poor people as the main objective followed by improving the conditions of the poor. A few respondents listed the schemes sponsored by the agency. The subsidy component attracted the attention of the target groups more than the other and more serious objectives associated with the schemes.

An analysis of the schemes (Table 3.8) extended to the beneficiaries in Medak reveals that 6.1 per cent of small and 5.0 per cent of marginal farmers got loans for the repair of old wells. 4.4 per cent of small and 2.2 of marginal farmers got oil engines and 16.1 per cent of small and 11.1 per cent of marginal farmers got electric motors. 5.0 per cent of small and 7.7 per cent of marginal farmers got other schemes pertaining to minor irrigation. In all 32.2 per cent and 27.8 per cent of the schemes are secured by the small and marginal farmers respectively. There are three agricultural labourers (1.7%) in Medak who secured schemes related to minor irrigation. Ironically they got included under either small farmers or marginal farmers category because they secured the scheme when they had land but having subsequently lost it they got pushed into the category of agricultural labourers. Under animal husbandry schemes 2.7 per cent of small and 3.3 per cent of marginal farmers got sheep units. The agricultural schemes are distributed as follows : 1.7 per cent of small and 1.1 per cent of marginal farmers got carts and bullocks, 4.4 per cent of small and 4.4 per cent marginal farmers and 0.5 per cent of agricultural labourers got plough bullocks, 3.3 per cent of small and 1.6 per cent of marginal farmers got agricultural implements, 3.3 per cent of small and 2.2 per cent of marginal farmers got land improvement schemes.

The data shows that in Medak it is only the small and marginal farmers who could avail themselves of the schemes while agricultural labourers remained neglected.

In East Godavari 2.6 per cent of small and 3.2 per cent of marginal farmers got new wells. From among the small farmers 1.3 per cent got loans for the repair of old wells, and 1.9 per cent got oil engine and none an electric motor. Under the animal husbandry programmes, 11.6 per cent of small and 27.2 per cent of marginal farmers and 22.7 per cent of agricultural labourers got milch cattle. 0.6 per cent of small and 1.3 per cent of marginal farmers got sheep units. 1.3 per cent of marginal farmers and 0.6 per cent of agricultural labourers secured poultry units.

TABLE 3.8 : **Scheme and category-wise benefit particulars**

District	Minor Irrigation						Animal Husbandry					Agriculture					Others		
Category	Well	Well dig-ging	Oil eng-ine	Electric motor	Ors.	Total	Milch cattte	Sheep	Poul-try	Ors.	Total	Cart & bul-locks	Plo-ugh & bul-locks	Sprayer	Land develop-ment	Total	Se-wing machine nylon nets	Total	Grand total
Medak																			
S F	14	3	8	29	9	63	5	10			15	3	8	6	6	23			101
(%)	13.9	3.0	7.9	28.7	8.9	62.4	5.0	9.9			14.9	3.0	7.9	5.9	5.9	22.8			100.0
M F	13		4	20	14	51	6	5		2	13	2	8	3	4	17			81
(%)	16.0		4.9	24.7	17.3	63.0	7.4	6.2		2.3	16.0	2.3	9.9	3.7	4.9	21.0			100.0
A L		1	1	1		3							1	1	1	3			6
(%)		16.7	16.7	16.7		50.0							16.7	16.7	16.7	50.0			100.0
Total	27	4	13	50	23	500	11	15		2	28	5	17	10	11	43			188
(%)	14.4	2.1	6.9	26.6	12.2	62.2	5.9	8.0		1.1	14.9	2.7	9.0	5.3	5.9	22.9			100.0
East Godavari																			
S F	4	2	3			9	18	3	2		23	4	3			7	5	5	44
(%)	9.1	4.5	6.8			20.5	40.9	6.8	4.5		52.3	9.1	6.8			15.9	11.4	11.4	100.0
M F	5					5	42	2			44	7	6			13	2	2	64
(%)	7.8					7.8	65.6	3.1			68.8	10.9	9.4			20.3	3.1	3.1	100.0
A L							35		1		36	1				1	11	11	48
(%)							72.9		2.1		75.0	2.1				2.1	22.9	22.9	100.0
Total	9	2	3			14	95	5	3		103	12	9			21	18	18	156
(%)	5.8	1.3	1.9			9.0	60.9	3.2	1.9		66.0	7.7	5.8			13.5	11.5	11.5	100.0
Total	36	6	16	50	23	13.1	10.6	20	3	2	131	77	26	10	11	64	18	18	344
(%)	10.5	1.7	4.7	14.5	6.7	38.1	30.8	5.8	0.9	0.6	38.1	4.9	7.6	2.9	3.2	18.6	5.2	5.2	10.0

Multiple Answers for Medak

From agricultural schemes 2.6 of agricultural labourers got carts and bullocks. 1.9 per cent of small and 3.9 of marginal farmers got plough bullocks. The schemes relating to agricultural implements, land improvement, demonstration plots did not figure at all.

The data from East Godavari shows that while minor irrigation and agricultural schemes were extended to small and marginal farmers, about 65.5 per cent of agricultural labourers, unlike those of Medak, were covered under livestock programmes.

When the non-beneficiaries were asked about their attempts to get any of these schemes (Table 3.9) 46.1 per cent in Medak and 36.8 per cent in East Godavari reported that they had applied for the schemes. A large number of marginal farmers and agricultural labourers did not apply for the schemes at all.

Further questioning revealed that among those of the non-beneficiaries who applied for the loans the propensity to seek

TABLE 3.9: **The respondents applied for the schemes**

Sl. No.	Name of the Village	Applied			Not Applied			Total
		SF	MF	AL	SF	MF	AL	
1.	Marpadga	5	6	1	4	3	9	28
	(%)	(17.8)	(21.4)	(3.6)	(14.3)	(19.7)	(32.1)	(100)
2.	Sirsingandla	8	6	3	1	6	5	29
	(%)	(27.6)	(20.7)	(10.3)	(3.4)	(20.7)	(17.2)	(100)
3.	Peddama-sanpally (%)	7	6	1	10	10	2	36
		(19.4)	(16.7)	(2.8)	(27.8)	(27.8)	(5.5)	(100)
	Total Medak Dist.	20	18	5	15	19	16	93
		(21.5)	(19.3)	(5.3)	(16.1)	(20.4)	(17.2)	(100)
4.	Shankavaram	7	8	5	6	6	9	41
	(%)	(17.0)	(19.5)	(12.2)	(14.6)	(14.6)	(22.0)	(100)
5.	Vajrakutam	2	2	2	9	7	8	30
	(%)	(6.7)	(6.7)	(6.7)	(30.0)	(23.2)	(26.7)	(100)
6.	Balarampuram	4	6	2	5	5	10	32
	(%)	(12.5	(18.8)	(6.3)	(15.6)	(15.6)	(31.2)	(100)
	Total East Godavari Dist.	13	16	9	20	18	27	103
		(12.6)	(15.5)	(8.7)	(19.4)	(17.5)	(26.2)	(100)
	Total of two districts	33	34	14	35	37	43	196
		(16.8)	(17.3)	(7.1)	(17.8)	(18.9)	(31.9)	(100)

loans was more pronounced in the income groups of Rs. 300 — Rs. 1500 while it was largely absent among the lowest income brackets, that is, Rs. 0 to Rs. 300 and higher income brackets, that is above Rs. 1,500. Against the land holding variable the data indicates that those who have land have greater desire to make use of the loan facility than the landless (Appendix III-17 & 18). From the landless category as many as 95.1 per cent did not apply for the loans at all. Thus it is clear that the members of the target group at the economic rockbottom have not been able to avail themselves of the benefits of the scheme. However, it is significant that 40.1 per cent of the scheduled castes, who have some land, did seek the loans.

The respondents who had not applied for the schemes were asked the causes for not seeking the schemes. A majority of them stated that they were not aware of the types of the schemes that they were eligible for. Quite a few of them complained that there was no one to inform them about the schemes. Thirdly, they approached the Sarpanch, Pyraveekar and officials but none was willing to help them. Fourthly, fear of initial expenditure involved in getting the schemes prevented them from applying. Fifthly, they reported that they were scared of government loans as they witnessed cases of recovery in which even the doors of the house were taken away. There are also a few repondents who said that they were not eligible as the land records were not updated. Others said that outstanding loans rendered them ineligible for the loans. A few said that nobody was willing to offer surety for the loan. Four respondents said that they were advised to join a Harijan as partners for getting the scheme sanctioned which course they did not adopt.

Those respondents who applied for the schemes but did not get them were asked at what stage their applications were held up. Except for a negligible number almost all of them said that their applications were under "consideration" ; only a few said that their applications were processed but the final decision was not taken.

The respondents who attempted to get the schemes were asked about the approach adopted in getting them. 11.6 per cent from Medak and 5.3 per cent from East Godavari tried on their own; 44.2 per cent from Medak and 7.9 per cent from East

TABLE 3.10: **Difficulties in getting the schemes**

Sl. No.	Name of the village	FACED			NOT FACED			
		SF	MF	AL	SF	MF	AL	Total
	Medak Dist.							
1.	Marpadga	30	28		24	20	1	103
	(%)	(29.1)	(27.2)		(23.3)	(19.4)	(0.9)	(100)
2.	Sirsingandla	7	3		4	2		16
	(%)	(43.7)	(18.8)		(25.0)	(12.5)		(100)
3.	Peddamasanpally	2						2
	(%)	(100)						(100)
	Total	39	31		28	22	1	121
		(32.2)	(25.7)		(23.1)	(18.2)	(0.8)	(100)
	East Godavari Dist.							
4.	Shankavaram	12	35	14	11	15	33	120
	(%)	(10.0)	(29.2)	(11.7)	(9.2)	(12.5)	(27.5)	(100)
5.	Vajrakutam	13	12	1	3	1		30
	(%)	(43.3)	(40.0)	(3.4)	(10.0)	(3.4)		(100)
6.	Balarampuram	3	1					4
	(%)	(75.0)	(25.0)					(100)
	Total	28	48	15	14	16	33	154
		(18.2)	(31.2)	(9.7)	(9.1)	(10.2)	(21.4)	(100)
	Grand Total	67	79	15	42	38	34	275
		(24.2)	(28.7)	(5.5)	(15.3)	(13.8)	(12.4)	(100)

Note : Figures in brackets indicate percentages.

Godavari through a middleman; 4.6 per cent from Medak and 65.8 per cent from East Godavari through the V.D.O.;* 13.9 from Medak and 13.2 per cent from East Godavari through friends and relatives; 25.5 per cent from Medak and 7.9 per cent from East Godavari through others which included village elders, sarpanch, karnam and so on.

Further analysis reveals that those who depend on the 'pyraveekar' are young, backward caste, marginal farmers in the income group of Rs. 300 to Rs. 900 belonging to nuclear families. But those who depend on the extension agency are middle aged, small and medium farmers, in the higher income

* One V.D.O. in East Godavari is virtually a middle-man. See the Chapter 6 on Pyraveekar.

groups belonging to forward castes and joint families. This indicates that those who are on the upper rungs of social and economic ladder depend more on the extension agency while those on the lower rungs depend on the 'pyraveekar'.

The impact of an agency depends not only on the giving of schemes but also on the way they were implemented and subsequently maintained and therefore, it is important to discuss the problems of getting and implementing the schemes.

The respondents were asked about the difficulties faced in getting the scheme. 57.9 per cent of them from Medak reported difficulties, while 42.1 per cent did not face any difficulty. Those who faced the difficulties constitute 32.1 per cent of small and 25.7 per cent of marginal farmers. But 23.1 per cent of small and 18.2 per cent of marginal farmers and 0.8 per cent of agricultural labourers did not face any difficulties. In East Godavari 59.1 per cent stated that they faced problems in getting the schemes while others did not face any difficulty. From both the districts 59.5 per cent reported obstacles in getting the schemes, while 41.5 per cent faced no difficulty (Table 3.10).

With regard to the obstacles faced in getting the scheme, castewise data indicates that while a majority from all the castes reported difficulties, the number of forward castes is more than that of the backward and the Scheduled Castes in this category. In terms of land and income the data suggests that the members from the landless and medium farmers category (5.1 acres-10 acres) faced lesser difficulties than marginal, small and better-off farmers. And in respect of the income groups also a similar tendency is noticed.

When asked to spell the type of difficulties which they faced in this regard, the respondents complained of pilferages at various points. Some of them reported that initially they had to mortgage their vessels or had to part with their savings in the hope of getting the scheme. The second type of complaints concerned the delay in getting the schemes sanctioned. It was stated that they had to go several times to government offices for getting the schemes. The third type of difficulties are related to technical problems such as location of the spot for a new well, delay in getting the report from geologist and initial clearance for the well. In the case of electric motors the lack of coordination between getting the electric motor and the securing of electric connection was reported.

A specific question was asked about the length of delay in getting the schemes. It ranged between one month to more than eighteen months. In Medak 16.4 per cent. of beneficiaries said that it took one month, 19.9 per cent three months and 22.3 per cent six months. From the rest 19.8 per cent of respondents reported that it took one year and 21.5 per cent of them more than one year. In East Godavari 42.2 per cent said that it took one month, 33.1 per cent three months, 13 per cent six months, 8.4 per cent one year and 3.2 per cent more than one year. The delay is more in Medak district than in East Godavari. On an average while it took 7½ months to get a scheme in Medak, it was only 3½ months in East Godavari (Table 3.11).

When looked at castewise, the delay was more in the case of backward castes followed by that of the Scheduled Castes. In the case of forward castes more than 44 per cent of the cases are disposed of in less than three months. Looked at from the stand point of income, the data indicates that the more the income the lesser is the delay. In the income group of Rs. 0 to Rs. 300, 56 per cent of the cases are disposed of in less than three months, and in the income bracket of Rs. 1,500 and above a large number of cases, that is 68.2 per cent took less than three months. From the angle of delay 28.8 per cent of the cases belonging to Rs. 0 to Rs. 300 income category reported delay of more than six months, and so also 13.6 per cent in the case of Rs. 1,500 and above income group. But similar trend is not seen in the case of land holdings. On the contrary 80 per cent of the cases of the landless labourers were disposed of in less than three months, whereas only 43 per cent of cases having five acres or more belonged to this category. Thus the delay appears to be more in the case of backward castes, low income groups than in others.

To a question about the difficulties in implementing these schemes, 79 per cent from Medak and 75 per cent from East Godavari stated that they encountered difficulties while 21 per cent from Medak and 25 per cent from East Godavari stated that they did not face any difficulty. Comparatively, it appears that implementation of the developmental schemes is fraught with more difficulties than securing them. In both the districts more than 75 per cent of the beneficiaries encountered difficul-

TABLE 3.11: **Time taken to get the scheme sanctioned**

Sl. No.	Name of the village	One month			Three months			Six months			One Year			More than			Total
		SF	MF	AL	SF	MF	AL	SF	MF	AL	SF	MF	AL	SF	MF	AL	
1.	Marpadga	9	10	—	9	9	1	15	7	—	9	9	—	12	13	—	103
	(%)	8.7	9.7	—	8.7	8.7	1.0	14.6	6.8	—	8.7	8.7	—	11.6	12.6	—	100
2.	Sirsingandla	—	—	—	3	2	—	4	1	—	4	1	—	—	1	—	16
	(%)	—	—	—	18.7	12.5	—	25.0	6.2	—	25.0	6.2	—	—	6.2	—	100
3.	Peddamasanpally	1	—	—	—	—	—	—	—	—	1	—	—	—	—	—	2
	(%)	50.0	—	—	—	—	—	—	—	—	50.0	—	—	—	—	—	100
	Medak Dist Total	10	10	—	12	11	1	19	8	—	14	10	—	12	14	—	121
	(%)	8.2	8.2	—	10.0	9.1	0.8	15.7	6.6	—	11.6	8.2	—	10.0	11.5	—	100
4.	Shankavaram	15	22	22	6	18	13	—	4	9	3	2	1	—	3	2	120
	(%)	12.5	18.3	18.3	50.0	15.0	10.8	—	3.3	7.5	2.5	1.6	0.8	—	2.5	1.6	100
5.	Vajrakutam	3	2	—	6	7	1	4	3	—	3	1	—	—	—	—	30
	(%)	10.0	6.6	—	20.0	23.3	3.4	13.3	10.0	—	100	3.4	—	—	—	—	100
6.	Balarampuram	1	—	—	—	—	—	—	—	—	2	1	—	—	—	—	4
	(%)	25.0	—	—	—	—	—	—	—	—	50.0	25.0	—	—	—	—	100
	East Godavari dist Total	19	24	22	12	25	14	4	7	9	8	4	1	—	3	2	154
	(%)	12.3	15.6	14.3	7.8	16.2	9.1	2.6	4.5	5.8	5.2	2.6	0.6	—	1.9	1.3	100
	Total of two Dist.	29	34	22	24	36	15	23	15	9	22	14	1	12	17	2	275
	(%)	10.5	12.4	80	8.7	13.1	5.4	8.4	5.4	3.3	8.0	5.1	0.4	4.4	6.2	0.7	100

ties in the implementation of schemes (Table 3.12).

Further analysis of the data pertaining to the difficulties shows that castewise all the groups faced difficulties although the number of persons experiencing difficulties declines as their composition goes up the caste ladder. Of all the occupational groups 84.9 of agricultural labourers had difficulties in utilising the schemes. In the case of land and income variables the data indicates that cent per cent from the landless, but only 62.5 per cent in the case of 5 acre to 10 acre category, and 42.5 per cent in the 10 acre category and 42.5 per cent in the 10 acres and above category stated that they had difficulty in utilising the scheme. A similar trend is noticed with regard to the income also. The number of persons who reported difficulty registered a decline as their income level rose. While all the categories experienced difficulties the respondents from forward castes having more land and higher income were slightly in a better position in utilising the schemes than the landless.

TABLE 3.12: **difficulties in implementation of the schemes**

Sl. No.	Name of the village	FACED SF	FACED MF	FACED AL	NOT FACED SF	NOT FACED MF	NOT FACED AL	Total
	Medak Dist.							
1.	Marpadga	44	39	1	10	9		103
	(%)	(42.7)	(37.9)	(0.9)	(9.7)	(8.7)		(100)
2.	Sirsingandla	9	2		2	3		16
	(%)	(56.2)	(12.5)		(12.5)	(18.8)		(100)
3.	Peddamasanpally	1			1			2
	(%)	(50.0)			(50.0)			(100)
	Total	54	41	1	13	12		121
		(44.6)	(33.9)	(0.8)	(9.9)	(9.9)		(100)
	East Godavari Dist.							
4.	Shankavaram	18	44	38	5	6	9	120
	(%)	(15.0)	(36.7)	(31.7)	(4.2)	(5.0)	(7.5)	(100)
5.	Vajrakutam	7	3	1	9	10		30
	(%)	(23.3)	(10.0)	(3.4)	(30.0)	(33.3)		(100)
6.	Balarampuram	3	1					4
	(%)	(75.0)	(25.0)					(100)
	Total	28	48	39	14	16	9	154
		(18.2)	(31.2)	(25.3)	(9.2)	(10.4)	(5.8)	(100)
	Grand Total	82	89	40	27	28	9	275
		(29.8)	(32.4)	(14.5)	(9.8)	(10.1)	(3.3)	(100)

Note : Figures in brackets indicate percentages.

As for the nature of the difficulties faced in the implementation of the programmes, the following are the key issues. On the economic front the loan amounts were found to be insufficient as the cost of fodder and oil had gone up to a point which they could not afford. On the technical side, several of them found technical assistance too inadequate. For instance technology could not overcome the difficulty when a rock sheet obstructed the digging of a new well or when an electric motor broke down. The milch cattle scheme was not supported by veterinary facilities. The availability of fodder for the animal and the market for the sale of milk were not taken care of. Quite a few of them reported that the animals die for want of veterinary facilities. The failure of monsoon caused a lot of difficulty in some schemes. The unsuitability of geo-climatic conditions also accounted for failure of milch cattle schemes. Complaints about infrastructural facilities relate to ineffective linkage of the schemes to the other necessary facilities. Even the programmes of poultry and sheep rearing faced crises because of the inadequate infrastructural facilities. In terms of the economy, the family poverty and other domestic demands like marriages, ill-health of family members, social and religious rites, and so on accounted for the diversion of funds meant for the schemes. In certain cases they reported that they diverted the funds because they got unwanted schemes.

The following reports are typical of those concerning the difficulties encountered in implementing the schemes which pinpoint them :

—"while I was digging a new well, the work could not proceed beyond fifteen feet because of a rock sheet found at that level. By then Rs. 1,400 of the loan amount was spent. I incurred an additional expenditure of Rs. 200 which I borrowed at 24 per cent interest". About the selection of the spot for the well he reported, "I dreamt of the spot where the well was to be dug and saw water in the well. I offered prayers and launched the scheme which proved to be unsuccessful because of the rock sheet".

—"My electric motor got burnt up. I incurred an expenditure of Rs. 300 for nothing. It was discovered that the engine was not of good quality. I was forced to incur consi-

TABLE 3.13 : **Purpose of utilisation of the scheme**

Sl. No.	Name of the village	Intended Purpose			Un intended Purpose			Total
		SF	MF	AL	SF	MF	AL	
	Medak dist.							
1.	Marpadga	48	39	1	6	9		103
	(%)	(46.6)	(37.8)	(0.9)	(5.8)	(8.7)		(100)
2.	Sirsingandla	9	3		2	2		16
	(%)	(56.2)	(18.8)		(12.5)	(12.5)		(100)
3.	Peddamasanpally				2			2
	(%)				(100)			(100)
	Total	57	42	1	10	11		121
		(47.2)	(34.7)	(0.8)	(8.2)	(9.1)		100
	East Godavari dist.							
4.	Shankavaram	20	45	45	3	5	2	120
	(%)	(16.1)	(38.1)	(38.1)	(1.7)	(4.2)	(1.7)	(100)
5.	Vajrakutam	12	8	1	4	5		30
	(%)	(40.0)	(26.6)	(3.4)	(13.4)	(16.6)		(100)
6.	Balarampuram	3	1					4
	(%)	(75.0)	(25.0)					(100)
	Total	35	54	46	7	10	2	154
		(22.3)	(35.5)	(30.2)	(3.9)	(6.9)	(1.3)	100
	Grand Total	92	96	47	17	21	2	273
		(38.3)	(35.2)	(17.3)	(5.8)	(7.7)	(0.7)	(100)

Note : Figures in brackets indicate percentages.

derable loss in the process".

—"The buffalow fell sick. I spent Rs. 50 on taking it to the hospital. The doctor suggested that it should be given good and adequate fodder which was not available in the village. As a result it went dry and became a liability. In the process the calf died".

—"I could secure an electric motor after three years of prolonged trials".

—"Our seven sheep died of a disease which could not be diagnosed. We sustained a major loss and did not even get the insurance amount as there was nobody to help us".

—"We were given cashew-nut plants but could not water them during summer".

—"We were given nylon nets but could not fish as there was a lot of grass in the tank".

The respondents were asked a direct question about the utilisation of the loan (Table 3.13) for the intended purpose. Eighty two per cent from Medak and 88 per cent from East Godavari stated that they utilised the loans for the intended purpose while 18 per cent from Medak and 12 per cent from East Godavari admitted that they diverted it to other purposes.

The respondents who diverted the loans were asked the purposes for which loans were diverted. They referred to various needs. The loan given for an oil engine was used for buying a milch cattle, the loan for milch cattle for buying oil engine, and the loan for digging a well for the purchase of an electric motor. In a large number of cases loans were diverted for the purchase of land. A few said that since they already had milch cattle the loans given for this purpose were used for some other purpose. There were also cases where the loans were used for meeting domestic demands such as daughter's marriage, father's death rites, the clearing off of earlier loans and medical attention for members of the family.

The respondents were asked the reasons for diverting the loan to other purposes : They stated that (1) there were some domestic necessities which compelled them to divert ; (2) the technical problems either in digging the well or in getting electric connection made them divert the scheme ; (3) the drought and scarcity of fodder accounted for diversion ; (4) the animals were sick and therefore, they had to be sold ; (5) the loan was not sufficient for the purpose. Some of them also said that they used them for more useful purposes like developing the land and building some permanent assets for the households.

The beneficiaries were asked a direct question as to whether they had been benefited by the scheme or not. Villagewise analysis indicates that in the villages which received the maximum and the minimum attention a large majority stated that they were benefited. Castewise analysis indicates that while a majority of the respondents from the Scheduled Castes and forward castes stated that they were not benefited, about 60 per cent from the backward castes said that they were benefited. Occupation analysis shows that about 51 per cent of cultivators and 21.8 per cent of agricultural labourers stated that they were benefited. Income analysis indicates that in the lower income bracket, that is Rs. 0 to Rs. 300, only 33 per cent reported benefited, whereas in the income bracket of Rs. 1,500 and above, 63 per cent reported that they were benefited. In the middle income groups, 55 per cent in Rs. 300 to Rs. 900 category and 40 per cent in Rs. 900 to Rs. 1,500 category were benefited. Land ownership analysis indicates that more than half of the respondents were not benefited in the categories of landless and marginal farmers, where as from small and medium farmers while half were benefited the other half were not. In the case of those having 10 acres and above, 57 per cent reported that they were benefited from the programmes. To derive the benefit from the schemes the economic variables are more important than the social variables. The majority from the forward castes were not benefited whereas the majority from the higher income group and larger land holding class which included Scheduled and backward castes reported as having been benefited.

A question about the impact of the schemes on the rural poor was posed to the non-beneficiaries (Table 3.14). Of them 57 per cent in Medak thought that the poor were benefited while 26 per cent thought that they were not benefited. Seventeen per cent could not answer the question. In East Godavari 57 per cent thought that the poor benefited and 26 per cent could not answer the question. It is interesting to observe that a majority of the respondents thought that the schemes benefited the poor, although they themselves were not the recipients of the benefits.

The beneficiaries were asked to state what the impact of the schemes had been in terms of increase in income and additional employment which were the main objectives sought to be achieved through the SFDA. With regard to employment 26.2 per cent of small farmers of Medak stated that it created additional employment while 28.1 per cent said that there was no additional employment. From among the marginal farmers 22.3 per cent said that there was no additional employment while 21.5 per cent reported additional employment on account of the schemes.

The responses from East Godavari show that 9.1 per cent of small and 16.2 per cent of marginal farmers stated that there was additional employment while 18.1 per cent of small and 25.3 per cent of marginal farmers said that there was no additional employment (Appendix-III 19, III 20, III 21). In respect of agricultural labourers in East Godavari half of them

TABLE 3.14 : **The benefit from the schemes—opinion of the non-beneficiaries**

Sl. No.	District	BENEFITED				NOT BENEFITED				DO NOT KNOW				Grand
		SF	MF	AL	Total	SF	MF	AL	Total	SF	MF	AL	Total	Total
1.	Medak	19	19	15	53	10	11	3	24	6	7	3	16	93
	(%)	(20.4)	(20.4)	(16.1)	(57.0)	(10.8)	(11.8)	(3.2)	(25.8)	(6.5)	(7.5)	(3.2)	(17.2)	(100)
2.	East Godavari	21	23	15	59	6	4	8	18	6	7	13	26	103
	(%)	(20.4)	(22.3)	(14.6)	(57.3)	(5.8)	(3.9)	(7.8)	(17.5)	(5.8)	(6.8)	(12.6)	(25.2)	(100)
	Total	40	42	30	112	16	15	11	42	12	14	16	42	196
	(%)	(20.4)	(21.4)	(45.9)	(57.1)	(8.2)	(7.7)	(5.6)	(21.4)	(6.1)	(7.1)	(8.2)	(21.4)	(100)

Note : Figures in brackets indicate percentages.

reported additional employment while the rest said that there was no additional employment.

TABLE 3.15 : **Additional employment generated by the scheme**

Sl. No.	Name of the village	Generated			Not Generated			Total
		SF	MF	AL	SF	MF	AL	
	Medak dist.							
1.	Marpadga	26	21		28	27	1	103
	(%)	(25.2)	(20.3)		(27.2)	(26.2)	(1.0)	(100)
2.	Sirsingandla	5	5		6			16
	(%)	(31.3)	(31.3)		(37.5)			(100)
3.	Peddamasanpally	2						2
	(%)	(100)						(100)
	Total	33	26		34	27	1	121
		(27.2)	(21.5)		(28.1)	(22.3)	(0.8)	(100)
	East Godavari dist.							
4.	Shankavaram	11	20	24	12	30	23	120
	(%)	(9.2)	(16.7)	(20.0)	(10.0)	(25.0)	(19.2)	(100)
5.	Vajrakutam	3	5		13	8	1	30
	(%)	(10.0)	(16.6)		(43.3)	(26.6)	(3.3)	(100)
6.	Balarampuram				3	1		4
	(%)				(75.0)	(25.0)		(100)
	Total	14	25	24	28	39	24	154
		(9.1)	(16.2)	(15.6)	(18.1)	(25.3)	(15.6)	(100)
	Grand Total	47	51	24	62	66	25	275
		(17.1)	(18.5)	(8.7)	(22.5)	(24.0)	(9.1)	(100)

Note : Figures in brackets indicate percentages

In the village of Shankavaram from East Godavari the feeling that the schemes did not generate additional employment was high among the marginal farmers; and so also among the small farmers in the village of Vajrakutam. From the village of Balarampuram the respondents reported that the scheme had no impact on their employment front.

In the village of Marpadga in Medak a large number of marginal farmers felt that there was no additional employment. In Sirsingandla while small farmers reported stagnation in employment, all the marginal farmers reported additional employment. Two small farmers from Peddamasanpally had additional employment.

If an overall view is taken, it may be seen that 17.1 per cent of small farmers commented favourably while 22.5 per cent commented adversely on the capacity of these schemes to generate additional employment. 18.5 per cent of marginal farmers had favourably commented and 24.0 per cent adversely. From among the agricultural labourers 8.7 per cent made favourable comments and 9.1 per cent adverse comments. It can be observed that in all the categories a majority of them expressed themselves against the schemes having the capacity to generate additional employment. This feeling is more pronounced among the small and marginal farmers than among the agricultural labourers.

An examination of the data concerning additional employment in relation to socio-economic indicators shows that while 48.9 per cent from the Scheduled Caste respondents stated that there had been additional employment, only 47 per cent in the case of backward castes and 38 per cent in the case of forward castes thought so. (Appendix in III. 22, III 23, III 24). Agewise, it conclusively indicates that the comments of the young were more favourable than that of the middle aged and old since 63 per cent from the young age group reported additional employment while only 24 per cent in the middle age group and 12 per cent in the old group did so. The land income particulars reveal that a majority from all the three target groups reported that the schemes did not generate additional employment. However, within the target groups the landless reported additional employment. From those of 10.1 and above acre group 85.7 per cent stated that there had been no additional employment. In the case of income it is found that the more the income the lesser is the employment that the schemes could generate. It appears that the schemes generated employment to the lower strata of the socio-economic group while the better placed groups reported no additional employment.

Those who stated that there was additional employment were asked to detail the nature of additional employment. Broadly, the responses throw up four trends ; one, they could pull themselves out from the hired labour class and were able to work on their own lands ; two, the schemes reduced physical drudgery such as drawing water from wells and divert the surplus time so saved to other agricultural operations ; three, members

TABLE 3.16: **Additional income generated by the scheme**

Sl. No. Name of the village	Increased			Not Increased			Decreased			Total
	SF	MF	AL	SF	MF	AL	SF	MF	AL	
Medak Dist.										
1. Marpadga	23	18	1	25	22		6	8		103
(%)	(22.3)	(17.4)	(0.9)	(24.3)	(21.3)		(5.8)	(7.8)		(100)
2. Sirsingandla	4	3		4	2		3			16
(%)	(25.0)	(18.7)		(25.0)	(12.5)		(18.7)			(100)
3. Peddamasanpally	1			1						2
(%)	(50.0)			(50.0)						(100)
Total	28	21	1	30	24		9	8		121
	(23.1)	(17.3)	(0.8)	(24.8)	(19.8)		(7.4)	(6.6)		(100)
East Godavari Dist.										
4. Shankavaram	6	12	15	5	19	12	11	19	21	120
(%)	(5.0)	(10.0)	(12.5)	(4.2)	(15.8)	(10.0)	(9.2)	(15.8)	(17.5)	(100)
5. Vajrakutam	8	10		6	3	1	2			30
(%)	(26.6)	(33.3)		(20.0)	(10.0)	(3.3)	(6.6)			(100)
6. Balarampuram				3	1					4
(%)				(75.0)	(25.0)					(100)
Total	14	22	15	14	23	13	13	19	31	154
	(9.1)	(14.3)	(9.7)	(9.1)	(15.0)	(8.4)	(8.4)	(12.3)	(13.6)	(100)
Grand Total	42	34	16	44	47	13	22	27	21	275
	(15.3)	(15.6)	(5.9)	(16.0)	(17.1)	(4.7)	(8.0)	(9.8)	(7.6)	(100)

Note : Figures in brackets show percentages.

of the family like son or wife who were working on other's fields could get additional work on their own land ; and four, some of them could employ additional labourers for their work. There were also a few respondents who stated that they were able to manage the fields on their own and could do away with servants.

The second aspect examined related to the rise in the income. For this purpose the target groups were asked about the additional income the schemes generated. In the district of Medak 23.1 per cent of small farmers reported rise in income while 24.8 per cent stated that there was no additional income. 17.3 per cent of marginal farmers said there was additional income, 19.8 per cent stated that they did not have any additional income. Interestingly, 7.4 per cent of small and 6.6 per cent of marginal farmers from Medak reported fall in their income due to these schemes. (Table 3.16)

In the district of East Godavari 9.1 per cent of small farmers reported additional income while 9.1 per cent said that there was no additional income. 14.3 per cent of marginal farmers stated that there was no additional income. From among agricultural labourers 9.7 per cent reported their having got additional income while 8.4 per cent said that there was no additional income. 8.4 per cent of small farmers, 12.3 per cent of marginal farmers and 13.6 per cent of agricultural labourers reported a fall in their income due to these schemes.

On the whole, the overall conclusion is that 15.3 per cent of small, 15.6 per cent of marginal farmers and 5.9 per cent of agricultural labourers reported having received additional income while 16.0 per cent of small and 17.1 per cent of marginal farmers and 4.7 per cent of agricultural labourers stated that there was no additional income. There is another group of 8.0 per cent of small and 9.8 per cent of marginal farmers and 7.6 per cent of agricultural labourers who reported decline in their income due to these schemes.

With regard to the rise in the income, castewise analysis indicates that while the respondents both from the Scheduled Castes and forward castes stated that the income had neither increased nor decreased, a majority from the backward castes indicated a rise in income. While 32.3 per cent of the Scheduled Castes and 33 per cent of the forward castes reported decrease in the income, only 11 per cent of backward castes reported decrease in the income. In the case of land and income the data reveals that 2/3rd of the respondents in all the land-holding categories, except those belonging to that of 10 acres and above, reported either no increase or no decrease in the income. In the 10 acres and above category 57 per cent reported rise in the income. On the contrary, 40 per cent of the landless category reported fall in their income. A comparison between the employment and income data reveals that there is no relation between them, since those socio-economic groups which reported additional employment did not report additional income. It was vice-versa in the case of better-off sections.

The income particulars are further analysed to assess the impact of the schemes on the target groups. For this purpose a probe is made to see how many members crossed the poverty line. The poverty line was drawn at Rs. 600 income level and another at Rs. 960 income level. The data reveals that before the scheme was given, 57.8 per cent were below the poverty line at Rs. 600 income level and 74.3 per cent below that of Rs. 960 income level. This indicates that ¼th of the respondents were above the poverty line. Due to the SFDA schemes as per the data 57 per cent were below the poverty line at Rs. 600 income level and 78 per cent below Rs. 960 income level. This means that 5.5 per cent of small farmers crossed the poverty line at Rs. 600 income level and 2.7 per cent at Rs. 960 income level. It may, therefore, be said that the impact of developmental schemes has been very marginal in helping the small farmers to cross the poverty line.

Among the marginal farmers before the scheme was given 58.1 per cent were below the poverty line at Rs. 600 income level and 81.2 below Rs. 960 income level. After the scheme had been sanctioned, 59.8 per cent were below the poverty line at Rs. 600 income level and 81.2 per cent below Rs. 960 income level. About ¼th of the members were above the poverty line when they got the schemes. The analysis of impact indicates that there has been virtually no impact of the schemes on marginal farmers' category. In fact, at Rs. 600 income level 1.7 per cent of additional marginal farmers are pushed down below the poverty line.

In the case of agricultural labourers 63.3 per cent were

below the poverty line at Rs. 600 income level and 85.7 per cent below Rs. 960 income level. This indicates that even in this category 15 per cent were above the poverty line at the time of receiving the benefit. After getting the scheme 67.3 per cent were below the poverty line at Rs. 600 income level and 89.8 per cent below the Rs. 960 income level. It can be noticed that ironically, due to the schemes additional 4 per cent of the agricultural labourers joined the below poverty line category.

The analysis reveals that the impact of the schemes on small farmers was negligible and on marginal farmers nil. In the case of agricultural labourers it was negative. Although 15.3 per cent of small and 15.6 per cent of marginal farmers and 5.9 per cent of agricultural labourers reported that there had been a rise in their income, the rise was not enough for them to cross the poverty line.

To assess the overall impact of the SFDA on the target groups, a comparison of income levels of the beneficiaries, and non-beneficiaries is done (Table 3.17). This would reveal the differences in the income levels between the two groups—one, benefited by the agency; and two, not covered by the agency.

The data shows that in the category of SFDA beneficiaries those who were getting less than Rs. 960 (treated as poverty line) constitute 78 per cent in Medak and 74 per cent in East Godavari (Table 3.18). In the category of non-beneficiaries the number of persons belonging to this cotegory was 81.2 per cent in Medak and 81.6 per cent in East Godavari. The difference between the number of beneficiaries and the non-beneficiaries above the poverty line works out to 3.2 per cent in the case of Medak and 6.2 per cent in the case of East Godavari. This means that although beneficiaries were recipients of SFDA schemes their income level was no better than that of their counterparts in the category of non-beneficiaries. This in turn establishes that the schemes have had no impact on the target groups.

IV

An examination of the impact of SFDA reveals that it could not make the intended impact on the target groups. An attempt is made to examine the phenomenon with the help of empirical data. This data includes secondary data pertaining to all the sixteen Small Farmers' Development Agencies in Andhra

TABLE 3.17 : **Scheme and categorywise benefit particulars**

District	Minor Irrigation						Animal Husbandry					Agriculture					Others		
Category	Well	Well digging	Oil engine	Electric motor	Ors.	Total	Milch cattle	Sheep	Poultry	Ors.	Total	Cart & bullocks	Plough & bullocks	Sprayer	Land development	Total	Sewing machine nylon nest	Total	Grand Total
Medak																			
SF	14	3	8	29	9	63	5	10			15	3	8	6	6	23			101
(%)	39	30	79	287	89	624	50	99			149	30	79	59	59	228			1000
MF	13		4	20	14	51	6	5		2	13	2	8	3	4	17			81
(%)	160		49	247	173	630	74	62		23	160	23	99	37	49	210			1000
AL		1	1	1		3							1	1	1	3			6
(%)		167	167	167		500							167	167	167	500			1000
Total	27	4	13	50	23	117	11	15		2	28	5	17	10	11	43			188
(%)	144	21	69	266	122	629	59	80		11	149	27	90	53	59	299			1000
Godavari	4	2	3			9	18	3	2		23	4	3			7	6	5	44
(%)	91	45	68			205	409	68	45		523	81	68			159	114	114	1000
MF	5					5	42	2			44	7	6			13	2	2	64
(%)	78					78	656	31			688	105	94			203	31	31	1000
AL							35		1		36	1				1	11	11	48
(%)							729		21		750	21				21	229	229	1000
Total	9	2	3			14	95	5	3		103	12	9			21	18	18	156
(%)	58	13	19			90	609	32	19		660	77	58			135	115	115	1000
Total	36	6	16	50	23	131	106	20	3	2	131	17	26	10	11	64	18	18	344
(%)	105	17	47	145	67	381	308	58	09	06	381	49	76	29	32	186	52	52	1000

TABLE 3.18 **Impact on target groups in crossing the poverty line**

		Poverty Line AT Rs. 600				Poverty Line AT Rs. 960				Total
		Before the Scheme		After the Scheme		Before the Scheme		After the Scheme		
		BPL	APL	BPL	APL	BPL	APL	BPL	APL	
Minor irrigation	SF	30 (57.7)	22 (42.3)	26 (50.0)	26 (50.0)	40 (76.9)	12 (23.1)	37 (71.2)	15 (28.8)	52
	MF	25 (60.9)	16 (39.0)	29 (70.7)	12 (29.3)	34 (82.9)	7 (17.1)	35 (85.4)	6 (14.6)	41
	AL	1	0	1	0	1	0	1	0	1
Animal husbandry	SF	24 (63.2)	14 (36.8)	22 (57.9)	16 (42.1)	28 (73.7)	10 (26.3)	29 (76.3)	9 (23.7)	38
	MF	31 (56.4)	24 (43.6)	33 (60.0)	22 (40.0)	45 (81.8)	10 (18.2)	45 (81.8)	10 (18.2)	55
	AL	20 (55.6)	16 (44.4)	25 (69.4)	11 (30.6)	29 (80.6)	7 (19.4)	32 (88.9)	4 (11.1)	36
Agriculture	SF	5 (35.7)	9 (64.3)	5 (35.7)	9 (64.3)	9 (64.3)	5 (35.7)	8 (57.1)	6 (42.9)	14
	MF	10 (55.6)	8 (44.4)	6 (33.3)	12 (66.7)	14 (77.8)	4 (22.2)	13 (72.2)	5 (27.8)	18
	AL	2	0	2	0	2	0	2	0	2
Others	SF	4	1	4	1	4	1	4	1	5
	MF	2	1	2	1	2	1	2	1	3
	AL	8 (80.0)	2 (70.0)	5 (50.0)	5 (50.0)	10 (100)	0	9 (90.0)	1 (100)	10
Total	SF	63 (57.8)	46 (42.2)	57 (52.3)	52 (47.7)	81 (74.3)	28 (25.7)	78 (71.6)	31 (28.4)	109
	MF	68 (58.1)	49 (41.9)	70 (59.8)	47 (40.1)	96 (81.2)	22 (18.8)	95 (81.2)	22 (18.8)	117
	AL	31 (63.3)	18 (36.7)	33 (67.3)	16 (32.7)	42 (85.7)	7 (14.3)	44 (89.8)	5 (10.2)	49

Note : Figures in bracket represents percentages.

APL : Above Poverty Line

BPL : Below Poverty Line

Pradesh and primary data concerning two Small Farmers' Development Agencies of East Godavari and Medak. In addition 613 respondents were covered in two selected blocks of these districts.

The sixteen agencies in Andhra Pradesh during the seventies ought to have covered 10 lakh persons but covered only 4.8 lakhs which accounts for 48 per cent of the total target. In the total coverage small farmers constitute 1.67 lakhs, the marginal farmers 2.23 lakhs and agricultural labourers 81.5 thousands. This means that the coverage of agricultural labourers accounts for only 17 per cent. A comparative analysis of the performance of these agencies in respect of identification and actual coverage indicates not only wide fluctuations over the years but also wide discrepancies between one district and another. The release of subsidy and the sanctioning of the loans followed no pattern. While a uniform physical and financial target was fixed for all the SFDAs, striking diversities are noticed in their achievement.

In the district of Medak the coverage accounts for 20 per cent of the total target which includes a negligible percentage of (0.2%) agricultural labourers. In East Godavari the coverage was about 40 per cent with a sizeable number of agricultural labourers. While the coverage has been far from the goal, the impact on those who are covered appear to be negligible.

When the awareness of the respondents about the developmental programmes was analysed, about 2/3rd of the respondents were aware of the Small Farmers' Development Agency and the ignorance of 1/3rd of the target groups could be traced to the absence of direct contact with the agency. About the objectives of the SFDA the largest number of respondents mentioned the subsidy component of the loan. Although 2/3rd of them know of the SFDA, the main purpose of the agency was not known to the members of the target group.

Although the schemes are extended to the target groups, the way the schemes are formulated, implemented, and subsequently sustained determines the outcome of the programmes. The data reveals that about 2/3rd of the respondents faced difficulties in getting the schemes. Further analysis reveals that a majority from the forward castes having more land and income reported difficulties rather than the lower strata in getting the schemes. The nature of difficulties related to pilferages at various points, initial expenditure, delay in the processing of the schemes, and so on. An investigation into the delays reveals that while in Medak, on an average, it ranged between seven to eight months, in East Godavari it has been three to four months. The delay appears to be more in the case of backward caste low income groups.

In both the districts more than $\frac{3}{4}$th of the respondents reported difficulties in the implementation of the developmental schemes. The socio-economic group which reported lesser difficulties in getting the scheme reported more difficulties in the implementation of the schemes, whereas the upper strata which had difficulties in getting the schemes reported lesser difficulties in the implementation of the schemes. The nature of difficulties can broadly be classified as follows: On the economic side, the loans were found to be insufficient; on the technical front, the schemes were not adequately backed by appropriate technology. The inadequacy of infrastructural facilities was another factor widely reported. Added to it domestic necessities and poverty accounted for diversion of the funds. All the factors collectively rendered the policy ineffective.

With regard to the rise in employment, the responses indicate that more than half of them expressed that there was no additional employment. This feeling is more pronounced in the case of small and marginal farmers than in the case of agricultural labourers. The schemes appear to have generated additional employment to the lower strata of socio-economic group while the better placed groups reported no additional employment. In those cases where it generated additional employment, the respondents reported that their family had additional work.

About the utilisation of the loan 15 per cent of the beneficiaries reported that they did not utilise the loans for the intended purposes. Observational data raised this figure to higher point. They offered different explanations for this diversion. Poverty figured prominently as the main cause. Some of them stated that they diverted the loan for better purpose.

With regard to rise in the income a majority of the respondents reported that there was no additional income. On the contrary ¼th of the respondents stated that their income declined because of these schemes. Most of the respondents from lower strata reported that there was either no rise in the income or decrease in it. This further indicates that there is no tangible correlation between the employment and income. While those socio-economic groups which reported additional employment did not report rise in their income, they on the contrary, reported a fall in their income. Whereas a few landed and better income groups who reported additional employment reported rise in income. This means certain schemes generate additional work to the lower strata, particularly the landless, without additional income. The schemes failed in most of the cases on account of the technical inadequacies, failure of monsoon, inadequate infrastructural facilities and rise in the cost of inputs and domestic problems.

An analysis of income on account of the schemes shows that the schemes have hardly had shown any impact on the target groups. Categorywise the impact on small farmers was very little and on marginal farmers negligible. In the case of agricultural labourers it resulted in further impoverishment of this class. For the number who could cross the poverty line is absolutely negligible. A comparison between the income levels of beneficiaries and those of non-beneficiaries further confirms that the schemes had no impact on the target groups.

The investigation on impact of the agency reveals that the coverage has been far from the expected. The target groups covered were not educated about the goals. They had faced difficulties in getting the scheme and greater impediments in implementation. Absence of appropriate technology and inadequate infrastructural facilities appear to be key factors in the failure of the schemes: they generated work in certain cases but not income. Those who could cross the poverty line on account of the schemes are negligible. On the contrary, the agricultural labour class suffered a decline in the income thereby revealing the counter-productive impact of the schemes on target groups.

4

The SFDA : Viability of the Schemes

A NUMBER of schemes have been sponsored under SFDA to enable the poor to cross the poverty line. Basically these schemes are of three types; namely, the land based schemes; the animal husbandry schemes, and other miscellaneous schemes. The present study focuses its attention mostly on the first two types of schemes. It attempted to examine whether these schemes proved to be viable from the standpoint of generation of additional income and of employment. The viability depends upon the nature of the scheme, the infrastructural facilities, the linkages and the other problems inherent in formulation of the scheme itself.

The land programmes mainly include loans for digging new wells or renovation of old ones, supply of oil engines and electric motors, pump sets and agricultural implements, and so on. These schemes can obviously be given only to those who own land. In fact, the Reserve Bank of India in its description of a viable farmer indicated that "the loans should be advanced to that category of persons whose agriculture is on a thin border line where some external help can enable them to produce surplus to cross the poverty line". According to this definition, only small farmers and, to some extent, marginal farmers can be covered. The commercial banks are also willing to advance loans to this category as they feel that there is lesser risk in advancing loans to those who own land. Land-based schemes when compared with other SFDA schemes had been more effective and helped in improving the conditions of the target groups, although these schemes were also not free from problems. Scheme-wise discussion would highlight the nature of the problems and processes inherent in each scheme.

The digging of new well or renovation of old well scheme, to a large extent, depends upon ground water table. It is generally experienced that the ground waterpotential is very low in the drought-prone areas. Therefore, the number of wells that can be taken up is extremely restricted. It is for this reason that the minimum physical distance between one well and another is stipulated. It is risky and futile to allow new wells to be dug in close proximity to the older ones. Generally, the banks along with a geologist have to assess the groundwater potential before new wells are sanctioned. But it is seldom that a geologist is involved in the process, and when involved, he views the whole process casually. In digging new wells farmers continue to be guided by hunches. There are instances of farmers consulting an astrologer or a *purohit* for the location of a spot to dig a new well. Inaccessibility of modern technology to a poor farmer is strikingly evident in this case.

The procedure for the sanctioning of the loan itself is fraught with a number of problems. First, in Medak district it is found that the land records are not up-to-date. In most of the cases the mutation of land has taken place. Most of the sale deeds have no legal validity as they come under benami transactions. As a result of defective land records, quite a large number of eligible farmers are eliminated from the benefits offered by the S.F.D.A. No measures have been initiated to update and to regularise the records. On being questioned, the revenue officials revealed that during the periodic surveys meant for updating the land records, the families concerned do not report the changes in the family. A senior revenue officer squarely put it: "How do we know that somebody in the family expired and the land is to be transferred in the name of his sons, unless this is brought to our notice?". The same officer added, "when people do not go far legal registration while entering the sale deed, how can we regularise the land records?".

Another defect in the maintenance of land records is the unscientific way they are maintained. For instance, the total land possessed by a family or a person is not recorded at one place in the record. This is split into several survey numbers which is partly a result of fragmentation of land in the village. In most of the cases persons own land in small pieces located in different corners of the village. As a result, locating the total land-holding of a particular person is quite difficult and the scope for manipulations is quite wide. For instance, "once a team for identification of members of target group went to a village, the *patwari* who was assisting the team was giving out the details of the ownership of land of an identified member. After giving a few details he paused and stared at the enquiry officer and asked whether the information was sufficient for the purpose of the loan". When asked what he meant by 'sufficient for the purpose', he replied that "if he gave out all the land-holding particulars, the member would cross the limits of eligibility fixed by the SFDA for the grant of loan". This explains how the land record and the principle of eligibility can be exploited at the lower levels because of unscientific nature of the land records.

The procedures followed by the SFDA and the multiple agencies that the beneficiaries have to contact, pose a number of problems to the beneficiaries. They have to get the details about their land ownership from the revenue department, get a certificate from the cooperatives that the land has not been mortgaged, get a clearance certificate from the registration department and panchayat samithi, and so on. Obtaining these particulars is an "art" by itself. This is one of the reasons why the members of the target groups are at the mercy of the middle-man *(Pyraveekar)*.

After the loans are sanctioned, the beneficiaries start encountering technical difficulties. For instance, in the well digging scheme failures may occur because of either paucity of water or the presence of a rock sheet and there are no readily available means to circumvent such difficulties. Moreover, the procedures are so cumbersome that the loanees are frightened of pursuing the matter.

The schemes relating to oil engine and electric motor also run into a number of difficulties. The procedural difficulties listed out in the case of well digging hold good in the case of these schemes also. In addition to those problems, the loanees of such schemes have to deal with a dealer. There are certain authorised dealers from whom the engines are to be bought.

The loanees complain that the dealers sell the engine at a higher cost than the actual market price. One project officer has wondered why this condition is imposed at all and stated that the subsidy component is virtually appropriated by the dealer.

In the case of electric motors the experience of the beneficiaries appear to be 'shocking'. The delays, the procedural rigmarole and the absence of coordination have become a part of the culture of 'electric power'. The beneficiaries have made a number of complaints against the Electricity Board. When an electric motor is to be sanctioned the banks insist on the loanee having the power connection before the actual sanction is made. And the Electricity Board insists on his possession of the electric motor before applying for a power connection. There are instances where the electric motors were kept unused for months as the farmers could not get the power connection on account of the Board's insistence on the fulfilment of a number of conditions for sanctioning a power connection. For instance, they say that a minimum number of wells with electric motors should be there in order that it may not be uneconomical to extend this facility, and to justify their stand they go on offering explanations to the effect that they do not have poles, wire, manpower, and so on. And the applicants feel that these are all pretexts. Again, after getting the connection there is the problem of irregular power supply for the purpose of cultivation. The supply sometimes is so erratic that it causes damage to the crops as the agricultural operations cannot be carried on in concurrence with the whims and the fancies of 'power'. Thus the modern facilities instead of solving the problems are creating some additional problems.

The increase in the number of oil engines and electric motors installed in rural areas is not matched by a commensurate development in the infrastructural facilities to take care of these modern tools of agriculture. Sometimes the farmers have to trek long distances if the engines go out of order as there are no technicians available in the villages to repair them. Thus the electric motor scheme is prone to a number of risks and the applicant is caught in a mesh of uncertainties.

In the case of animal husbandry programmes, the nature of problems is different. This is so because in a large number of cases these programmes have been given to those who either do not have land or have small pieces of land. In fact, the schemes are primarily meant to assist agricultural labourers. It is reported that innumerable problems are thrown up in the course of the implementation of the schemes. These problems are more complex than those of land based schemes; they arose because of procedural difficulties. It is reported that there are several unhealthy practices concerning the purchase of animals: for instance, when the purchasing committee visits the local shandy, the beneficiary has to pay for the transport, lodging and food of the committee members and other expenses. In addition, there are a number of malpractices involved in the rural markets. The applicant is generally anxious to buy the animal as the scheduling of another visit of the purchasing committee not only is difficult but also involves additional expenditure. Knowing the predicament of the buyer, the dealers push up the price of the animal. It is reported that sometimes the cost of the animal is raised to such a point that the entire subsidy amount is swallowed up by it.

Of all the animal husbandry programmes the milch cattle scheme suffered most. This is a scheme which requires an integrated approach and considerable infrastructural facilities. Right from the stage of buying an animal to the stage of income generation there are several processes which the scheme has to pass through. The survival of the animal, the survival of the calf, the right type of fodder, availability of grazing land, regular milk yield, adequacy of veterinary facilities, the transport and marketing of milk, the maintenance of the animal during the dry period, etc., are some of the problems which make the scheme complicated. Inadequate attention to any of the problems will make the scheme ineffectual.

In the milch cattle scheme, the policy itself is creating bottlenecks. It is found that the banks are insisting on the applicant being given either Murra buffalo or Jersey cow in order he might cross the poverty line. The original scheme proposed was to give two cows so that one would generate income when other went dry. But it was found that this was not followed at all when this proposal came up for discussion in East Godavari. It seems that the officials, more so the grass-roots officials, were not favourably inclined towards it. The banks maintain that the insistence of this type of animal being given to the loanee is in accordance with the instructions received from the Reserve Bank. Experience with such schemes reveals that the maintenance of these animals is difficult as they need a different type of fodder on the one hand and technical competence to maintain them on the other. Most of the villagers are found to be lacking the requisite experience to maintain such animals. The programme succeeded only in those cases where the beneficiaries possessed grazing-land and in all other cases the schemes proved to be a failure. It is added that the geo-climatic conditions in these areas are also found to be uncongenial for these animals.

Marketing is yet another problem faced by the beneficiaries. It is reported that where the villages are not linked with the milk route, the beneficiaries faced the difficulty of marketing their milk. This is not because there is nobody to drink milk in those areas but because they do not have the purchasing power to do so.

Another aspect of the programme is its technical dimension. The technical opinion maintains that during the lactation period an animal can be impregnated without any adverse effect on the milk yield, but most of the villagers think that pregnancy affects the milk yield and reduces the lactation period. This information lag proved to be detrimental to the implementation of the scheme. Once the lactation period is over, the animal becomes liability to the owner as it has to be fed during this period without any returns.

It is reported that there have been quite a number of cases where the beneficiaries diverted the loan amount to other purposes. There are instances where the beneficiary and the dealer in collusion played the drama of 'selling and buying a buffalo' without actually doing so for record purposes. This includes cases where the beneficiary put his own animal in the rural local market with the help of somebody and 'purchase' it in the presence of purchasing committee. In the cases of such sales the loans are diverted and utilised for other purposes.

The sheep and goat rearing scheme is found to be relatively more successful. It is successful particularly in the case of the shepherd caste which has been traditionally associated with it. This caste enjoys a good deal of credibility with the banks. Several banks are willing to finance these schemes as they are confident of securing the repayment of the loan. The caste also enjoys a high reputation for its prompt repayment of the loan. However, the scheme could not make the same impact on the Scheduled Caste and Scheduled Tribe recipients.

The reasons advanced for the relative success of the programme are : (a) the shepherds are very particular about repayment of the loan which facilitates the process of recovery ; (b) this professional group can handle sheep units with care and efficiency as they are experienced ; (c) the sheep and goat units hardly require any expenditure for maintenance but generate regular income ; (d) the beneficiaries at additional income from wool ; (e) this scheme also generates income as the sheep units are engaged for the purpose of penning. In addition to these multiple benefits it has built-in flexibility as far as repayment is concerned. For instance, they can sell a couple of sheep at any moment and pay the instalment—a flexibility that most of the other schemes do not have. This scheme appears to be effective if restricted only to shepherds. This programme, however, highlights that schemes with built-in flexibility backed by people's traditional wisdom, skills and proper attitudes are likely to succeed. This scheme, it is reported, has also suffered in certain cases due to inadequate veterinary and other infrastructural facilities.

In the case of poultry units, although the programme raised hopes and had a good beginning, it appears to have become entangled in the same cobwebs as the other programmes have. It is noticed that monopolistic tendencies are rapidly developing in poultry industry. Therefore, it seems that an unit becomes viable if it comprises at least a hundred or two hundred birds. But, strangely, even units with five hundred birds are becoming uneconomical. It is also reported that poultry farming is becoming increasingly risky on account of the possibility of an epidemic breaking out killing the birds in hundreds. Therefore, the poultry units should be backed by adequate veterinary facilities. Some of the large, privately managed units have a full time veterinary doctor to attend on the birds. Obviously, the poor and backward beneficiaries of the SFDA cannot provide for such services and the existing veterinary facilities are too meagre to meet the growing needs of such an industry.

There are also complaints to the effect that the poultry

industry has been facing the same acute problem of marketing as the milch cattle programme. There are also complaints about the cost of the feed having steeply gone up. To overcome this difficulty the agency has started supplying the feed at subsidised rates. But it is observed that the feed sometimes does not reach the units in time. They are also facing the problem of transportation of eggs. As a result, the poultry programme is becoming uneconomical and unpopular with the target group.

The experience with the fisheries scheme is no different. It is reported that the benefits are cornered off by a few influential and prominent fishermen. The supply of nylon nets and modernised boats did not have the desired impact. Several instances of fishermen selling away the nylon nets and boats have come to light. It is alleged that after the introduction of modern boats, the fishermen have not been putting in as much of hard work and industry as they did earlier. There are also cases of diversion of loans for other purposes. There is thus the feeling that it has not had much impact on the target groups.

The above discussion indicates that the SFDA schemes have not been formulated with an integrated thrust and necessary linkages. The policy has been incremental in scope, ad-hoc in nature and inadequate in content. Any public policy should aim at an integrated approach taking several variables into account during its formulation. It should envisage a number of alternative measures to face the unforeseen or unintended consequences that a policy may give rise to in implementation. This requires not only a thorough theoretical and conceptual exercise but also experimentation on a pilot basis so as to understand the problems that possibly would arise during the course of implementation. Unfortunately, the present policy has been neither properly conceived nor implemented with any seriousness.

An analysis of various schemes and their viability was done in respect of the districts of Medak and East Godavari. This empirical data, it is hoped, would throw more light on the schemes and help us in understanding how a developmental policy works.

II

An analysis of the schemes so far extended to various categories of the beneficiaries reveals that of 188 schemes* given in Medak 14.4 per cent concerned the digging of new wells, 2.1 per cent loans for repair of the old wells, 6.9 per cent oil engines, 26.6 per cent electric motors. In East Godavari nine schemes were given to small farmers and five to marginal farmers under minor irrigation schemes. In both the districts taken together, of 344 schemes 72 (20.9%) minor irrigation schemes went to small farmers, 56 (16.3%) to marginal farmers and three to agricultural labourers (see for details Chapter 3).

Here an attempt is made to find out whether minor irrigation schemes proved to be viable enough to enable the rural poor to cross the poverty line. For this purpose the beneficiaries were asked a few questions on the basis of which an analysis of the scheme is attempted.

As regards the additional employment that the schemes was to generate, while 19.8 per cent of small farmers from Medak said that they had additional employment, 15.7 per cent said that there was no additional employment. From among the marginal farmers 12.4 per cent said that they had additional employment while 17.3 per cent said that they did not have any additional employment. In East Godavari the number of beneficiaries of the minor irrigation programmes, as stated earlier, is a negligible fourteen. All the nine small farmers and the five marginal farmers reported that the minor irrigation schemes did not generate any additional employment. However, the data indicates that under this scheme small farmers had an advantage over the marginal farmers. It means that for these schemes to prove beneficial the size of the land-holding is important. These schemes, it is evident, cannot generate any additional employment in the case of very small holdings (Table 4.1).

The beneficiaries of minor irrigation were asked another question with regard to the additional income that schemes generated, income being another key component of viability. (Table 4.2). In the district of Medak 20.2 per cent of small farmers said that they got additional income while 18.1 per cent said that there was no additional income and 7.4 per cent reported that their income decreased because of these schemes. From

* The number of schemes do not tally with the number of beneficiaries since some of the beneficiaries got more than one scheme.

among the marginal farmers 16.0 per cent said that there was additional income while 16.0 per cent reported that there was no additional income and 7.4 per cent said that their income decreased.

In East Godavari of 14 recipients of minor irrigation schemes nine were small farmers. Of these, four said that their income increased while five said that their income did not increase. From among the five marginal farmers four said that the income did not increase while one said that his income decreased.

With regard to increase in the income under all types of minor irrigation schemes there has been no addition to income in a majority of the cases. In all the schemes 3/5th of the respondents reported that there was no addition to income because of these schemes. And under well development 1/5th of the respondents and under oil engine 1/3rd of the respondents reported that their income decreased because of the schemes.

An analysis of the impact of minor irrigation schemes on the income of the target groups shows that of 36 small and marginal farmers covered under the new well scheme 20 were below the poverty line at Rs. 600 income level and 38 at Rs. 960 income level thereby indicating that the scheme had an adverse impact as two recipients of the scheme were pushed below the poverty line. Owing to this scheme per capita rise in the income was 2.7 per cent in the case of small and 10.4 per cent in the case of marginal farmers. Although there had been a slight rise in the income it was so small that it could not help them in crossing the poverty line (Table 4.3).

In the case of well development or well repair schemes all the six respondents were below the poverty line at Rs. 600 income level. After the implementation of the scheme two respondents crossed the poverty line at Rs. 600 income level and one could cross even the Rs. 960 level. One marginal farmer, it is to be noted, became an agricultural labourer. The per capita income rise due to this scheme was 42.3 per cent, but in spite of it none of the recipients under this scheme could cross the poverty line.

Under the oil engine scheme, of the ten recipients of the scheme four were below the poverty line at Rs. 600 income level and seven at Rs. 960 income level. After the implementation of the scheme one small farmer could cross the poverty line but one marginal farmer went down below the poverty line

TABLE 4.1 : **Generation of employment by the schemes**

District	Minor Irrigation								M.I.	Animal Husbandry								A.H.
	Generated				Not Generated				TOTAL	Generated				Not Generated				Total
	SF	MF	AL	Total	SF	MF	AL	Total		SF	MF	AL	Total	SF	MF	AL	Total	
1	2	3	4	5	6	7	8	9	10	11	12	13	14	15	16	17	18	19
Medak	24	15	1	40	19	21	—	40	80	7	8	—	15	10	3	—	13	28
	(30)	(19)	(1)	(50)	(24)	(26)		(33)	(100)	(25)	(29)		(54)	(36)	(11)		(46)	(100)
East Godavari	—	—	—	—	9	5	—	14	14	11	23	16	50	10	21	20	51	101
					(64)	(36)		(100)	(100)	(11)	(23)	(16)	(49)	(10)	(21)	(20)	(50)	(100)
Total	24	15	1	40	28	26	—	54	94	18	31	16	65	20	24	20	64	129
	(25)	(16)	(1)	(43)	(30)	(28)		(57)	(100)	(14)	(24)	(12)	(50)	(15)	(19)	(15)	(50)	(100)

TABLE 4.1 : (*Contd.*)

District	Agriculture									Others									
	Generated				Not Generated				AGR.	Generated				Not Generated				Oth.	Grand
	SF	MF	AL	Total	SF	MF	AL	Total	TOTAL	SF	MF	AL	Total	SF	MF	AL	Total	Total	Tocal
1	20	21	22	23	24	25	26	27	28	29	30	31	32	33	34	35	36	37	38
Medak	1	3	—	4	6	3	—	9	13	—	—	—	—	—	—	—	—	—	121
	(8)	(23)		(31)	(46)	(23)		(69)	(100)										(100)
East Godavari	—	2	—	2	7	11	1	19	21	—	—	8	8	5	2	3	10	18	154
		(9)		(9)	(33)	(52)	(5)	(90)	(100)			(44)	(44)	(28)	(11)	(17)	(56)	(100)	(100)
Total	1	5	—	6	13	14	1	28	34	—	—	8	8	5	2	3	10	18	275
	(3)	(15)		(18)	(38)	(41)	(3)	(82)	(100)			(44)	(44)	(28)	(11)	(17)	(56)	(100)	(100)

Note : Figures in brackets indicate percentage.

TABLE 4.2 : **Minor irrigation schemes—Impact on income**

	Increased				Not Increased				Decreased				Grand
	SF	MF	AL	Total	SF	MF	AL	Total	SF	MF	AL	Total	Total
1. Medak	19	15	1	35	17	15	—	32	7	7	—	14	81
(%)	(20.2)	(16.0)	(1.1)	(36.2)	(18.1)	(16.0)		(34.0)	(7.4)	(7.4)		(14.9)	(85.1)
2. East Godavari	4	—	—	4	5	4	—	9	—	1	—	1	14
(%)	(4.3)			(4.3)	(5.3)	(4.3)		(9.6)		(1.1)		(1.1)	(14.9)
Total	23	15	1	39	22	19	—	41	7	8	—	15	95
(%)	(24.5)	(14.9)	(1.1)	(40.4)	(23.4)	(20.2)		(43.6)	(7.4)	(8.5)		(16.0)	(100.0)

at Rs. 600 income level and there was no difference at Rs. 960 income level. The per capita rise in the income was 25.7 per cent for small farmers and 37.9 per cent for marginal farmers. Interestingly, while 25.7 per cent rise could make one small farmer cross the poverty line, even 37.9 per cent rise could not do so in the case of marginal farmers.

In the case of electric motor schemes, of 42 respondents 26 were below the poverty line at Rs. 600 income level and 34 below the Rs. 960 income level. After the implementation of the scheme, of those at Rs. 600 income level two small farmers crossed the poverty line while two marginal farmers slipped below the poverty line. At Rs. 960 income level two small farmers also could cross the poverty line while one marginal farmer went down below the poverty line. The per capita rise in the income due to this scheme was 8.8 per cent for small farmers and 11 per cent for marginal farmers.

The schemes could not make the expected impact due to various problems faced by the recipients of these schemes. Scheme-wise analysis of the difficulties experienced in getting the scheme indicates that under all the four minor irrigation programmes there had been difficulties. However, while more than half of the respondents of all the schemes reported difficulties, only ⅓rd reported difficulties under well development schemes which showed that getting a loan for well development was relatively simpler.

With regard to the time consumed in getting a scheme, the data indicates that ⅔rd of the respondents under all the schemes except those of well development reported that it took more than six months to get the scheme. In the case of well development 77 per cent said that they got it in less than three months. The delay is maximum in the case of electric motor scheme, since it took six months or more in the case of 26 per cent of the respondents and more than one year in the case of 42 per cent of them.

The recipients of these programmes were asked whether they had any difficulty in implementing the schemes (Table 4.4). The problems in implementation would provide an insight into the viability of the schemes and the causes for its success or failure. From Medak 41.3 per cent of small farmers said that they had difficulty in implementing these schemes while 12.5 per

TABLE 4.3: **Impact of the schemes in crossing the poverty line**

		Poverty line at Rs. 600				Poverty line at Rs. 960				Average Additional income	No. of Respondents
		Before the Scheme		After the Scheme		Before the Scheme		After the Scheme			
		BPL	APL	BPL	APL	BPL	APL	BPL	APL	%	
New	SF	10 (55.1)	8 (44.4)	11 (61.1)	7 (38.9)	13 (72.1)	5 (27.9)	13 (72.1)	5 (27.9)	2.7	18
well	MF	10 (55.1)	8 (44.4)	11 (61.1)	7 (38.9)	15 (83.3)	3 (16.7)	15 (83.3)	3 (16.7)	10.4	13
Well dee-	SF	5 (100.0)	0	3 (60.0)	2 (40.0)	5 (100.0)	0	4 (80.0)	1 (20.0)	42.3	5
pening	AL	1	0	1	0	1	0	1	0	0	1
Oil	SF	3 (37.5)	5 (62.5)	2 (25.0)	6 (75.0)	5 (62.5)	3 (37.5)	5 (62.5)	3 (37.5)	25.7	8
Engine	MF	1	1	2	0	2	0	2	0	37.9	2
Electric	SF	12 (57.1)	9 (42.9)	10 (47.6)	11 (52.4)	17 (81.0)	4 (19.0)	15 (71.4)	6 (28.6)	8.8	21
Motor	MF	14 (66.7)	7 (33.3)	16 (76.2)	5 (23.8)	17 (81.0)	4 (19.0)	18 (85.7)	3 (14.3)	11.0	21
Milch	SF	13 (56.6)	10 (43.5)	12 (52.2)	11 (47.8)	15 (65.2)	8 (34.8)	16 (69.6)	7 (30.4)	-6.6	23
Cattle	MF	24 (50.0)	24 (50.0)	26 (54.2)	22 (45.8)	38 (79.2)	10 (20.8)	38 (79.2)	10 (20.8)	1.4	48
	AL	20 (57.0)	15 (42.9)	25 (71.4)	10 (28.6)	29 (82.6)	6 (17.1)	32 (91.4)	3 (8.6)	-13.6	35
Poul-	SF	0	2	0	2	0	2	0	2	0	2
try	AL	0	1	0	1	0	1	0	1	0	1
Sheep	SF	11 (84.6)	2 (15.4)	10 (76.9)	3 (23.1)	13	0	13	0	34.6	13
	MF		0	7	0	7	0	7	0	11.2	7

TABLE 4.3: (*Contd.*)

		Poverty line at Rs. 600				Poverty line at Rs. 600				Average Additional income	No. of Respondents
		Before the scheme		After the scheme		Before the scheme		After the scheme			
		BPL	APL	BPL	APL	BPL	APL	BPL	APL		
Cart &	SF	2	1	2	1	3	0	2	1	8.0	3
Bullo-	MF	2	2	1	3	3	1	3	1	26.7	4
cks	AL	1	0	1	0	1	0	1	0	76.9	1
Plough	SF	3 (33.3)	6 (66.7)	3 (33.3)	6 (66.7)	5 (55.6)	4 (44.4)	5 (55.6)	4 (44.4)	—0.9	9
Bullo-	MF	8 (57.1)	6 (42.9)	5 (35.7)	9 (64.3)	11 (78.6)	3 (21.4)	10 (71.4)	4 (28.6)	21.0	14
cks	AL	1	0	1	0	1	0	1	0	0	1
L D	SF	1	1	1	1	2	0	2	0	0	2
Sprayer	SF	0	1	0	1	0	1	0	1	0	1
Mango	SF	1	0	1	0	1	0	1	0	0	1
	MF	2	0	2	0	2	0	2	0	—18.4	2
Cashew	SF	3	0	3	0	3	0	3	0	0	3
	MF	0	1	0	1	0	1	0	1	0	1
Nylon nets	AL	8 (80.0)	2 (20.0)	5 (50.0)	5 (50.0)	10 (100.0)	0	9 (90.0)	1 (10.0)	40.2	10

BPL=Below Poverty Line APL=Above Poverty Line LD=Land Development

Note : Figures in brackets indicate percentage.

TABLE 4.4 : **Difficulties faced in implementing the schemes**

District	Minor Irrigation									Animal Husbandry								
	Faced				Not Faced				M.I.	Faced				Not Faced				A.H
	SF	MF	AL	Total	SF	MF	AL	Total	TOTAL	SF	MF	AL	Total	SF	MF	AL	Total	TOTAL
1	2	3	4	5	6	7	8	9	10	11	12	13	14	15	16	17	18	19
Medak	33	30	1	64	10	6	—	16	80	15	7	—	22	2	4	—	6	28
	(41)	(37)	(1)	(80)	(12)	(7)		(20)	(100)	(54)	(25)		(79)	(7)	(14)		(21)	(100)
East Godavari	5	—	—	5	4	5	—	9	14	15	38	30	83	6	6	6	18	101
	(36)			(36)	(28)	(36)		(64)	(100)	(15)	(38)	(30)	(82)	(6)	(6)	(6)	(18)	(100)
Total	38	30	1	69	14	11	—	25	94	30	45	30	105	8	10	6	24	129
	(40)	(32)	(1)	(73)	(15)	(12)		(27)	(100)	(23)	(35)	(23)	(81)	(6)	(9)	(5)	(19)	(100)

TABLE 4.4 : (*Contd.*)

District	Agriculture									Others									Grand
	Faced				Not Faced				AGR.	Faced				Not Faced				Oth.	
	SF	MF	AL	Total	SF	MF	AL	Total	TOTAL	SF	MF	AL	Total	SF	MF	AL	Total	Total	Total
1	20	21	22	23	24	25	26	27	28	29	30	31	32	33	34	35	36	37	38
Medak	6	4	—	10	1	2	—	3	13	—	—	—	—	—	—	—	—	—	121
	(46)	(31)		(77)	(8)	(15)		(23)	(100)										(100)
East Godavari	4	4	—	8	3	9	1	13	21	5	1	8	14	—	1	3	4	18	154
	(19)	(19)		(38)	(14)	(42)	(5)	(62)	(100)	(28)	(6)	(44)	(78)		(6)	(17)	(22)	(100)	(100)
Total	10	8	—	18	4	11	1	16	34	5	1	8	14	—	1	3	4	18	275
	(29)	(23)	—	(53)	(12)	(32)	(3)	(47)	(100)	(28)	(6)	(44)	(78)		(6)	(17)	(22)	(100)	(100)

Note : Figures in brackets indicate the percentage.

cent stated that they had no difficulty. 37.3 per cent of marginal farmers and 1.3 per cent of agricultural labourers faced difficulties. In East Godavari of the nine small farmers five said that they had difficulties while the other four said that they had no difficulty. All the five marginal farmers reported that they had difficulties in availing themselves of the programme.

In all 80 per cent of the beneficiaries experienced difficulties while 20 per cent had no problems in implementing the minor irrigation schemes. It is obvious that minor irrigation programmes are fraught with a number of difficulties in respect of their implementation. It is interesting to note that while 60 per cent had difficulties in getting the schemes, 80 per cent had no difficulty in implementing them. Scheme-wise 56 per cent of them faced difficulties in getting the loan for a new well but 90 per cent of them experienced difficulties in implementing the scheme. In the case of well development 33 per cent had difficulties in getting the scheme while 55.5 per cent had no difficulty in implementation. In the case of oil engine and electric motor schemes too ⅔rd of them had difficulties in getting the scheme while ¾th had difficulties in implementing the scheme.

An attempt is made to analyse the types of difficulties which the beneficiaries faced under minor irrigation schemes. (Appendix-IV.1). The types of difficulties are broadly categorised into economic, technical, geo-climatic, infrastructural and personal. The data reveals that in Medak 5.8 per cent of small farmers faced economic difficulties, 13.0 per cent technical difficulties, 5.8 per cent geo-climatic difficulties, 4.3 per cent infrastructural difficulties and 4.3 per cent personal difficulties. And in the case of 13 per cent of them the types of difficulties were more than one, but it was the technical difficulties that figured frequently among them. Among the marginal farmers 17.4 per cent faced technical difficulties, 2.9 per cent infrastructural difficulties and about 17.4 per cent a combination of these difficulties. In East Godavari 4.3 per cent faced geo-climatic problems, 4.3 per cent infrastructaral problems and another 4.3 per cent a combination of these difficulties.

In all 5.8 per cent of small farmers reported economic problems, 13 per cent technical problems, 4.3 per cent personal problems, 7.2 per cent geo-climatic problems, 5.8 per cent infrastructural problems, and 2.5 per cent other problems. From among the marginal farmers 17.4 per cent faced technical problems, 4.3 per cent personal problems, 4.3 geo-climatic problems, 5.8 per cent infrastructural problems and 18.8 per cent more than one type of difficulties or problems.

This data reveals that the beneficiaries faced different types of difficulties. However, a majority of the small and marginal farmers reported technical difficulties in implementing the schemes. The geo-climatic and infrastructural problems that were reported also relate to technical difficulties. This suggests that the minor irrigation schemes sponsored by the SFDA are devoid of adequate technical support. As a result, their impact on the target groups has been poor.

Animal husbandry programmes

The animal husbandry programme is the second major programme taken up by the SFDA. This includes the milch cattle, sheep and goat rearing, poultry, and so on. It is proposed to examine whether these schemes had the intended impact on the target groups. While in Medak the emphasis was laid on minor irrigation, in East Godavari it was mostly on livestock schemes.

To the question whether livestock programmes generated any additional employment (see Table 4.1) 25 per cent of small farmers from Medak said that it created additional employment while 35.7 per cent stated that there was no additional employment; 28.6 per cent of marginal farmers said that it had created additional employment while 10.7 per cent said that it did not create any additional employment. In East Godavari 10.9 per cent of small farmers said that it created additional employment while 9.9 per cent said that it did not create any additional employment. 22.8 per cent marginal farmers stated that it generated additional employment while 20.8 per cent said that it did not create any additional employment. From among the agricultural labourers 15.8 per cent said that it created additional employment, while 19.8 per cent said that it did not generate any additional employment.

In all, 14 per cent of small and 24 per cent of marginal farmers and 12.4 per cent of agricultural labourers said that there was additional employment, while 15.5 per cent of small farmers, 18.6 per cent of marginal farmers and 15.5 per cent of agricultural labourers said that there was no additional employment. However, animal husbandry programmes appear to have a slight edge over minor irrigation schemes as they could generate additional employment to a larger number of the respondents than minor irrigation schemes.

Of the animal husbandry schemes the most important comprise milch cattle and sheep rearing units. A few were given poultry units. Of the 129 livestock beneficiaries 46.2 per cent, 65 per cent and 100 per cent of milch cattle, sheep and poultry unit beneficiaries respectively reported additional employment. This indicates that sheep and poultry units have greater potentiality to generate additional employment than the other schemes.

Let us now turn to the question of increase in the income of the recipients of animal husbandry programmes (Table 4.5). 9.3 per cent of small farmers said that there was additional income while 12.4 per cent said that there was no additional income and 7.8 per cent said that there was decrease in income. Of marginal farmers 13.2 per cent said that there was additional income, 14.7 per cent reported no additional income while 14.7 per cent said that there was decrease in income. From among the agricultural labourers 3.1 per cent said that there was additional income, 9.3 per cent reported no additional income and 15.5 per cent said that there was a decline in their income.

As per the analysis of the impact of the scheme on poverty conditions, among the 106 milch cattle beneficiaries 57 were below the poverty line and 49 above the poverty line at Rs. 600 income level whereas 82 were below the poverty line and 24 above the poverty line at Rs. 960 income level before the scheme was sanctioned. After the implementation of the scheme 63 are found below the poverty line at Rs. 600 income level and 86 below at Rs. 960 income level. This shows that six persons went down below the poverty line at Rs. 600 income level and four below Rs. 960 income level. Category-wise analysis reveals that from among small farmers one person crossed the poverty line at Rs. 600 income level and at Rs. 960 income level too. From among the marginal farmers two and from among agricultural labourers four went down below the poverty line at Rs. 600 income level and one below the Rs. 960 income level. The per capita income rise analysis indicates that small farmer s and agricultural labourers experienced a decline in their

TABLE 4.5: **Animal husbandry schemes—impact on income**

District	Increased				Not Increased				Decreased				Grand
	SF	MF	AL	Total	SF	MF	AL	Total	SF	MF	AL	Total	Total
Medak	5	4	—	9	10	6	—	16	2	1	—	3	28
	(3.9)	(3.1)		(7.0)	(7.8)	(4.7)		(12.4)	(1.6)	(0.8)		(2.3)	(21.7)
East Godavari	7	13	4	24	6	13	12	31	8	18	20	46	101
	(5.4)	(10.1)	(3.1)	(18.6)	(4.7)	(10.1)	(9.3)	(24.0)	(6.2)	(14.0)	(15.5)	(35.7)	(78.2)
Total	12	17	4	33	16	19	12	47	10	19	20	49	129
	(9.3)	(13.2)	(3.1)	(25.6)	(12.4)	(14.7)	(9.3)	(36.4)	(7.8)	(14.7)	(15.5)	(38.0)	(100.0)

Note : Figures in brackets indicate the percentage.

income to the tune of 6.6 per cent and 13.6 per cent respectively. However, the marginal farmers gained 1.4 per cent of additional income. This shows that the milch cattle scheme had an adverse impact on the target groups in general and agricultural labourers in particular. Due to this scheme four to six members of the target groups slipped into below-the-poverty-line group and their income declined considerably. The scheme on the whole failed to make any favourable impact and indeed, caused further impoverishment among the agricultural labourers.

From among the twenty recipients of the sheep unit scheme eighteen were below the poverty line and two above the poverty line at Rs. 600 income level and all of them were below the poverty line at Rs. 960 income level before the scheme was sanctioned. After the sanctioning of the scheme only one from among the small farmers could cross the poverty line at Rs. 600 income level and none at Rs. 960 income level. The per capita rise in the income for small farmers was 34.6 per cent and for marginal farmers 11.2 per cent. Although the rise in the income was considerable it was not sufficient to enable the members of the target group to cross the poverty line.

With regard to the poultry scheme of the three beneficiaries all of them were above the poverty line at Rs. 960 income level. This indicates that the schemes were given to only those who were above the poverty line.

Scheme-wise details indicate that in the case of milch cattle one-fourth of the respondents and slightly more than half of the respondents under sheep units scheme reported additional income. All the respondents under poultry scheme stated that there was no additional income. Under the milch cattle scheme half of the respondents stated that their income declined on account of the scheme.

With regard to the question whether they were benefited by the livestock scheme, ⅔rd of the respondents stated that they had not benefited by the schemes. The scheme-wise analysis indicates that while 70.8 per cent under the milch cattle scheme and all the respondents under poultry scheme stated that they were not benefited by the scheme. However, 75 per cent under sheep unit scheme reported that they had been benefited by the scheme.

The unimpressive performance of the schemes, particularly

the milch cattle schemes, needs an explanation. With this in view the respondents were asked about the difficulties in getting and implementing the scheme. Schemewise analysis indicates that under all the three schemes the majority had difficulties in getting the schemes; which includes 51.9 per cent of milch cattle beneficiaries, 80 per cent of sheep unit beneficiaries and 66.7 per cent of poultry beneficiaries. With regard to the delay in getting the scheme the data reveals that 90.6 per cent under the milch cattle scheme were given in less than three months while under the sheep and poultry schemes ⅔rd reported that it took more than six months to secure the scheme. Although 90 per cent of the respondents under milch cattle stated that they got the scheme in less than three months, 55 per cent of them reported that they had difficulties in getting the scheme. This includes other types of difficulties such as those related to the market, purchasing, malpractices, and so on.

Thus the above mentioned data shows that in all the categories, irrespective of their regional background and the type of scheme, the majority had faced difficulties in getting the animal husbandry scheme.

As for the difficulties in implementing the schemes, 81.4 per cent of the respondents under the livestock schemes reported difficulties. It appears that implementation of the scheme is more difficult than getting it. 82.1 per cent under milch cattle, 75 per cent under sheep unit and all the respondents under poultry schemes stated that they had difficulties in the implementation of the schemes.

As regard the nature of difficulties, the data shows (Appendix-IV.2) that in the district of Medak while a majority of the small farmers faced geo-climatic problems followed by personal problems, a majority of the marginal farmers encountered economic difficulties. In East Godavari the small farmers faced geo-climatic problems and infrastructural problems, and an overwhelming majority of the marginal farmers faced infrastructural difficulties. From among the agricultural labourers also a majority of them faced infrastructural difficulties. The data indicates that more than 41 per cent had faced infrastructural difficulties followed by economic and geo-climatic problems. Those who faced technical difficulties were not many. 34.9 per cent of them faced more than one type of difficulty is indicative of multi-dimensional nature of the difficulties in implementing the schemes.

The data suggests that animal husbandry programmes suffered more due to the inadequacy of the infrastructural and geo-climatic problems. It also indicates that these schemes are fraught with multiple problems. This shows the inadequacy of the schemes in terms of financial support and effective linkages which severely affected the viability of the schemes.

Agricultural schemes

The third major programme taken up by the SFDA is that of helping the target groups by extending agricultural schemes (Appendix IV-3). In Medak thirteen schemes were sanctioned about which 30.8 per cent of them thought that there was additional employment while 69.2 per cent of them thought that there was no additional employment. In East Godavari twenty-one schemes were given about which 90.5 per cent reported that there had been no additional employment. In the case of agricultural schemes, unlike the other two types of schemes, an overwhelming majority stated that there had been no additional employment.

As regards the agricultural development schemes, 91.7 per cent under plough bullock schemes, 75 per cent bullock and cart schemes reported that there had been no additional employment. But cent per cent of them under land development schemes reported that there was additional employment.

To the question whether these schemes added any additional income to the household (Table 4.6), from Medak 20.6 per cent held that there was additional income while 17.6 per cent thought that there was no additional income. In East Godavari 35.3 per cent stated that income had gone up, 14.7 per cent said that there had been no additional income while 11.8 per cent reported that their income declined.

Scheme-wise analysis indicates that 58.3 per cent under plough and bullock scheme and 62.5 per cent under cart and bullock scheme reported additional income. But 4.2 per cent under plough and bullock scheme, 12.5 per cent under cart and bullock scheme reported decline in their incomes. All the respondents under the land development reported decline in income.

TABLE 4.6: **Agricultural schemes—Impact on income**

Districts	Increased				Not Increased				Decreased				Grand
	SF	MF	AL	Total	SF	MF	AL	Total	SF	MF	AL	Total	Total
Medak	4	3	—	7	3	3	—	6	—	—	—	—	13
	(11.8)	(8.8)		(20.6)	(8.8)	(8.8)		(17.6)					(38.2)
East Godavari	3	8	1	12	—	5	—	5	4	—	—	4	21
	(8.8)	(23.5)	(2.9)	(35.3)		(14.7)		(14.7)	(11.8)			(11.8)	(61.8)
Total	7	11	1	19	3	8	—	11	4	—	—	4	34
	(20.6)	(32.4)	(2.9)	(55.9)	(8.8)	(23.5)		(32.4)	(11.8)			(11.8)	(100.0)

Note : Figures in brackets indicate the percentage.

On the whole, as per the data, in the case of small farmers the income of 20.6 per cent increased, that of 8.8 per cent stagnated and that of 11.8 per cent got decreased. In the case of marginal farmers 32.4 per cent had additional income and 23.5 per cent had no additional income. From among the agricultural labourers 2.9 per cent had additional income. It is significant that while in the case of animal husbandry schemes there was additional employment but not income, in the case of agricultural programmes there was not much of additional employment but there was an increase in the income.

Of the 34 recipients of agricultural development schemes 16 were above the poverty line at Rs. 600 income level and eight members above Rs. 960 income level. Under the cart and bullock scheme, of eight recipients five were below the poverty line at Rs. 600 income level and six below at Rs. 960 income level. On account of the implementation of the schemes, from among the small farmers one crossed the poverty line at Rs. 960 income level. From among the marginal farmers one crossed the poverty line at Rs. 600 income level and none at Rs. 960 income level. The condition of the only agricultural labourer among them remained the same. The per capita rise in the income indicates that for the small farmers it was 8 per cent, for marginal farmers 26.7 per cent and for agricultural labourers 76.9 per cent. The scheme could generate additional income but except one small farmer no one could cross the poverty line. It is interesting to observe that although the scheme generated 76.9 per cent of additional income, the agricultural labourer could not cross the poverty line—which is indicative of the depth of poverty.

Of 24 recipients of plough bullock scheme half of them were below the poverty line at Rs. 600 income level and seventeen below the Rs. 960 income level. After the implementation of the scheme there was no change in the status of the small farmers and agricultural labourers. In the case of marginal farmers three of them crossed the poverty line at Rs. 600 income level and one could cross it even at Rs. 960 income level. The per capita income details reveal that the small farmers suffered 0.9 per cent of decline in their income. However, for the marginal farmers there was a rise in the income to the tune of 21 per cent.

In the case of land development schemes, the impact was nil

on the target group.

The agricultural developmental schemes such as cart and bullock brought about a rise in the income of marginal and small farmers. The plough and bullock scheme brought about a rise in the income of marginal farmers and agricultural labourers, while it caused a decline in the income to small farmers. The rise in the income of marginal farmers and agricultural labourers due to the scheme was reasonably good, yet it could not be of much help to them in crossing the poverty line. The land development scheme has had no impact. Thus no scheme proved to be capable of becoming viable.

To a question about the difficulties in getting the scheme about 3/4th of them opined that they had difficulties. However, scheme-wise analysis indicates that about 75 per cent under plough and bullock scheme and 62.5 per cent under cart and bullock scheme stated that they had difficulties in getting the scheme. An overwhelming majority who received land development and other schemes had to face the brunt of the difficulty in getting the scheme.

With regard to the difficulties in implementing the scheme about 52.9 per cent reported difficulties in implementation. 45.8 per cent under plough and bullock scheme, and 62 per cent under cart and bullock scheme stated that they faced difficulties in implementing the scheme. All respondents under land development and other schemes reported problems in implementation. The analysis indicates that land development and other schemes are fraught with more difficulties than plough and bullock or cart and bullock schemes. With regard to the overall benefit, of 34 beneficiaries 20 reported they have been benefited under plough and bullock scheme, 14 out of 28 are benefited under cart and bullock scheme, of 8 recipients five are benefited under the land development scheme.

The nylon nets scheme was implemented in the district of East Godavari. For the purpose of analysis a sample of ten respondents were undertaken. As the scheme does not fit into the broad categories of agricultural schemes, a separate analysis would help in not only understanding the dynamics of the scheme but also in formulating schemes for a large number of fishermen living along the coast of Andhra Pradesh. The other schemes include cashewnut, mango trees, and so on.

(Appendix IV-4)

With regard to employment from among the 18 recipients of the schemes 44.5 per cent of the beneficiaries reported additional employment while 55.5 per cent stated that there had been no additional employment. As per scheme-wise details seven out of ten nylon net beneficiaries and four mango beneficiaries stated that they had additional employment. All others reported that they had no additional employment.

As per income-wise details, 55.6 per cent of them stated that the schemes had generated additional income 33.3 per cent reported that no additional income and 11.2 per cent said that there was a decline in their income.

As per scheme-wise details, all the ten nylon net beneficiaries stated that there was a rise in their income. Two beneficiaries from mango tree and three from cashew scheme reported that there was no rise in their income. An analysis of the impact of the schemes on the target groups shows that of the ten recipients of the scheme three crossed the poverty line at Rs. 600 income level and that one could cross at Rs. 960 income level also. The mango and cashew schemes have had no impact on the income level of the target groups. The analysis of the per capita rise in the income reveals that in the case of nylon net beneficiaries there had been 40.2 per cent rise in the income. It is significant that all the recipients under this scheme were agricultural labourers. In the case of mango scheme the marginal farmers suffered a fall of 18.4 per cent in their income, but in the case of cashewnut scheme there was no impact on the income. This indicates that the nylon net scheme has enough potential provided the quantum of assistance is further raised.

When asked about the difficulties in getting the scheme all the nylon net respondents replied that there was no difficulty in getting the scheme, while the recipients of mango and cashew schemes stated that they faced difficulties. In respect of the time taken 80 per cent of the recipients under all the schemes stated that they got the schemes in less than six months. Although they said that they had no difficulty in getting the scheme, 77 per cent of them reported that there were difficulties in implementing the scheme. In spite of implementational difficulties 72.7 per cent of respondents stated that they had been benefited by the schemes. Thus nylon net scheme like sheep units scheme stand as an exception as it had a positive impact on the target groups. In the case of other schemes more than half of the respondents reported that there was a rise in their income although more than half stated that there was no additional employment. Thus the data indicates once again that the relation between income and employment need not be positive.

III

This part is devoted to a discussion on related programmes which are compared with the SFDA schemes. The related programmes also include schemes like milch cattle, bullocks, oil engine, electric motor, poultry, and so on (Appendix IV-5). These schemes are sponsored either by governmental departments or co-operative agencies such as Cooperative Central Bank and Agricultural Development Bank. In addition, the government sponsored certain other anti-poverty schemes which included the giving of house-sites, loans for purchase of fertilisers, rehabilitation of bonded labour, and so on. Since these sponsored schemes lie outside the SFDA framework, it is attempted to see whether the schemes sponsored by the special agency have greater chances of proving viable and successful than those sponsored by either the bureaucratic or co-operative agencies.

The respondents under related programmes were asked whether they faced any difficulty in getting the schemes (Table 4.7) 74 per cent from Medak said that they faced difficulties while 26 per cent said they did not face any difficulty. Those who faced difficulties were more among marginal farmers and agricultural labourers than among the small farmers. The small farmers had an edge over the others. 69.5 per cent faced difficulties while 30.5 per cent did not face any difficulty. In the case of the SFDA the number of respondents who faced the difficulty were 58.5 per cent. Compared to 72.7 per cent of the related programmes, the beneficiaries under SFDA had less difficulty.

The socio-economic indicators reveal that under related programmes 75 per cent of Scheduled Castes and 78 per cent of backward castes reported difficulties in getting the schemes

TABLE 4.7 : **Other schemes—impact on income**

District	Increased				Not Increased				Decreased				Grand Total
	SF	MF	AL	Total	SF	MF	AL	Total	SF	MF	AL	Total	
Medak	—	—	—	—	—	—	—	—	—	—	—	—	—
East Godavari	—	—	10 (55.6)	10 (55.6)	4 (22.2)	2 (11.1)	—	6 (33.3)	1 (5.6)	—	1 (5.6)	2 (11.2)	18 (100.0)
Total	—	—	10 (55.6)	10 (55.6)	4 (22.2)	2 (11.1)	—	6 (33.3)	1 (5.6)	—	1 (5.6)	2 (11.2)	18 (100.0)

Note : Figures in brackets indicate the percentage.

whereas only 46 per cent of forward castes reported that they had any difficulty. However, under the SFDA a large number of forward castes reported difficulties while the number of Scheduled Castes and backward castes who reported difficulties are less by 20 per cent. In relation to income and land the data indicates that in the case of related programmes the more is the income the more are the number of persons facing difficulty. In the case of the SFDA the number of respondents reported difficulty is less in the higher income groups than in the lower income groups. In relation to land under the SFDA only 33 per cent landless labourers reported they were having difficulties whereas they constituted a large percentage under the related schemes which is as high as 73 per cent.

The respondents under related programmes were asked about the nature of difficulties in getting and implementing the schemes. In getting the scheme the common difficulties faced are: pilferage at various levels; delays in getting the scheme; going round the offices and getting unwanted schemes. A few of them also complained that they had spent a good deal of money on pyraveekar without any return.

With regard to the implementation of the related programmes 61 per cent faced difficulties and 39 per cent did not, whereas under the SFDA the number of persons who faced difficulties was as high as 74.9 per cent. Caste-wise analysis indicates that 74 per cent among the Scheduled Castes, 53 per cent from the backward castes and 42 per cent of the forward castes faced difficulties under related programmes. In the case of the SFDA 85 per cent of the Scheduled Castes, 77 per cent of backward castes and 68 per cent of other castes faced difficulties. While all the castes were facing difficulties under the SFDA sponsored schemes, under the schemes sponsored by other agencies a lesser number of forward castes and backward castes faced difficulties. A majority of the Scheduled Castes faced difficulties under both the SFDA and the related programmes in implementation.

The income-wise analysis indicates that for better income groups under both the patterns there was no significant difference. In the case of lower income groups a larger number of recipients of the SFDA schemes reported difficulties than those of related schemes. Land-wise analysis reveals that from among the landless 69.6 per cent reported difficulties under related programmes while 86 per cent of them reported difficulties under the SFDA schemes. Similarly, a large number of farmers reported difficulties under the SFDA sponsored schemes as compared to the related schemes.

About the nature of difficulties in implementing the scheme, (Appendix-IV.6), the respondents complained that the amount given was not adequate to construct the houses; two, there was a lot of delay in grounding the schemes; three, the recipients of cattle complained that there was the problem of supply of fodder; and four, failure of monsoon. There were also instances of either the bullocks or buffalo dying. In the case of agricultural inputs, there has been delay in the delivering of fertilisers, seeds and pesticides. Under the minor irrigation programmes they faced the difficulties concerning the presence of a rock sheet while digging the new well or paucity of water in the new well. Most of the respondents under the housing programme complained that they could neither construct the house nor get a house in a good condition allotted to them.

Despite the difficulties in getting and implementing the schemes, the beneficiaries were asked whether they felt benefited from the scheme (Appendix-IV.7). 58.6 per cent from Medak stated that they were benefited while 41.4 per cent said that they did not. From East Godavari 76.4 per cent said that they were benefited while 23.6 per cent said that they did not. This indicates that a larger number of beneficiaries under related programmes feel benefited than the recipients of SFDA schemes.

When the respondents were asked to indicate the nature of the benefit they derived, most of them said that there was an increase in their total produce and an addition to their income. Those who said that they got house sites felt that they were benefited, as they had a piece of land for constructing a shelter for their families. A few felt benefited as they could avail themselves of the loan amount for consumption purposes, daughters' marriages and other domestic needs.

With regard to their opinion about the overall impact of these schemes on target groups, under related programmes 61 per cent reported that they had been benefited while under SFDA only 46 per cent reported that the target groups were benefited. Caste-wise analysis reveals that 52 per cent of the Scheduled Castes under the related programmes felt benefited while it was only 37 per cent under the SFDA. The income-wise details reveal that from among the beneficiaries of the lower income groups under related programmes 64 per cent felt benefited while it was only 34 per cent under the SFDA. In the income groups of Rs. 900—Rs. 1,500, 60 per cent reported they having been benefited under related programmes while it was only 40 per cent under the SFDA. The land-wise analysis indicates that from among the landless labourers 42 per cent reported their having been benefited under the SFDA while it was 70 per cent under related programmes. This is true of marginal farmers and medium farmers too. Thus the related schemes sponsored by the regular governmental agencies and co-operatives appear to have left a better impression than the SFDA—a special agency created for the purpose.

Those respondents under the related programmes who stated that they were not benefited by the schemes were asked to state the reasons for it. The pattern of responses is as follows; they did not receive the whole amount meant for the scheme; the amount given was not sufficient for the purpose it was given; the animals died because of inadequate veterinary facilities; the implements given were defective; the infrastructural facilities for the scheme were inadequate; inputs given for agriculture were not of good quality; the failure of the monsoon damaged agriculture and the domestic needs and difficulties compelled them to divert the loans, and so on.

The analysis reveals that the related programmes had some impact on the target groups. Schemes like house-sites, release of bonded labour and land distribution do not involve much of a loan component. Therefore, most of the recipients of these schemes naturally feel benefited by them. This indicates that any benefit in the shape of a physical asset is percieved as a positive gain by the target groups. Those respondents who complained against the schemes were recipients of the type of schemes which were identical with those of the SFDA. Therefore, the kind of difficulties associated with the SFDA schemes are also experienced by the beneficiaries of related programmes too.

The viability of all the SFDA and non-SFDA schemes is

sought to be analysed with the help of secondary data pertaining to the loan recovery position furnished by the co-operative and commercial banks working within the jurisdiction of the two blocks. This includes Co-operative Agriculture Development Bank, State Bank of India, Andhra Bank, State Bank of Hyderabad, Co-operative Central Banks (Table 4.8). Regular repayment of the loans can be treated as one of the indicators of viability of the schemes.

The data reveals that in Siddipet block the average loan amount advanced under the minor irrigation, animal husbandry and agricultural schemes by all the banks was 54 per cent, 36 per cent and 10 per cent respectively. The recovery position under minor irrigation, animal husbandry and agriculture was 54 per cent, 50 per cent and 35 per cent respectively. This shows that the recovery of loans is slightly better in the case of minor irrigation schemes than in the case of animal husbandry and agricultural schemes. Under animal husbandry schemes the repayment is the highest in the case of sheep units. The recovery is lowest in as far as agricultural schemes are concerned. On an average the recovery has been 46 per cent.

In Shankavaram block State Bank of India, Cooperative Agriculture Development Bank and Andhra Bank advanced loans while the State Bank of Hyderabad and Cooperative Central Bank did not advance loans. From these loans 38 per cent of the amount is advanced for minor irrigation, 20 per cent for agricultural schemes and more than 42 per cent for animal husbandry schemes. The recovery of the loans shows that under minor irrigation it is 51.7 per cent, under agricultural schemes it was 38 per cent and under animal husbandry schemes it was 65 per cent. This indicates that in Shankavaram block on an average the recovery has been slightly more than 51 per cent.

An attempt is made to compare the income levels of the beneficiaries under various types of schemes (Table 4.9). The data reveals that under minor irrigation schemes 43.6 per cent of the small farmers and 17 per cent marginal farmers were found to be above the poverty line. Under agricultural schemes 61.6 per cent of the small and 25.0 per cent of the marginal farmers were above the poverty line. Under animal husbandry schemes 37 per cent of small and 20.4 per cent of marginal farmers and 11.2 per cent of the agricultural labourers were above the poverty line.

TABLE 4.8 : **The loan recovery position under different banks**

Name of Bank	No. of villages covered by each bank		Advance Rs. lakhs		Recovery (%)		Scheme wise Advance							Scheme wise Recovery					
	Medak	E.G. Dist	Medak	E.G. Dist	Medak	East Godavari Dist	Medak			E.G. Dist				Medak			E.G. Dist		
							MI %	Ag %	AH %	MI %	Ag %	AH %	Ors %	MI %	Ag %	AH %	MI %	Ag %	AH %
1. SBI ADB	21	76	10.5	45.0	50	50	30	30	40	10	20	70	—	70	30	60	60	50	65
2. CADB	149	140	45.3	17.0	40	20	90	—	10	80	5	10	5	40	—	50	30	20	—
3. Andhra Bank	27	13 (FSCS)	14.0	5.0	89	78	55	—	45	25	35	40	—	60	—	40	65	60	—
4. SBI	3	—	4.0	—	60	—	55	10	35	—	—	—	—	60	40	70	—	40	—
5. C.C.B.	59	—	11.0	—	30	—	40	—	60	—	—	—	—	40	—	35	—	20	—

There is none in this category under the other schemes. Under all the schemes small farmers have an edge over the marginal farmers and agricultural labourers. If the number of persons above the poverty line is any indication the data suggests that it is not determined by the type of the schemes because large number of the beneficiaries under all the schemes were below the poverty line. A comparison of the beneficiaries above the poverty line indicates the other categories. This shows that the generation of additional income is linked more with the category of the beneficiary and the land they own than with the type of the schemes.

IV

An examination of viability of the schemes is crucial to the policy analysis. For the schemes which proved to be economically viable should be strengthened while the schemes that do not stand the test should either be discarded or redesigned. The small farmers' development agency sponsored broadly three types of schemes, namely minor irrigation schemes, livestock schemes and agricultural schemes. In addition there were related programmes sponsored by various other governmental agencies. An observational analysis reveals that all these schemes are fraught with a number of problems and difficulties. These problems include procedural difficulties, unscientific land records, inadequate infrastructural facilities, poor technical support and unfavourable geo-climatic conditions.

As regards employment and income, the viability is sought to be examined in respect of minor irrigation schemes. A majority of the beneficiaries under all the schemes reported that the schemes did not generate any additional employment (Appendix-IV.8). In respect of income the data reveals that half of the small farmers and one-third of marginal farmers reported their having received additional income.

The minor irrigation schemes include four schemes, namely the new well, well development, oil engine and electric motor. None of the schemes could generate additional employment and income (Appendix-IV.9).

An analysis of additional income generated indicates that the minor irrigation schemes did not have any significant impact. No minor irrigation scheme could be categorised as viable in

TABLE 4.9 : **Income levels of beneficiaries under different schemes**

Income Range	Minor Irrigation								Agriculture							
	Medak				E. Godavari				Medak				E. Godavari			
	SF	MF	AL	T	SF	MF	AL	T	SF	MF	AL	T	SF	MF	AL	T
1	2				3				4				5			
0-300	10	14	—	24	—	—	—	—	—	1	—	1	—	—	—	—
%	19.6	35.9	—	26.7	—	—	—	—	—	14.3	—	6.7	—	—	—	—
301-600	23	15	—	38	—	3	—	3	—	1	—	1	—	7	1	8
%	45.1	38.5	—	42.2	—	50.0	—	20.0	—	14.3	—	6.7	—	50.0	100	40.0
601-900	8	3	—	11	2	2	—	4	4	3	—	7	1	4	—	5
%	15.7	7.7	—	12.2	22.3	33.3	—	26.7	50.0	42.9	—	46.7	20.0	28.6	—	25.0
901-1200	5	5	—	10	4	—	—	4	—	1	—	1	2	1	—	3
%	9.8	12.8	—	11.1	44.4	—	—	26.7	—	14.3	—	6.7	40.0	7.1	—	15.0
1200	5	2	—	7	3	1	—	4	4	1	—	5	2	2	—	4
%	9.8	5.1	—	7.8	33.3	16.7	—	26.7	50.0	14.3	—	33.2	40.0	14.3	—	20.0
Total	51	39	—	90	9	6	—	15	8	7	—	15	5	14	1	20
%	100	100	—	100	100	100	—	100	10.0	100	—	100	100	100	100	100

Income Range	Animal Husbandary								Others							
	Medak				E. Godavari				Medak				E. Godavari			
	SF	MF	AL	T	SF	MF	AL	T	SF	MF	AL	T	SF	MF	AL	T
1	6				7				8				9			
0-300	6	3	1	10	3	7	14	24	—	—	—	—	3	—	1	4
%	26.1	23.1	100	27.0	13.0	16.3	40.0	23.8	—	—	—	—	50.0	—	9.1	22.2
301-600	7	4	—	11	5	14	10	29	—	—	—	—	2	1	7	10
%	30.4	30.8	—	29.7	21.7	32.6	28.6	28.7	—	—	—	—	33.3	100	63.6	55.6
601-900	4	4	—	8	4	12	7	23	—	—	—	—	1	—	3	4
%	17.4	30.8	—	21.6	17.4	27.9	20.0	22.8	—	—	—	—	16.7	—	27.3	22.2
901-1200	3	2	—	5	2	5	2	9	—	—	—	—	—	—	—	—
%	13.0	15.4	—	13.5	8.7	11.6	5.7	8.9	—	—	—	—	—	—	—	—
1200	3	—	—	3	9	5	2	16	—	—	—	—	—	—	—	—
%	13.0	—	—	8.1	39.1	11.6	5.7	15.8	—	—	—	—	—	—	—	—
Total	23	13	1	37	23	43	35	101	—	—	—	—	6	1	11	18
%	100	100	100	100	100	100	100	100	—	—	—	—	100	100	100	100

terms of its capacity to generate additional income. For although there was a rise in the income due to these schemes, it was not sufficient to enable the members of the target groups to cross the poverty line. Comparison of the performance of different schemes reveals that well development scheme proved to be a better scheme for the small farmers and oil engine to marginal farmers than others. In contrast, the new well scheme proved to be too feeble to create any additional income.

Further probing into the causes for such an unimpressive performance has shown that respondents under all the categories of minor irrigation schemes, except well development had faced difficulties in getting and implementing the schemes. In most of the cases it took more than six months to get the scheme itself. It is interesting to observe that while 60 per cent of the respondents reported difficulties in getting the scheme, 80 per cent stated that they had difficulties in implementing the schemes (Appendix-IV.10). These difficulties relate to absence of technological support, unsuitability of the geo-climatic conditions and insufficient infrastructural facilities.

The second major programme taken up by small farmers' development agency is animal husbandry schemes. An examination of viability reveals that animal husbandry schemes generated more additional employment than minor irrigation schemes. In the case of agricultural labourers, however, there had been no additional employment in either of the districts. With regard to income a majority of small and marginal farmers reported either stagnation or a fall in the income.

Of the three livestock schemes, namely, milch cattle, sheep rearing and poultry, the milch cattle schemes generated lesser employment than the sheep and poultry units. With regard to income the milch cattle and poultry caused a decline in the income. Under the milch cattle scheme half of the respondents suffered a decline in their income. The sheep schemes generated a rise in their income. Some of the schemes generated additional employment but not income.

Livestock schemes are regarded as one of the most vital schemes, particularly to those groups who do not have land. The agricultural labourers were not extensively covered. The net impact of the scheme on them was that a few agricultural labourers who had been above the poverty line slipped into below the poverty line group. Agricultural labourers as a class suffered a fall of 13.6 per cent in their incomes due to these schemes.

None of the livestock schemes proved to be economically viable. Of the three schemes sheep breeding could generate additional income. Yet it was not sufficient to enable the members of the target groups to cross the poverty line. On the contrary the other schemes caused further impoverishment of agricultural labourers.

This disastrous performance of the schemes can partly be traced to the difficulties in getting and implementing the schemes. Although milch cattle schemes were sanctioned in less than three months they floundered badly in respect of implementation (Appendix-IV.11). The livestock schemes suffered in implementation mainly due to the inadequacy of infrastructure and unsuitability of geo-climatic conditions. In addition the schemes suffered from problems of multi-dimensional nature.

Coming to agricultural schemes, the recipients reported additional income but not employment. The agricultural development schemes such as cart and bullock schemes resulted in effecting a rise in the income of marginal and small farmers. The plough and bullock scheme resulted in effecting a rise in the income of marginal farmers and agricultural labourers but caused a fall in the income of small farmers. Although land development schemes generated additional income, they also did not prove viable as they could not help the members of the target group to cross the poverty line.

With regard to the difficulties in getting the scheme the majority had faced difficulties. Scheme-wise details indicate that recipients of plough and bullock scheme relatively had lesser difficulties. In respect of the implementation of the scheme too they faced difficulties although the situation was slightly better in the case of plough and bullock scheme.

The other schemes that the SFDA sponsored were the supply of nylon nets to the fishermen and other schemes. The respondents under nylon net scheme like those under a few other schemes had no difficulty in getting the scheme but faced difficulties in implementing them (Appendix-IV-12). In spite of implementational difficulties the majority reported that they had been benefited by the schemes. The scheme generated

40.2 per cent of additional per capita income and a few beneficiaries could cross the poverty line. In contrast, under the mango tree scheme the beneficiaries suffered a fall in their incomes. Although nylon net scheme has potentiality to become viable, it needs greater support if it has to help the members to cross the poverty line.

A comparison between the related programmes and the SFDA scheme is made to assess whether a special agency is better suited to the task. The analyses reveal that while the SFDA could deliver the schemes in a slightly smoother fashion, particularly to the Scheduled Castes and backward castes, its schemes encountered more difficulties in implementation than others. In terms of gain the target groups feel that the related programmes have been more beneficial than the SFDA schemes. This is partly on account of the fact that under the related programmes the benefit was in terms of physical assets such as house-sites or land. The target groups perceive that a physical asset is a better form of benefit than other forms of benefits.

The viability of the schemes is also examined from stand point of the repayment position of the loans to the banks. The recovery was made in about 50 per cent of the cases. On the whole the recovery was slightly better in the case of minor irrigation schemes than in case of livestock schemes. The position under the agricultural development schemes appear to be quite bleak. Comparatively, the recovery position in East Godavari is slightly better than Medak district.

The last indicator used for comparison is that of income levels of the beneficiaries under various schemes. The data reveals that under all types of schemes a majority were found to be below the poverty line (Appendix-IV.13). One-third of small farmers and about one-fourth of marginal farmers, irrespective of the type of the scheme, were found to be in the above-poverty-line group. The number of agricultural labourers belong to this category is negligible.

A relative assessment of various schemes shows that under minor irrigation schemes well development and electric motor and under animal husbandry sheep rearing units and the nylon net scheme proved to be potentially viable. Milch cattle scheme proved to be counter productive. Physical assets like cart and bullock, plough and bullock, house-sites have had a favourable impact on the target groups. A further probing revealed that land, traditional skills, and physical asset oriented schemes were relatively more promising than other types of schemes. In the case of those schemes which did not make much impact, the inadequate support of technology, gaps in infrastructure, unsuitability of geo-climatic environment account for the failure of the schemes.

In sum all the schemes proved to be non-viable, when looked at from the point of "crossing the poverty line". The rise in income and employment that a few schemes could generate was not enough to enable the target groups to cross the poverty line—the main objective of the small farmers' development agency.

5

The SFDA : Rural Bureaucracy

IN THE implementation of the anti-poverty programmes, there has been increasing reliance on the bureaucratic machinery. Bureaucracy has become one of the vital instruments in translating public policies into realities and the Small Farmers' Development Agency programmes is no exception to this phenomenon. Therefore, a critical analysis of the role of bureaucracy in development is essential. This analysis includes a study of organisational process to study the existing administrative structures with an emphasis on co-ordination, the social composition, the attitudinal disposition, and public image of the rural bureaucracy. It also attempts to discern the characteristics of the rural bureaucracy and their impact on developmental process.

As pointed out earlier the Small Farmers' Development Agency came into existence in the wake of target group oriented development strategy for the removal of poverty. The Government of India launched a number of projects in various parts of the country. Each project is confined to one revenue district and proposes to cover 50,000 beneficiaries during a five year period of operation adopting a compact area approach within the adopted district. There is an outlay of Rs. 150 lakhs for each project for a five year period coterminous with the plan period which has to be implemented within this outlay. No further break-up of expenditure is indicated to provide flexibility to the agency in implementing the programmes by taking the local variations into account. This has been one of the reasons for the creation of an autonomous organisation at the district level.

For the purpose of implementing this programme the organisation that has been created is as follows. At the Central level, the Department of Rural Re-construction is responsible for formulating the policies and providing guidelines for implementing various schemes. The Department also reviews progress of the project. At the state level there is a State-level Sanctioning Committee which sanctions the schemes and guides the implementation. The Secretary to Government, Forest and Rural Development Department is the Chairman and Secretaries/Directors of the Development Departments are members of the State-level Committee. The Joint Secretary/Deputy Secretary of Forest and Rural Development is the convener of this committee.

At the field level the Collector is in-charge of Coordination; he is the Chairman of the agency. The success of the scheme very much depends on this office which continues to enjoy the authority and prestige at the district level. Since the state administration leans heavily on the Collector most of the district heads respond to his decisions and demands. For an agency like the SFDA which has to depend largely on the existing machinery, the role of a coordinator is all the more important. The agency needs his interest rather than his interference. But, it is observed that in some of the districts, there is too much of interference and in some others they are not able to find time for this task. In the districts where the Collectors evinced keen interest and provided scope for the initiative to the project director, the performance of the agency is stated to be good. As one Project Director put it, "the Collector must repose confidence in me to such a point where I can decide matters on the spot without any hesitation. This can quicken the process of development". He added that, "effective rapport between the Project Director and District Collector can produce remarkable results". Thus the institution of District Collector plays a vital role in the SFDA schemes.

The Project Officer who is redesignated as Project Director under the new District Rural Development Agency is the king-pin of the scheme. In the instructions from Government of India the state governments were called upon to depute only dynamic and active persons with the necessary aptitude for this kind of work. The Project Director is a full-time man. He is generally drawn from development departments such as agriculture, cooperatives, animal husbandry, and so on, or belongs to the All India Services. He is provided with a full compliment of staff in his office at the district level consisting of eight to nine officers of Assistant Director rank drawn from development departments such as agriculture, veterinary, cooperatives, fisheries, industries, statistics and planning and so on. As senior officers are involved, in the programme, the Project Director needs to possess higher level of leadership qualities. It is observed that not much attention has been paid to the selection of persons for this position. Most of them are chosen on considerations other than their leadership qualities. A few of them are not interested in the job and try for their repatriation. In a few cases it is noticed that the choice was based on right considerations. This assumes importance in view of the experience of Himachal Pradesh where a dynamic Project Director could give a good account of himself.*

The Block Development Officer is the third important functionary in the SFDA programmes. The BDO being the leader of the team, occupies a crucial position. He is the key channel of communication between the district authorities and field administration. He is responsible for processing the loan applications of the SFDA and forwarding them to the district level. The BDO is to exercise an overall supervision over the field functionaries and also to see that the schemes are implemented properly. Some of the BDOs argue that since they are shouldering the entire burden of the SFDA, the whole process can be decentralised so that they can decide at their level about the schemes and watch their implementation.

The Village Development Officers (VDOs) and the Extension Officers (EOs) provide the link between the administration and the target groups at the grass-roots level. They carry the message of development, collect information, help in identifying members of the target group, process their applications and push them upwards for action. It is these functionaries who are to help the beneficiaries in getting the schemes grounded. Therefore, the rural bureaucracy operating at the cutting edge largely determines the outcome of the SFDA schemes.

---

* See Chapter-I for the details.

The District Collector, Project Director and his associates, BDOs and his extension team constitute thus, the heart of the development machinery and it is on them, the effective working of SFDA depends. The existing organisational structure is shown in the Charts 1 and 2.

With a view to achieving the targets, the Small Farmers Development Agency has been given autonomous status unlike most other government departments. This autonomy can be exercised in selecting the area or fixing up the priorities and in assessing the needs of each area. The autonomy while offering certain advantages, creates also a new set of problems. This aspect deserves a detailed analysis. The separation of an agency from the main organisation network at the district level and below is looked upon with suspicion by all other agencies. Some of the district and block level officers argue that there is no justification for an autonomous organisation at the district level when it is entirely dependent on the existing agencies for technical and administrative support. Most of the government departments do not accept the programmes of SFDA and feel that it is an additional burden thrust on them. These officers maintain that the regular departments also can produce the same, if not better results. This feeling is articulated more at the field level. At the Panchayat Samithi level it is argued that the SFDA has merely added one more level to the decision making process contributing to delay in the implementation of developmental programmes. They further argue that if the funds are placed at the disposal of Panchayat Samithi, which is accessible to the people, most of the delays could be avoided and implementation speeded up.

These being the feelings, no wonder there will be problems in their administration. The most important is the problem of coordination. This is the result of inadequate integration, absence of effective linkages and paucity of coordinating points in the administrative pyramid. For implementing the developmental programmes of SFDA the support and cooperation of a number of agencies like agriculture, animal husbandry, fisheries, industries, revenue, registration, cooperatives, panchayati raj, banks is necessary. Except the District Collector there is no other institution with the necessary authority to secure coordination among these various developmental agencies. Even the

CHART 1

THE VERTICAL LINKAGES OF SMALL FARMERS DEVELOPMENT AGENCY/DRDA

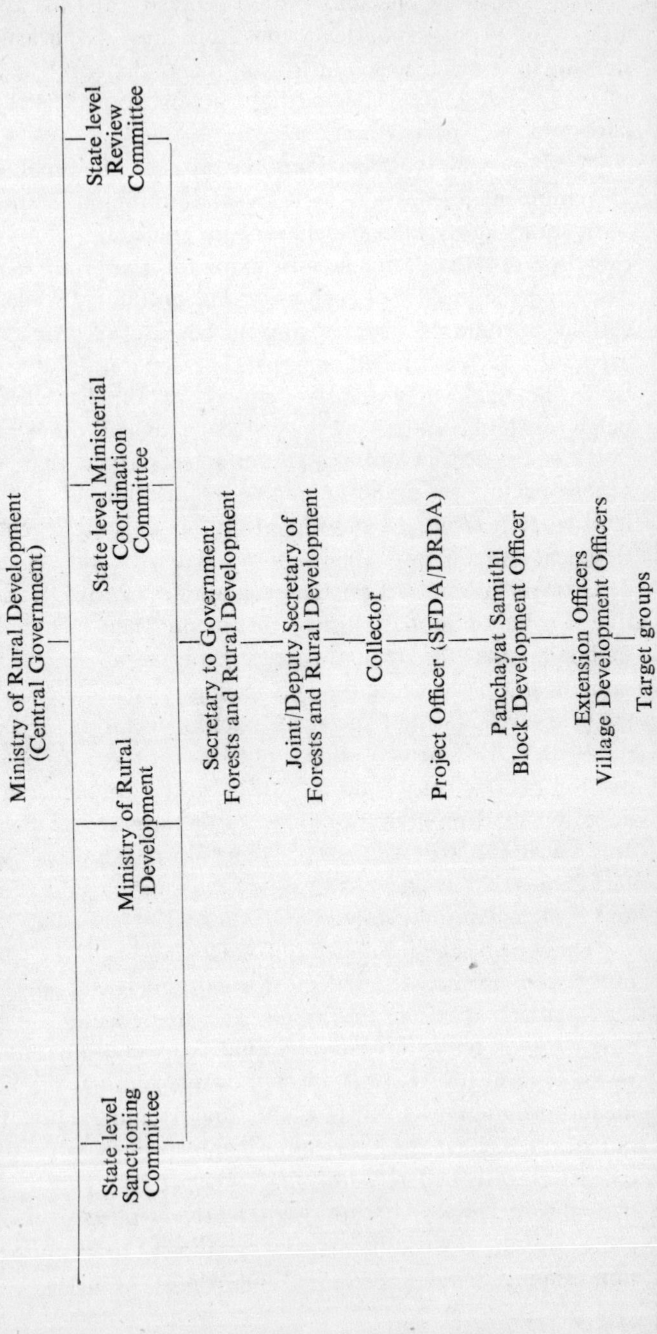

CHART 2

ORGANISATION OF SFDA/DRDA

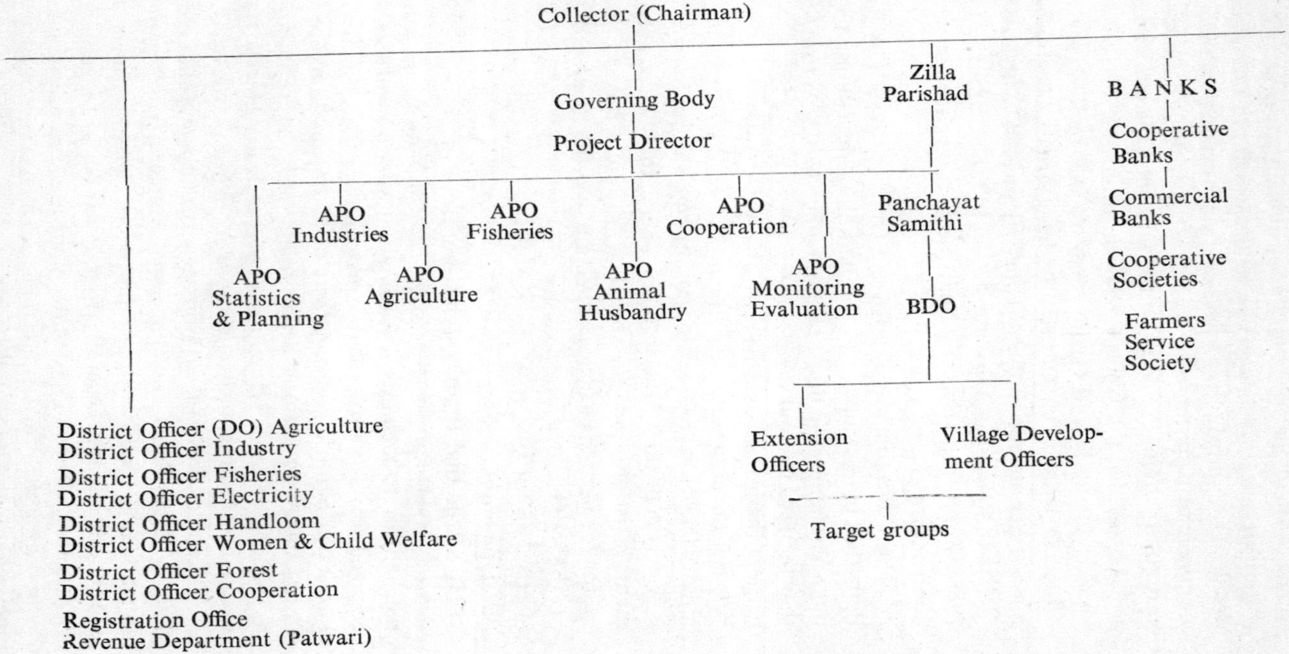

office of the Collector is finding it difficult to secure the cooperation of certain agencies like banks which are not placed under its direct control. For instance, one branch manager of a commercial bank referring to a District Collector said: "I would not mind lending 50 lakhs to the District Collector for disbursement, provided the Collector takes upon the responsibility to recover the loans and repays them to the bank regularly". He added that "mere enthusiasm of the District Collector cannot be a guarantee to the public money deposited with banks". The Collectors go on coaxing the banks to take helpful attitude but there is no formal institutional mechanism through which their cooperation can be ensured.

The Collectors and the Project Officers of SFDA complain that the banks have not been voluntarily coming forward to finance schemes for the rural poor. The banks, in turn, complain that the revenue and development departments have not been helping them in the recovery of the loan amount. The conflict between the electricity department and banks, between engineering departments and banks and among various other agencies is widely reported. One instance where the "electricity department insisting that the beneficiary should possess the electric motor for getting electric connection and the banks demanding of the beneficiary to produce first electric meter for getting electric motor", epitomises the crisis of coordination in rural development.

It is true that there is some semblance of coordination at the district level but at the lower levels, there is no institutional mechanism to facilitate coordination among various agencies engaged in an anti-poverty programme like the SFDA. The Panchayat Samithi has no effective institutional linkage with the functionaries of various departments such as revenue, animal husbandry, electricity, banks, cooperatives. The BDO is the weakest joint among the various agencies at that level.[1]

The breakdown of co-ordination is almost total at the village. The Village Panchayat has no control over a number of functionaries working at that level. The sarpanch and the village officer[2] are generally found to be at loggerheads with each other. The VDOs state that the revenue functionaries exhibit an unhelpful attitude. The VDO at the village level is the weakest link in the developmental chain. He has neither the powers nor the prestige to secure the co-operation of other functionaries. Added to it most of the functionaries at the village level think that they have no stakes in the outcome of these schemes. It is such institutional and attitudinal patterns that hamper the developmental process.

That the SFDA does not have even one functionary at the field level is a striking gap in the whole organisational arrangement. They entrust the overall responsibility of the SFDA work to one Extension Officer and two or three VDOs in some of the samithis of Medak district.[3] This staff, instead of being offered additional incentives, are deprived of even the rural allowances. For instance, all the Extension Officers and VDOs are entitled to fixed travelling allowances (FTA) every month. The functionaries on deputation to the SFDA have not been getting the FTA ever since they were entrusted with SFDA work. The concerned officers state that there has not been an adequate provision in the SFDA budget for this purpose.[4] Another limitation has been the adequacy of staff. It is observed that the Panchayat Samithis covered under SFDA have not had even full compliment of regular development staff which is evident from the Table 5.1.

TABLE 5.1: **Staff particulars**

Staff	Siddipet Samithi		Shankavaram Samithi	
	Budgeted Position	Existing Position	Budgeted Position	Existing Position
Extension Staff				
Block Development Officer	1	1	1	1
Extension Officer	12	12	11	10
Village Development Officer	21	17	20	11
Ministerial Staff				
Manager	1	1	1	1
Upper Division Clerk	2	2	4	2
Junior Assistant	8	7	7	4

The problem of co-ordination is also manifest in the inadequate infrastructure for the development programmes launched by the SFDA. While the milch cattle are given, the marketing facility and milk route are not taken care of. While the poultry farms are encouraged, the feed supply is not looked into. The animal husbandry programmes are stepped up but commensurate veterinary facilities and grazing land are not provided for. Several such instances can be cited from the field experience which go to prove that coordination is a missing element in the development strategies.

This inadequate integration of the total process of development cannot be corrected by creation of an autonomous agency like the SFDA without the necessary changes in the other institutions. Therefore, success of these programmes largely rests with the dynamism of individual officers. There are some examples of Projects Officers like the Project Officer of East Godavari who through his personal and informal contacts strives to fill in the gaps in coordination. The Project Officer opined that "the scope for personal initiative depends on the other officers in general and the attitude of the District Collector in particular". He added that "the confidence that Project Director enjoys with the District Collector largely determines the success of the former."

In an anti-poverty programme intended for creating viable schemes, monitoring and evaluation should form an indispensable component for the scheme. There is a need for considerable technical expertise not only to select right type of programmes which are economically viable but also to monitor and evaluate them continuously. Absence of monitoring and evaluation keeps the policy formulator and the implementor in the dark about the impact of the schemes on the target groups. In fact in an anti-poverty programme like the SFDA it is not enough that the members of the target groups cross the poverty line but the members should not lapse into it again. Under the SFDA scheme there was no provision for this function. The DRDA is provided now with an officer for monitoring and evaluation. This cannot be considered an adequate arrangement as a single functionary has to monitor the schemes in the entire district. In a district like East Godavari with twenty blocks covering an area of 10,807 sq. kms. and a population of 37,01,714, it is physically not possible to do the job. Such gaps render the machinery inefficient in achieving its objective.

Thus, the SFDA is fraught with a number of structural problems. Although it is autonomous, its autonomy is not looked upon favourably by the other district officers. The agency is considered a sixth finger to the coach of the district administration. Added to it the mechanism at various points to secure coordination is inadequate and ineffective. The agency has no staff at the grassroots level to implement the programmes, nor is there any provision for monitoring and evaluation. This indicates that the existing administrative structure of the SFDA is not cast for the role that is assigned to it.

II

As stated earlier, SFDA is entirely dependent on the existing administrative machinery at the levels below the district. Therefore, the effectiveness of the agency depends upon the vitality of this machinery. The administrative vitality depends upon the smooth structure, proper behavioural orientation and a conducive environment. It is proposed here to discuss these major dimensions and internal processes of rural bureaucracy and assess whether the existing set-up, on which SFDA is entirely dependent, is capable of achieving the goals. These observations are based on case studies, informal discussions with the concerned officials, perusal of official records and observations of the bureaucracy at work.

The structural dimensions of the rural bureaucracy deserves a detailed critical analysis. The important trends perceived in the operation of the structure are presented here.

One of the major trends in the rural bureaucracy has been its propensity to centralise decision-making. The whole bureaucratic ethos support increasing centralisation of decision-making. For instance, all the application forms relating to the SFDA schemes, instead of getting processed at the block level, are sent to the district and the decision for sanctioning of the loans is taken at that level. Another instance relates to the inclusion of a scheme wherein the SFDA East Godavari had to seek clarification whether coconut plants could be included under social forestry. In an anti-poverty programme like this, there is a greater need to decentralise the decision making to the lower levels so that the decisions could be taken on the spot. For greater access to decision making levels to the people is one of the prerequisites for effective implementation of developmental programmes. This point is not adequately appreciated.

The increasing centralisation has led to a number of consequences adversely affecting the programmes. One, centralisation resulted in reliance on top down communication blocking the other channels of communication. Each lower level depends upon and waits for instructions from the higher level and does not display any sense of initiative. That absence of free and frank communication stifles the feed-back mechanism is not realised at all. Feed-back is essential in a complex rural situation where anti-poverty schemes are being implemented. In such a context continuous learning from experience is warranted. The existing mechanism ignores the field experience and depends heavily on the ideas and some times fads of the functionaries sitting at the 'top' ignoring those who are down the ladder.

Centralisation and absence of proper communication result again in distorted reporting from the field. There are quite a few instances where the records are manipulated for the consumption of the higher levels, who are in no position to verify physically the figures furnished. For instance, it was discovered that "those who were included in the list of the beneficiaries did not even know about it". When this was brought to the notice of the concerned officials, they reported that the subsidy was released but the banks in turn did not release the loan amount. In a sample of 296 there were 21 such cases. But for the purposes of record all of them are listed under the category of beneficiaries. Some of the officials openly admitted these practices and asked "what else do you expect when the targets are thrust on us?" And added, "higher levels are not prepared to listen to our difficulties in the field".

Centralisation has yet another dimension. The programmes and priorities are frequently altered without any adequate notice and information to the field level. It is not uncommon that suddenly a new programme is thrust on the field functionaries while they are engaged in some other programme. For instance, when the field functionaries were engaged in special component programme meant for the Scheduled Castes, they were asked to give priority to family planning programme. This sort of adhocism is widespread in the case of most of the developmental policies, and the SFDA programme is no exception.

The second major trend noticed in the rural administrative structure is the proliferation of the institutions at the grass-roots level. As pointed out earlier, at the level of the samithi and below there is no mechanism to secure co-ordination. There are several agencies such as Panchayati Raj, agriculture, co-opera-ives, revenue, banks which operate with strong vertical linkages. These vertical structures, instead of taking the shape of a pyramid, emerge as parellel ladders each operating in its own style and jurisdiction. They do not share any common purpose or perspective. Their understanding of a development policy like small farmers' development is different from and sometimes even contradictory to. Added to it, there is no collective respons-ibility in implementing the development policy. This resulted in two negative consequences; (1) the rural poor are made to go from pillar to post to have access to the benefit that the policy offers to them; and (2) the agencies sometimes operate at cross purposes neutralising the developmental effort.

The third trend in rural bureaucracy has been the criss-cross linkages. Functionaries placed at various levels in the formal administrative ladder have 'non-formal' linkages. As a result the formal arrangement is put to severe test. Sometimes an indivi-dual placed at a particular point in the hierarchy, because of his 'non-formal' linkages with the top officers or influential leaders of the ruling party, emerge as a power centre in the organisa-tion. As a result the immediate higher level officer instead of supervising the work of the subordinate ignores his shortcom-ings, if not submit himself to his supervision.

Another aspect of these relationships has been the tendency on the part of higher levels to lean on one or two members of the group instead of the entire team. These individuals, it is observed, wield extra-institutional influence. It is noticed that the relations between members of the team are based not on the formal structure but on various extraneous considerations such as caste, region, religion, language and sometimes "common interests". This sort of non-formal linkages cause tensions in human relations. In one Samithi the Progress Assistant who belonged to clerical cadre was found wielding considerable influence because of his "outside" linkages. This was widely resented by the Extension Officers. In another instance, an engineering supervisor was feared by his colleagues because of his linkages with the Samithi President. An Assistant Project Officer was considered important as the project director leaned on him very heavily. There are quite a large number of such instances which strain human relations and upset the 'hierarchical' arrangement.

The rural administrative structure has also developed stresses since the relations between the line and the staff are strained. The line functionaries are responsible for achieving the targets in the field while the staff agency is expected to help the line to achieve the goals. Contrary to this assumption the clerical staff confined to the office wield considerable authority. They delay payment of T.A. and D.A. and sometimes even salaries of staff. This is done to establish their supremacy. They make the field functionaries go round them a number of times even for small and routine matters. The field functionarics, on the other hand, look down the office staff as men of no consequence. They give them extra respect when they have work and ignore them at other times. There have been several such instances which divided these two sets of functions almost into two hostile camps. This lack of positive attitudes on the part of each other makes the workplace tension ridden and team-work difficult.

Yet another trend of the rural bureaucracy has been the absence of reward and punishment system. It is rare that a hard working man is rewarded duly and a defaulter punished severely. Instances are not lacking where the officers at higher levels go out of the way to safeguard 'the interests' of even those who are guilty of either violation of the rules or negligence. The success in achieving the target is the least important consideration in the evaluation of the performance of a functionary. There is also an impression among the functionaries that it is not the work that is important but the intimacy and the linkages with key persons that matter. As a result tale-carrying, flattery, sycophancy, personal favours, looking after the domestic work of the officers or influential leaders, arranging dinners and playing cards to please the officers are becoming increasingly important in the bureaucratic culture in the rural areas. This indicates that the bureaucratic machinery is spending its time on matters which are not relevant to development work.

Another trend that is strikingly evident is the expansion of the bureaucracy at the mid-points and not at the cutting edge. For instance the SFDA and the present DRDA has a number of officers of the rank of Assistant Director with a full-time

Project Director. This expansion should be viewed as an expansion in the workload on the administration. If this is so, this additional load will fall on the field functionary who has to directly deal with the target groups. But there has not been addition of even a single development functionary at the grass-roots level. This expansion can partly be traced to the pressure that the organised sector of employees apply for expansion of the promotional avenues. The expansion in the middle levels at the cost of the field level can be checked if it is accepted that a promoted employee need not necessarily be shifted from the field to the office. In fact retaining more experienced functionaries in the field can be of help in the implementation of the developmental programmes. This would also strengthen the field machinery which directly deals with the target groups.

In the rural administration the level of competence—administrative and technical—of the bureaucracy is largely inadequate to the tasks that it is entrusted with. This is partly a result of the promotional system which pulls experienced persons into the offices and retains relatively junior, inexperienced and less qualified ones in the field, and partly due to over emphasis on generalist administrators. There are instances where an extension officer of agriculture is not being able to diagnose a pest, and a veterinary doctor fails to treat an animal. The failure of an engineering supervisor to plan any construction with available local resources is yet another example. In fact the schemes initiated by the SFDA are so varied that they call for higher degree of technical competence. The fact that the schemes were launched without adequately improving the competence of the functionaries and providing adequate technological support speak of the lopsidedness in the organisational arrangement for developmental policy.

Lastly, most of the precious time of the functionaries is swallowed up by the meetings and paperwork. Several of them think that most of the paperwork can either be simplified or reduced. For instance, the three VDOs and one extension officer who are associated with SFDA work in Siddipet Samithi hardly find time to go to the field; most of the time they are locked up in the paperwork. It is felt that there is considerable duplication in it. Although huge data is available at the state and district levels, frequent demands are made by the higher ups for some kind of information or other. There is a need to systematise the total paperwork through modern techniques. This would relieve the functionaries of unnecessary burden and the time so saved can be invested in the field work.

The second important dimension of the rural bureaucracy is its behavioural complexities. As mentioned earlier, it is not only the smooth structure but also the behavioural and attitudinal pattern that determines the performance and outcome of developmental programmes, more so of an anti-poverty programme like small farmers development. Therefore, a detailed analysis of behavioral problems is presented here.

An intelligent study of the administration at work in the rural areas reveals that the total development effort is guided neither by any concern for the poor nor any clear cut social purpose. It has become common in the meetings that the key officers invoke the name or office of the superior level and caution that the higher ups would become unhappy if the programmes are not implemented. It is this sort of "personality cult" devoid of social purpose that makes the field functionaries feel that they are 'servants' of a few personalities and not of the public. This in turn perpetuates a tendency to treat the rural poor more as subjects and not as the deserving and needy members of the target groups.

Lack of social purpose breeds pessimism, if not cynicism, among the functionaries. Such comments as 'this country will not develop', 'it is impossible to improve the conditions of the poor', 'the development programme can never succeed', 'all the help is a waste of national resources' and so on, indicate the pessimistic attitudes of the functionaries. Such an attitude is bound to be counter-productive in the case of developmental programmes and more so in the programmes that are intended for the rural poor.

Another striking tendency is the widespread elitist bias of the rural bureaucracy. Most of these functionaries think that the benefits are doled out to the poor, they feel that these benefits are unnecessarily extended to them. There are persons who maintain that if some of these developmental schemes are extended to the medium and rich peasants they would not only make better use of them but step up production. They maintain that poor can never improve. They add that increasing quantum of assistance that government extends to these backward people will have no impact on them.

It is widely complained that officers contact only the influential persons in the village.* It is these persons who decide whether a person should get a scheme or not. The officers confirmed this feeling and maintain that it is physically not possible to contact every villager in person. They add that implementing the programmes without the support and cooperation of the village leaders is difficult. A few of them comment that they are compelled to go to the houses of rich people in the village as there is not even a tea stall in most of the villages. As a result, the elite groups in the villages enjoy a unique position and an added advantage.

Yet another aspect of behavioural complexity has been its "de-personalised nature". The Weberian norms expect the bureaucracy to be impersonal for reasons of objectivity and impartiality. Impersonal bureaucracy may have some advantages but in an anti-poverty programme such as the SFDA there is a need for commitment and personal rapport with the target groups. On the contrary, the rural bureaucracy is depersonalised which is manifest on its indifference and hostile attitude towards the target group. Making a poor villager go round a number of offices, deliberately delaying the decisions and so on., are symptomatic of depersonalisation of rural bureaucracy.

There are a number of problems arising within the bureaucracy on account of relations based on authoritarianism among various functionaries. The higher levels, in matters of supervision and guidance, resort to authoritarian tendencies preventing the field functionary from frankly articulating his opinion. There is a widespread feeling among the subordinate levels that free and frank expression will invite the wrath of higher levels. Therefore, they silently accept the decisions coming from above knowing fully well that most of them cannot be implemented. Another consequence of such practice would be widespread fear psychosis among the functionaries. This can be observed from the way they behave in meetings and in their personal 'encounter' with the higher levels. There are several instances where some of the functionaries are found flattering

* The details are discussed in the III part of this chapter.

the officers whom they almost hate in the same breath.

Organisation climate of this kind causes information-lags and one-way-traffic approach. As a result the inputs into the decision making are fed by the fads and fancies of the higher levels and the outputs are conditioned by the feasibility and physical realities at the lower levels. The higher levels, most of the times, are engaged in fault-finding and not in fact-finding. Consequently, the lower levels cook the information in such a way that it tastes good to the bosses. The manifestations and consequences of authoritarian approach are not appreciated and understood by the supervisory staff. It is interesting to notice that each level suspects its lower level and exhibits authoritarian outlook, in the same breath resenting such behaviour from their immediate superior level.

Localism—the tendency of belonging to the local area—has become a part of the rural bureaucratic model. Most of the grass-roots functionaries are drawn from the villages of the same Samithi and are engaged in agriculture, business or some other subsidiary occupation. In some cases they treat these occupations as primary occupations and their regular jobs as part-time headaches. This also encourages favouritism to their kith and kin. In the process, the most needy members of the target groups may get either neglected or ignored.

It is also observed that most of the employees are obsessed with their own self-development. They are rarely found discussing and exchanging their experiences with developmental programmes. In fact most of the time they are engaged in discussing questions of D.A., T.A., pay revision, chances of their personal promotions and comparison of their lot with the lot of employees of other departments. Sometimes it appears that each functionary is an island upto himself in the office. This is also a result of growing economic crisis in the larger system on the one hand and absence of a shared goal or purpose on the other.

An analysis of the capacity of the bureaucracy to comprehend the developmental phenomenon reveals that they never attempt to go to the root of the problems. It is this poor and superficial understanding of the causal relations that accounts for ascribing the failure of scheme solely to the target groups. They offer different types of explanations for the failures but rarely examine them in the larger socio-economic context.

This also explains their incapacity to throw up new ideas and alternatives.

There is a widely shared feeling that the subsidy schemes accentuated the unhealthy practices in the rural areas. The practice of giving fixed percentage of "commission" for functionaries for sanctioning the schemes is an open secret. It appears that pilferages in all facets of administration in general are being institutionalised.

The third dimension of the rural bureaucracy that deserves a detailed discussion is the environmental culture. The bureaucracies are largely shaped by the culture in which they operate. For the culture can stimulate or strangulate the bureaucracy. In view of its importance certain emerging trends are pointed out based on field observations.

Owing to the increasing focus of public policy on the rural poor during the last three decades the rural administration has been interacting with the rural people at several points. There has been a shift in public policies aimed at rural development from time to time and every successive policy gave rise to new hopes. The overall performance has not been commensurate with the publicity and propaganda. There has been growing disappointment among the rural poor with the governmental performance. The net result of this approach has been increasing erosion of credibility of the bureaucracy. The low credibility has its own consequences to the bureaucratic performance.

Another environmental constraint on the bureaucratic machinery is the unresolved conflict between the officials and public representatives. The public representatives have a number of complaints and blame the administrative machinery for the failure of programmes. The officials in their private discussions bitterly complain against the non-officials and maintain that they interfere with the programmes beyond the desirable limits. It is true that structurally the demarcating line between the public representatives and the civil servants has not been clear. Behaviourally there is a gap in the social composition of these two groups. However, there are instances where non-officials hesitate to interfere unduly with the administration when they know that the officer is strong-willed and rule minded. Among the officers there are different types. There are officers who consider public representatives as important persons and view their pressure not as interference but as a part of the democratic process. There are also a set of officers who go completely out of the way to subserve the interests of the politicians. On the whole the roles of and relations between these two sets of functionaries are in turmoil. While non-officials fail to appreciate the formalised methods of functioning, the officials lack professional code among themselves. The net effect of the whole process is stresses and strains on the developmental process.

It is observed that the gap between people and the developmental machinery in the rural areas gave rise to middle-men (*pyraveekars*) in a number of villages. This institution assumed considerable importance on account of subsidy based anti-poverty schemes. The institution of middle-man is rooted in the social, political, economic and cultural ethos of the rural society.* This institution is a result of bureaucratic procedural rigmarole. The gap between bureaucracy and the rural people added vigour to this institution. The field observations reveal that bureaucracy indirectly encourages the institution of middle-man for various reasons. This gives rise to doubt about the preparedness of administration at the grass-roots level to take up the responsibility of directly dealing with the target groups.

Another tendency that is gaining momentum in the rural areas has been the growing consciousness of the people resulting in increasing articulation of their demands. They are found vocal and critical of the administrative system. There are instances of the rural poor demanding the benefits of developmental schemes. An administrative system which lacks the culture of accountability to the people is bound to be shocked by the growing awareness of the masses. The field functionaries are found bitterly complaining against the rural people and more so against the scheduled castes and backward classes. The growing consciousness calls for changes both in the structure and the attitudes of the bureaucratic functionaries. In the absence of such a preparedness the system will get increasingly paralysed.

The growing consciousness among the people leads to

* There is a full length discussion on this institution in the VI chapter.

increasing social conflict in the rural areas. For the people in the rural areas are divided into various groups on the basis of caste, traditional feuds and classes of haves and have-nots. The administrative machinery has to do a tight-rope walking which is an extremely difficult exercise. This calls for higher degree of tact, understanding and strategy in order to cast their support in favour of the poor even at the risk of antagonising the other groups. Whether bureaucracy can play this historical role in social transformation is a question that awaits an answer.

Thus the rural bureaucracy is faced with problems arising out of the existing structural arrangement and overall behavioural patterns appear to be not conducive to meeting the growing challenge thrown up by public policies for rural development with an anti-poverty thrust. The role of bureaucracy is further constrained by an environmental culture in which it has to operate.

III

As a part of empirical analysis, an attempt is made here to examine the social composition of the field machinery in the districts of Medak and East Godavari. The social background largely shapes their outlook. Therefore, its examination is necessary. For this purpose, the particulars of age, education, caste, service, rural/urban origins, occupational background are analysed. An attempt is also made to examine the attitudes of the functionaries towards the developmental programmes. This would provide an insight into their attitudinal pattern. For the purpose of analysis a questionnaire was canvassed to the extension officers and village development officers who directly deal with SFDA programmes. The officers at higher levels were interviewed through informal conversational method.

The data about social composition is presented in Table 5.2. They indicate that the field functionaries are middle-aged. They mostly belong to the forward castes and are not highly qualified. Origins reveal that slightly more than 50 per cent come from the urban areas. Out of 21 field functionaries covered by this survey only $\frac{1}{3}$rd of them are from agricultural occupation and another $\frac{1}{3}$rd are from professional groups.

The service particulars in the Table 5.3 indicate that a majority of them belong to Panchayat Raj Department and have

TABLE 5.2 : **Social background of field functionaries**

Sl. No.	Variable	Frequency	%	Frequency	%	Frequency	%	Frequency	%
1.	Age	25-40 yrs.		41-55 yrs.		—		—	
		9	42.9	12	57.2				
2.	Caste	O.C.		B.C.		S.C.		—	
		13	61.9	7	33.3	1	4.8		
3.	Qualification	Matric		Inter		Graduate			
		11	52.4	7	33.3	3	14.3		
4.	Origin	Rural		Urban					
		10	47.6	11	52.4	—			
5.	Father's occupation	Agriculture		Business		Service		Others	
		7	33.3	2	9.5	10	47.7	2	9.5

TABLE 5.3: **Service particulars of field functionaries**

Sl. No.	Variable	Frequency	%	Frequency	%	Frequency	%
1.	Parent department	Panchayat Raj 19	90.4	Other development department 2	9.6	—	
2.	Promotions secured	One promotion 2	9.5	Nil 19	90.5	—	
3.	Service in years	Below 10 2	9.6	10 to 20 5	23.8	Above 20 14	66.7
4.	Opinion about joining the job	Do not regret 6	28.6	Regret 15	71.4	—	
5.	Willing to change the job	Willing 13	61.9	Not willing 8	38.1	—	

TABLE 5.4: **Development perception of field functionaries**

Sl. No.	Variable	Frequency	%	Frequency	%	Frequency	%
1.	Development schemes	Success 2	9.5	Partly success 15	71.4	Failure 4	19.1
2.	S.F.D.A.	3	14.3	16	76.2	2	9.5
3.	Difficulties in getting the schemes	Yes 21	100.0	No Nil		—	
4.	Difficulties in utilising the schemes	Yes 20	95.2	No 1	4.8	—	
5.	S.F.D.A. approach	Appropriate 2	9.5	Not Appropriate 19	90.5	—	

put in more than twelve years of service. In fact ⅔rd of them have put in more than 20 years of service. Their career pattern reveals that except for a negligible 10 per cent, none could secure even a single promotion. This highlights the total stagnation in the rural administration at the grass-roots level causing considerable frustration.

To examine the morale, the field functionaries were asked the reasons that made them enter this job. Most of them stated financial and family necessities as the major reason. Quite a few of them felt that they had no alternative except taking up this job. Only negligible number were found interested in the job related to agriculture and only one functionary could find the job interesting and suitable to his aptitude.

To another question whether their decision to join the department was a right one, more than 70 per cent replied in the negative. When asked for the reasons, an overwhelming majority stated absence of promotional opportunities as the main reason and a few of them mentioned lack of job satisfaction. A few of them reported that the work was strenuous as job chart lacked clarity. Some of the following typical responses put the opinions in a sharp focus.

—"I think, it is my misfortune that I am in this job. There are no promotional avenues. My whole life is spoiled. A classmate of mine who joined as a clerk in revenue department became a tahsildar while I continue to be in the same position".

—"We have become victims of the community development policy. We feel deceived by S. K. Day and Nehru".

—"Our work has no purpose as there is no job chart. There are 25 types of jobs as a result of which there is no job satisfaction."

—"The job is so strenuous that it is beyond what I could imagine".

To a third question, about their willingness to change the present job, about 65 per cent of them answered in the affirmative. Most of them gave 'inadequate promotional opportunities' as the main cause for their willingness to quit the job. A few of them remarked that "this is the worst job" and "I am fed up with the job". When asked about their alternative preference quite a few of them were vague about choices but

TABLE 5.5: **Visit to government offices by the respondents**

Sl. No.	Name of the village	Visited Frequency	Visited %	Not Visited Frequency	Not Visited %	Total
	Medak Dist.					
1.	Marpadga	115 (60.5)	65.7	75 (39.5)	57.7	190 (100)
2.	Sirsingandla	36 (55.4)	20.6	29 (44.6)	22.3	65 (100)
3.	Peddamasanpally	24 (48.0)	13.7	26 (52.0)	20.0	50 (100)
	Total	175 (57.4)	100	130 (42.6)	100	305 (100)
	East Godavari Dist.					
4.	Shankavaram	111 (59.0)	71.6	77 (41.0)	50.3	188 (100)
5.	Vajrakutam	31 (44.3)	20.0	39 (55.7)	25.5	70 (100)
6.	Balarampuram	13 (26.0)	8.4	37 (74.0)	24.2	50 (100)
	Total	155 (50.3)	100	153 (49.7)	100	308 (100)
	Grand Total	330 (53.8)		283 (46.2)		613 (100)

TABLE 5.6: **Number of offices visited by the respondents**

Sl. No.	Name of the village	Number of Offices: One		Two		Three		Four		Five and above		Total	
		Fre.	%	Fre.	%	Fre.	%	Fre.	%	Fre.	%	Fre.	%
	Medak Dist.												
1.	Marpadga	57 (49.6)	59.4	30 (26.1)	69.8	13 (11.3)	72.2	12 (10.4)	80.0	3 (2.6)	100	115 (100)	65.7
2.	Sirsingandla	23 (63.9)	24.0	8 (22.2)	18.6	2 (5.6)	11.1	3 (8.3)	20.0	—	—	36 (100)	20.6
3.	Peddamasanpally	16 (66.7)	16.6	5 (20.8)	11.6	3 (12.5)	16.7	—	—	—	—	24 (100)	13.7
	Total	96 (54.9)	100	43 (24.6)	100	18 (10.3)	100	15 (8.6)	100	3 (1.6)	100	175 (100)	100
	East Godavari Dist.												
4.	Shankavaram	82 (73.9)	82.0	12 (10.8)	52.2	13 (11.7)	50.0	2 (1.8)	50.0	2 (1.8)	100	111 (100)	71.6
5.	Vajrakutam	11 (35.5)	11.0	10 (32.3)	43.5	8 (25.8)	30.8	2 (6.4)	50.0	—	—	31 (100)	20.0
6.	Balarampuram	7 (53.8)	7.0	1 (7.7)	4.3	5 (38.5)	19.2	—	—	—	—	13 (100)	8.4
	Total	100 (64.5)	100	23 (14.8)	100	26 (16.8)	100	4 (2.6)	100	2 (1.3)	100	155 (100)	100
	Grand Total	196 (59.4)		66 (20.0)		44 (13.3)		19 (5.8)		5 (1.5)		330 (100)	

were quite unhappy with the existing job.

When asked to mention some of their happy experiences in their present job, the field functionaries narrated their achievements in the early stages of their career. They gave the instances of introduction of new high yielding varieties, helping the people in natural calamities, construction of tanks, bridges, houses for the poor and school buildings. That they did not have happy experiences in the recent past indicates the declining morale. About unhappy experiences, political interference, humiliation at the hands of their bosses and political leaders, routine nature of the job, cases of being cheated, not being able to keep the promises to the people and delays in getting their salaries and other emoluments, were cited as instances of unhappy experiences.

About their assessment of the developmental programmes a very negligible number of functionaries thought that development programmes were successful. Quite a large number of them felt that either the schemes were a failure or only partially successful. All of them agreed that members of the target groups faced difficulties in getting and utilising the loans. They also felt that the approach of SFDA was not an appropriate one.

IV

An attempt was made to elicit the opinions of members of the target groups about the rural bureaucracy. This provided an understanding of working of the bureaucracy in rural areas and the emerging public image of the rural bureaucracy.

To the question whether the respondents had gone to any government office, out of 613 respondents as many as 53.8 per cent said they had visited government offices while 46.2 per cent had not gone to any government office (Appendix-V.1). The analysis revealed that in the district of Medak 57.4 per cent and in East Godavari 50.3 per cent had visited government offices.* Out of 330 respondents who had visited the government offices, 196 had visited one office, 66 two, 66 three, 19 four and five visited five or more offices. Further probing revealed that most of the respondents who had visited one government office had

* It should be remembered that the sample consists of a large number of beneficiaries of SFDA schemes.

TABLE 5.7 : **Outcome of the visit (respondent's experience)**

Sl. No.	Name of the Village	Work completed Frequency	Work completed %	Work not completed Frequency	Work not completed %
	Medak Dist.				
1.	Marpadga	78	63.9	37	69.8
	%	(67.8)		(22.2)	
2.	Sirsingandla	26	21.3	10	18.9
	%	(72.2)		(27.8)	
3.	Peddamasanpally	18	14.8	6	11.3
	%	(75.0)		(25.0)	
	Total	122	100	53	100
		(69.7)		(33.0)	
	East Godavari Dist.				
4.	Shankavaram	87	71.3	24	72.2
	%	(78.4)		(21.6)	
5.	Vajrakutam	27	22.1	4	12.1
	%	(87.1)		(12.9)	
6.	Balarampuram	8	6.6	5	15.2
	%	(61.5)		(38.5)	
	Total	122	100	33	100
		(78.7)		(21.3)	
	Grand Total	244		86	
		(73.9)		(26.1)	

Note : Figures in brackets indicate percentage.

gone either to Panchayat Samithi or the bank to receive the benefit leaving the main task to middlemen. The respondents who had visited four to five offices were those who pursued the cases on their own without the help of a middleman.

Analysis of village data shows that the respondents who visited government offices have been more from those villages which received better coverage than from the neglected villages. For from Marpadga and Shankavaram 62 per cent and 57 per cent respectively had visited the offices while from Peddamasanpally and Balarampuram—the neglected villages—48 per cent and 26 per cent respectively had visited the government offices. (Appendix-V.2) Castewise, 55 per cent from the scheduled castes, 58 per cent from the forward castes and 50 per cent from backward castes visited the government offices. Income details indicate that while in the lower income groups about 50 per cent visited the government offices, from the better income groups it is slightly more than 60 per cent. The land holding analysis indicates that while 37 per cent visited the offices from the landless labourers category around 56 per cent from the small and marginal farmers visited the offices. From the 5 acres and above category the number of persons who visited is more than 75 per cent. Thus of all the variables land appears to be an important factor in relation to the visit to the government offices.

To another question whether their work was completed or not, from those respondents who visited government offices 73.9 per cent replied that their work was done while 26.1 per cent stated that their work was not attended to. Further probing reveals that the reasons for incompletion of the work are: indifference, lack of influence, corruption and complicated office procedures and rules. When asked what they did when their work was not attended to, the respondents replied that they returned home helplessly. A few of them said that they approached influential persons and a few others bribed the officers for getting their work done.

The respondents who did not go to the government offices were asked about the reasons for not going to the government offices. The typical responses are as follows: "We never needed to go to government offices". "We do not know where the government offices are located". "We are afraid that nobody would care for us if we go to government offices". "They do

TABLE 5.8 : **Attitude of officers (respondents' view point)**

Sl. No.	Name of the Village	Helpful Frequency	Helpful %	Not Helpful Frequency	Not Helpful %	Do not know Frequency	Do not know %
	Medak Dist.						
1.	Marpadga	50 (26.3)	57.5	85 (44.8)	72.6	55 (28.9)	54.4
2.	Sirsingandla	23 (35.4)	26.4	17 (26.1)	14.6	25 (38.5)	24.8
3.	Peddamasanpally	14 (28.0)	16.1	15 (30.0)	12.8	21 (42.0)	20.8
	Total	87 (28.5)	100	117 (38.4)	100	101 (33.1)	100
	East Godavari Dist.						
4.	Shankavaram	49 (26.1)	70.0	65 (34.6)	65.0	74 (39.3)	53.6
5.	Vajrakutam	18 (25.7)	27.7	17 (24.3)	17.0	35 (50.0)	25.0
6.	Balarampuram	3 (6.0)	4.3	18 (36.0)	18.0	29 (58.0)	21.0
	Total	70 (22.7)	100	100 (32.5)	100	138 (44.8)	100
	Grand Total	157 (25.6)		217 (35.4)		239 (39.0)	

Note : Figures in brackets indicate percentage.

not care for people in dirty clothes". "There are others who do our job in the offices". "If we are to go to the government offices we have to forego our wage for that day". "We do not have money to go round the government offices". These responses broadly indicate that the respondents are not confident that officers would respond positively to their problems. Their poverty and the expenses involved in visiting these offices are the other causes for their avoiding visits to the government offices.

The respondents were asked to comment on the general behavioural style and outlook of the government functionaries towards them. To this question 25 per cent of them said that the officers were helpful, and 35 per cent felt that their attitude was unhelpful. About 39 per cent would not comment on this aspect as they did not come in contact with any government official. Castewise, the opinion about the officers' attitude (Appendix-V.3) is equally distributed among the respondents of all the castes. Income analysis indicates that the degree of resentment is more as there is rise in the income. In the lower income groups 30 per cent stated that officers were unhelpful, from the better income group around 49 per cent held this view. Land ownership details indicate that from the small and marginal farmers about 27 per cent reported that they were helpful and 37 per cent unhelpful. From the medium farmers about ⅓rd said helpful and about 45 per cent said unhelpful. From agricultural labourers only 16 per cent held that officials show helpful attitude and 22 per cent stated that they were not helpful and more than 60 per cent reported that they did not know about their attitude. The minimum interaction between the landless labourers and the officials is evident from the data.

Those respondents who held that officers were helpful observed that they were benefited from the positive attitude of the officers. They said that they got the house sites, milch cattle, plough bullocks, bullocks and carts, loans for digging wells and other benefits. However, quite a few of them qualified their response with comments such as "they are helpful when they are bribed". "They are positive but the vested interests in the village do not allow them to help us". "They extended us the benefits when we approached them through a middle-man". "They talk to us in a very sweet tone but do not actually help".

TABLE 5.9 : **Officers' personal contact (respondents' experience)**

Sl. No.	Name of the village	Personally contacted		Personally not contacted	
		Frequency	%	Frequency	%
	Medak Dist.				
1.	Marpadga	54 (28.4)	68.4	135 (71.6)	60.2
2.	Sirsingandla	16 (24.6)	20.3	49 (75.4)	21.7
3.	Peddamasanpally	9 (18.0)	11.3	41 (82.0)	18.1
	Total	79 (25.9)	100	226 (74.1)	100
	East Godavari Dist.				
4.	Shankavaram	35 (18.6)	47.3	153 (81.4)	65.4
5.	Vajrakutam	31 (44.3)	41.9	39 (55.7)	16.7
6.	Balarampuram	8 (16.0)	10.8	42 (84.0)	17.9
	Total	74 (24.1)	100	234 (75.9)	100
	Grand Total	153 (25.0)		460 (75.0)	

Note: Figures in brackets indicate percentage.

About unhelpful attitudes the respondents remarked; "they are careless", "talk but do not implement", "accept bribes and yet do not help", "get annoyed and lose temper unnecessarily", "advise us not to come directly and go through a middle-man", "make us go round the offices" and so on. About tackling such attitudes, most of them said that they could get the things done by bribing them. A few of them stated that they sought the help of a few influential persons or middlemen to have access to the benefits of development schemes.

It was sought to know whether the government officers directly met the respondents to discuss the schemes and their priorities when they visited the villages. For this purpose, they were asked whom did the government officers meet when they visited the village. An overwhelming majority said that officers met village karnam/patwari/the malipatel/munsif, sarpanch, samithi president, ex-samithi president, landlords, *pyraveekar* and village elders. When asked whether any officer met them personally about 25 per cent of them answered in the affirmative while 75 per cent answered in the negative. Castewise the data indicates (Appendix-V.4) that from all the castes more than 70 per cent reported that officers did not meet them personally. From those who reported that officers met them personally the scheduled castes constitute 29 per cent, the backward castes 19 per cent and forward castes 26 per cent. The income particulars reveal that from the lower income group 22 per cent reported that officers met them personally which slightly increased in the case of other income groups and touched 36 per cent in the income groups getting Rs. 1,500 and above. The land holding data reveals that the officials do not meet the landless labourers and meet only those who have more than 10 acres of land. For more than 85 per cent of the landless labourers stated that officers did not meet them personally and from the small and marginal farmers $\frac{3}{4}$th reported similar experience. From the group owning 10 acres and above 55 per cent stated that officers met them personally. This indicates that possession of land is an important variable.

When asked to give the reasons for failure of the officers to contact them personally the responses followed the earlier pattern of response. The main reason, according to them, is that "they are poor". The other reasons include; "why should the officers

TABLE 5.10: **Loaning procedure (respondents' view point)**

Sl. No.	Name of the village	Convenient		Difficult		Do not know	
		Frequency	%	Frequency	%	Frequency	%
	Medak Dist.						
1.	Marpadga	33 (17.4)	63.4	111 (58.4)	64.2	46 (24.2)	57.4
2.	Sirsingandla	16 (24.6)	30.8	30 (46.2)	17.3	19 (29.2)	23.8
3.	Peddamasanpally	3 (6.0)	5.8	32 (64.0)	18.5	15 (30.0)	18.8
	Total	52 (17.1)	100	173 (56.7)	100	80 (26.2)	100
	East Godavari Dist.						
4.	Shankavaram	46 (24.5)	80.7	80 (42.6)	62.5	62 (32.9)	50.4
5.	Vajrakutam	9 (12.9)	15.8	31 (44.2)	24.2	30 (42.9)	24.4
6.	Balarampuram	2 (4.0)	3.5	17 (34.0)	13.3	31 (62.0)	25.2
	Total	57 (18.5)	100	128 (41.6)	100	123 (39.9)	100
	Grand Total	109 (17.8)		301 (49.1)		203 (33.1)	

Note : Figures in bracket indicate percentage.

come to poor peoples' houses", "we are not useful to them", "we are small people". A few of them said that "village elders do not allow them to meet us". They also added that they are arrogant and think that "it is below their dignity to visit the houses of the poor people". "We are not clean and are in dirty clothes", "they do not treat us as equals". The consciousness on the part of the poor that they are not cared for is increasing. This indicates that the gap between the rural bureaucracy and the poor is on an increase.

About the procedures for getting the loans 17 per cent stated that they were not very difficult while 49 per cent found them difficult to get loans for developmental purposes. However, 33 per cent could not comment as they did not have any direct experience with governmental machinery. About their experience with the loaning procedures, they pointed out innumerable instances of delay, multiplicity of agencies, inconvenient conditions, inaccessibility to land records, bribing, wide time lag between release of the first instalment and the subsequent instalments, difficult procedures for repayment, high rate of interest, inexplicable procedures, heavy expenditure in getting loan, delay in release of subsidy, failure to get insurance amount when the animal died etc. These responses broadly indicate the procedural rigmarole in the rural bureaucracy which is resented by the people. They feel that they are put to difficulties because they are ignorant, illiterate and poor. This indicates the wild scope for improving the procedures which can provide accessibility to the benefits without many of these "administrative pangs".

The above analysis broadly indicates that while the interaction between the rural poor and the bureaucracy has been increasing their experience appears to be unhappy. The poor in both the districts think that government officers meet only the village elders and influential persons and do not care for the poor. The rural poor are equally bitter about the role of money, unhelpful attitudes and procedural rigmarole in the developmental schemes. This shows the growing gap between expectation of the rural poor and performance of the administrative machinery intended to serve them. Lack of confidence in the bureaucratic machinery has a deleterious effect on an anti-poverty programme like small farmers development.

V

The small farmers development agency is basically an administrative institution devised for purposes of covering specific target groups under anti-poverty schemes. An autonomous agency is created to insulate it from the bureaucratic culture. The agency is given a fixed amount and the target is expected to be achieved within a stipulated time. The agency has had to implement the schemes with the help of other district level departments and the bureaucratic machinery available at the grass-roots level. In fact all the functionaries of SFDA including the project director are drawn from various state government departments. Thus this agency has to operate with the functionaries drawn from the regular bureaucracy and implement the schemes through regular field administration. We find that "a new agency is called upon to operate through the old structures and their functionaries".

An autonomous agency like SFDA should enjoy flexibility in the decision making process. The observations reveal that the disadvantages outnumber the advantages. For it is faced with a new set of problems. Most of the district officers are not happy with the creation of the agency. This had added strain to the process of coordination. The total burden of coordination rests on the office of the District Collector, which is already overburdened with multiplicity of functions and roles. The process of coordination is more chaotic at the levels below the district. At the village level there is none to whom one can look to for coordinating the developmental activities. Thus the existing arrangement indicates two trends; one, the rural administrative pyramid is devoid of coordinating points; two, the trend confirms Riggsian observation that while differentiation is occurring very fast, the integration of the system is lagging far behind.

That the SFDA scheme is not conceived properly is evident from absence of any field staff of its own. Further, the nature of the schemes sponsored by the agency is such that it calls for large scale infrastructural arrangements. But neither were attempts made to build up the infrastructure nor were effective linkages provided within the existing infrastructure. Thirdly, there has been no provision for effective monitoring and evaluation of the schemes, which is an indispensable condition for an anti-poverty programme like the small farmers development.

Lastly, the management of the programme is entirely left to the rural bureaucracy at the grass-roots level.

The trends that are emerging in the style of working of the bureaucratic organisations in the rural sector do not fit into any existing conceptual framework. The goals for the bureaucracy at the grass-roots level are set ambitiously but the structure suffers from innumerable infirmities. The growing centralisation of decision making, proliferation of the agencies, criss-cross and non-formal linkages among the functionaries characterise the structure of the organisation. Further, absence of reward and punishment, expansion at midpoints, low-level of technical and managerial competence and wastage of time in the routine meetings and paperwork render the organisation so feeble that it cannot cope with the dynamic social system where the process of social change is triggered through conscious design. In these conditions, structures of this kind are likely to develop inverse relationship with the developmental tasks.

The structural infirmities can be countered only when the behavioural pattern is adequately geared to the tasks of the organisation. The rural bureaucratic behaviour is largely characterised by absence of concern for the poor which breeds pessimism, if not cynicism. The elitistic bias, authoritarian attitudes and a depersonalised approach to the people are likely to prove counter productive. Added to it, growing 'localism', obsession with self-development, superficial understanding of the magnitude of the problems lead to negative disposition harming the purpose of organisation.

While the structural infirmities and bureaucratic disposition have not been in consonance with the goals of bureaucratic organisation, the rural socio-economic environment has been undergoing qualitative changes throwing up new challenges. The growing aspirations and political consciousness result in increasing conflict in demands on the scarce resources of the society. This gives rise to new institutions like *pyraveekar* as a part of the support structure outside the framework of bureaucratic organisations. As the environment keeps on changing—it is indeed changing rapidly—the bureaucratic organisation would get increasingly paralysed.

An empirical analysis reveals that the rural bureaucracy consisting of the middle aged, forward caste functionaries with unimpressive educational qualifications suffers from low morale. They regret having joined the present job as they could not secure a single promotion and are prepared to quit if any alternative is available. Added to it they are dissatisfied with the developmental experience and do not appear convinced with the logic of developmental policy.

The weaker sections cannot be happy with such type of bureaucracy. A large number of respondents reported that their experience with the bureaucracy has not been a happy one. A sizeable number never visited the government offices and among those who visited a majority visited only once to receive the loan amount which was pursued and secured by the pyraveekars. Those who visited more than once and secured the loan are largely from those who possessed land. Such persons offered favourable comments on the functioning of the bureaucracy. With regard to officers' personal contacts, the responses indicate that the officers meet only those who have land. The landless poor of all the castes resented the indifference of the officers towards them. They stated that officers did not care for the poor whose living conditions and environment are not attractive. They also reported that the officers suffer from a number of complexes and are arrogant in their behaviour towards the poor. The respondents complained about the procedural difficulties. They pointed out instances of delay, multiplicity of the agencies, inconvenient conditions, inaccessibility of records and widespread corruption in the bureaucratic machinery. Thus they hold a strong negative image of the administrative system.

From this it is clear that the rural bureaucracy lacks smooth structure, behavioural preparedness and cultural conduciveness. Its morale is very low. We also see the signs of the poor articulating their demands and registering their resentment at the bureaucracy. Those who own land seem to be more happy with the rural bureaucracy. Consequently, the gap between the bureaucracy and the rural poor is getting widened rendering one of the vital instruments of public policy for anti-poverty programmes largely ineffective.

REFERENCES

1. When a B.D.O approached a bank for information about the loans given in the samithi, they flatly refused to furnish the information and he was asked to get-out of the office.
2. Village officer is Popularly known as patwari in Telangana region and Karnam in Andhra region.
3. For a similar arrangemgnts in all the other blocks, when the district collector asked the district officers to spare the services of one of its extension officers, none of them was inclined to spare 'their' functionary. On the other hand they argued that it would adversly affect their regular work implying that thi, is an additional work.
4. These functionaries drew the attention of the research team to this problem several times.

6

The SFDA : Pyraveekar

THE SCHEMES sponsored by SFDA for the benefit of the target groups involve multiple agencies and several procedural formalities. The target groups, being poor and backward, need to be initiated into the process and assisted till the schemes become viable so that they can cross the poverty line. The administrative system, as pointed out in the earlier chapter, has been found inadequate for the task. The existing decision making levels, that are located either at the block or the district levels, are inaccessible to the target groups living in villages spread over vast areas. The administration which is largely alienated from the poor* is also spatially separated from them. This calls for effective institutional linkages and involves establishment of a number of intermediate institutions through which the communication is facilitated and technology transmitted. Generally in a developing system the political parties should act as channels of communication and ensure mass mobilisation in support of development. The role of bureaucracy should be confined to the administration of programmes and transmission of the latest technology, In the absence of a well developed political system bureaucracy is not only called upon to act as channel of communication but mobilise peoples' support for programmes. In the developing countries where the institutions —both political and administrative—are not adequately developed there is a gap between the people and the developmental

* This is discussed in the Chapter 5.

process. The institutions such as SFDA which intend to provide economic help to the poor further accentuate the gap. This gives rise to new institutions or transformation of certain traditional institutions which step into the new roles. The institution of pyraveekar or middle-man or fixer is one such institution which assumed added importance in the wake of the new development strategy with a focus on specific target groups.

The link between the rural bureaucracy and the people is the middle-man who is popularly known as pyraveekar in Telangana region of Andhra Pradesh. His main role is to provide a contact point between the administrative machinery and its clientele. He pursues the cases, chases the files, goes round the offices in pursuit of the schemes promised to the target groups. Thus the pyraveekar has come to assume considerable importance in SFDA schemes. An examination of a public policy would be incomplete if all the institutions that affect it are not analysed. It is for this reason that the institution of pyraveekar is analysed in detail in this study.

The origin of the institution can be traced to the feudal phase when the relations between the state and the people had been indirect from all the angles. It was for the intermediaries to provide links and channels of information between the state and the people. In the process of gradual transformation the feudal institutions are being replaced by democratic structures. Although democratisation enlarged the base of the elite groups, it remained restricted to narrow circles. But the interaction between the government and the people increased mani-folds because of a number of developmental schemes. While the scope for interaction has enlarged, the capacity and level of awareness of the people has not increased in commensurate measure. There is thus a vacuum which is filled by the pyraveekar or middle-man or 'the fixer'.

The administrative structures and procedures, through which the state operates, are devised to formalise the processes and rationalise, if not legitimise the working of government administration. Further, the western bureaucratic models, which were evolved in a different socio-economic setting and cultural value set-up, had been borrowed by most of the countries. This gave rise to new combination of socio-economic forces. It was Fred

W. Riggs who in his work on ecological influences, brought out the tremendous influence that the larger socio-economic system leaves on the working of the government and its administrative system. For in the interaction between administrative system and the society one is bound to influence the other. Riggs further explained that prismatic societies, which are in the process of transition, developed their own peculiar institutions. This is a result of combination of tradition and modernity. The institution of 'pyraveekar' with its roots in the traditional nature of the system stepped into the new roles. This can be considered as one of the products of prismatic culture.

The people in developing societies like India are coming in increasing contact with governmental machinery and its complex operations. Earlier their interaction with the village socio-economic system and its elite groups was based on non-formalised structures of action. Further the rural poor who were hitherto dealing with one or two agencies are now to deal with a large number of agencies which came into existence in the wake of new developmental process. The people lack necessary experience and exposure to deal with complex processes. As a result they depend on pyraveekar to negotiate with new and emerging situation.

In the past the position of the pyraveekar was largely manned by the Karnam or the village officer who held formal position of village elder in whom people had confidence. Of late the institution seems to have acquired a new political dimension. This fixer has to maintain political linkages with leaders at higher levels and use those contacts to do pyravi.[1] And the politicians use their contacts with pyraveekars for purpose of elections. Thus their dependence is mutual—one institution reinforcing the other. There are also instances of pyraveekars turning into politicians. In fact pyravi has become one of the means through which persons are initiated into rural politics. Because of the traditional nature of rural politics the roles of politician and pyraveekar appear to be overlapping.

The middle-man also cultivates different government officers

1. Pyravi is an equivalent or a combination of 'pursuit' 'lobbying', 'influence peddling', 'pleading', and so on. See BPR Vithal, Vithal's Laws of Indirect Pyravi, *Swarajya*, August 26, 1979.

with the help of whom he 'delivers the goods'. He employs different techniques to strike rapport with them. These techniques include; one, looking after the needs of the officials visiting the village; two, invoking the names of important political leaders; three, making the leaders 'to put in a word' to the officers and lastly, using vocal chords either to please or threaten the officers depending upon the demands of the situation.

It is also noticed that bureaucracy discourages direct approach by members of the target groups to government offices. This lends strength to the institution of pyraveekar. The officials maintain that it is difficult to deal with a mob and view it as a waste of time. They also argue that it is difficult to explain to the rural poor some of the administrative procedures which they think are beyond their comprehension. Instead, they think that dealing with a few middle-men would be easy as they are considered to be well informed about the programmes. Officers think that procedural difficulties can be explained without much difficulty to the middle-men who in turn can communicate to the people in the language they understand. This explains favourable disposition of bureaucracy towards the institution of pyraveekar.

The need for the institution of pyraveekar arises, as pointed out earlier, on account of the inability of the rural poor to understand the complex administrative mechanism. Added to it the rural poor feel that they would not be properly treated by officials and they suffer from diffidence. In addition the number of forms and procedures to be completed and offices to be contacted are so cumbersome that they cannot handle it on their own. And a visit to government office involves expenditure without any assurance of the results. It is surely not economical—to lose their wages, incur the expenditure on transport and stay at the headquarters—all to no purpose. Therefore, they leave the matters to the pyraveekar in the hope that he would complete the task. There are also instances of pyraveekars meeting the initial expenditure and deducting it at the time of receipt of loan amount or subsidy.

The institution of pyraveekar acquired added significance and wider role in the wake of the introduction of subsidised schemes. The subsidy, from the point of view of a poor man in rural areas, is an amount doled out by the government. Although there is a heavy loan component, he would be too willing to pay 'commission' to the middle-man. In a number of cases it is the middle-man who carried the information about the schemes to the rural poor and goaded them to apply. The rural people feel obliged for this 'favour'. In a society where paying of 'commission' is accepted as an integral part of its socio-cultural ethos, the commission for the pyraveekar goes well with the prevailing rural ethics.

The institution of pyraveekar, however, caused certain unintended consequences to SFDA schemes. Firstly, the rural poor are made to apply for the needs not felt by them because of the subsidy component in the loan. This has had deleterious effect on the outcome of the schemes. Secondly, the 'commission' of the middle-man cuts into even the loan component of the scheme, defeating the purpose of the subsidy. Thirdly, instances are not lacking where the beneficiaries were not even aware of the total loan amount sanctioned; they were committed to more amount than was given to them. Fourthly, some of the pyraveekars passed on distorted information to the target groups. This distortion went to the extent of creating an impression that the loans would be written off.* Fifthly, pyraveekars being a part of the village socio-political framework, adopted partisan attitudes and helped only those members who were loyal to their groups, there are instances of middle-man lefusing even to give information to some of the members not belonging to their group in the village. Sixthly, it is observed that subsidy based schemes are used for political ends. Lastly, most of the pyraveekars had no interest in the welfare of the poor; therefore, their role in SFDA schemes can only be of dysfunctional nature.

On balance, it appears that while the pyraveekar filled the gap caused by the absence of intermediate institutions—political and administrative—their role created confusion about the schemes, largely defeated the purpose of subsidy and introduced distortions in the schemes. This is one example of how a public policy can go off the track, if it is not backed by adequate institutional arrangements.

* Some of the beneficiaries maintained that the amount was sent by Mrs. Gandhi, who would not ask them to give it back.

II

An attempt is made here to examine the phenomenon of pyraveekar with the help of empirical data. For this purpose both the Government officials and members of the target groups were interviewed.

One important aspect examined (Table 6.1) is the background of pyraveekars. The respondent choose their pyraveekars according to their background and the influence they may have with the higher-ups. In all, 19 types of pyraveekars are there in the field. And most of them are non-officials associated with rural institutions such as panchayat, cooperatives etc. In East Godavari there are ten types of pyraveekars, the most predominant types are the VDOs, elite of the village followed by sarpanch. This indicates that while in Medak the pyraveekars come from non-officials, in East Godavari a large number of respondents depend on the Village Development Officer. The VDO in the area covered by this study works as a pyraveekar in the sense he does the pyravi—goes round the offices and gets the things done. In the process, he exhibits certain characteristics of the pyraveekar and is found using some of their techniques.

An attempt is made to find out how many of the beneficiaries depended on pyraveekars to secure the schemes. Out of the total of 417 beneficiaries of SFDA and related programmes 88.6 per cent from Medak and 72.2 per cent from East Godavari depended on them. Out of 196 non-beneficiaries 63.4 per cent from Medak and 23.3 per cent from East Godavari approached pyraveekars for help and the rest did not approach anybody. This is indicative of the degree of dependence on the pyraveekar in the rural areas for getting the developmental schemes.

Further analysis (Appendix-VI. 1, 2, 3, 4, 5 and 6) reveals that dependence on the middle-man is equally distributed among all the age groups in both the regions. Caste data indicate that 91.3 per cent from the scheduled castes, 93 per cent from the backward castes and 60 per cent from the forward castes in Medak are dependent on the pyraveekar. In East Godavari also the trend is largely the same. 86.6 per cent from the scheduled castes, 76 per cent from the backward castes and 62.8 per cent from the forward castes depended on him. From the non-

TABLE 6.1: **Background of Middle-men—Assistance taken by respondents**

Sl. No.	Types of Pyraveekar	Medak		East Godavari	
		Frequency	%	Frequency	%
1.	Village Development Officer	26	8.6	112	56.2
2.	Panchayat Member	79	26.3	1	0.5
3.	Ex-Samithi President	50	16.6	—	—
4.	Educated youth	33	11.0	—	—
5.	Elite of the Village	13	4.3	36	18.1
6.	Village Officers	31	10.3	4	2.1
7.	Sarpanch	19	6.3	24	12.1
8.	Ex-Vice President	13	4.3	—	—
9.	Co-operative Society President	13	4.2	5	2.5
10.	Caste Elders	3	1.0	6	3.0
11.	Friends	5	1.6	3	1.5
12.	Close Relatives	4	1.3	5	2.5
13.	Co-operative Supervisors	3	1.0	3	1.5
14.	Teachers	3	1.0	—	—
15.	Ex-Sarpanch	1	0.3	—	—
16.	M.L.A.	1	0.3	—	—
17.	Samithi President	1	0.3	—	—
18.	Outside Elite	1	0.3	—	—
19.	Office Attender	1	0.3	—	—
	Total	300	100	199	100

TABLE 6.2 : **Respondents who took assistance from middle-man**

Name of the District	SFDA & Related beneficiaries			Non-Beneficiaries		
	Yes	No	Total	Yes	No	Total
Medak	188 (88.7)	24 (11.3)	212 (100)	59 (63.4)	34 (36.6)	93 (100)
East Godavari	148 (72.2)	57 (27.8)	205 (100)	24 (23.3)	79 (76.7)	103 (100)
Total	336 (80.6)	81 (19.4)	417 (100)	83 (42.3)	113 (57.7)	196 (100)

Note : Figures in brackets indicate percentage.

TABLE 6.3 : **Necessity of middle-man—respondents' opinion**

Name of the District	SFDA & Related beneficiaries			Non-beneficiaries		
	Necessary	Not necessary	Total	Necessary	Not necessary	Total
Medak	156 (73.6)	56 (26.4)	212 (100)	48 (51.6)	45 (48.4)	93 (100)
East Godavari	138 (67.3)	67 (32.7)	205 (100)	33 (32.0)	70 (68.0)	103 (100)
Total	294 (70.5)	123 (29.5)	417 (100)	81 (41.3)	115 (58.7)	196 (100)

Note : Figures in brackets indicate percentage.

beneficiaries in Medak 42.8 per cent from the scheduled castes, 57.7 per cent from the backward castes and 50.0 per cent from the forward castes approached the pyraveekar. In East Godavari 62.5 per cent from the scheduled castes, 14 per cent from the backward castes and 38.4 per cent from the forward castes apprcached the middle-man. The data suggests that the dependence of the beneficiaries on the pyraveekar has been very high among all the castes. Even from the non-beneficiaries a sizeable number approached him, although it is not as high as in the case of the beneficiaries.*

Examined against the educational background the data from Medak reveals that from the less educated, which includes the illiterate and near illiterates, (primary and less than primary) more than 90 per cent are dependent on the middle-man. Whereas from those who completed their primary education, only 40 per cent dependant on the middle-man. In East Godavari 76.8 per cent illiterates and 55.0 per cent near illiterates are dependent on the middle-man. Interestingly the dependence has gone up in the case of respondents who completed upper primary education. Thus while in Medak a significant relation is found between education and the dependence on the middle-man, in East Godavari there appears to be no relation between these two variables. Among the non-beneficiaries both in Medak and East Godavari, no significant relation is found between the level of education and the degree of dependence on the middle-man.

An analysis of the occupational background reveals that in Medak 90.1 per cent of the small farmers, 91.3 per cent of the marginal farmers took the help of the pyraveekar, but only 57.9 per cent of the agricultural labourers took his help. In East Godavari 63.8 per cent of the small farmers, 63.0 per cent of the marginal farmers and 83 per cent of agricultural labourers took his help.

The income analysis reveals that in Medak a majority from all the income groups depended on the pyraveekar. However, the dependence on him is 93.3 per cent in the lowest income group of Rs. 101 to Rs. 900 while it is 79.5 per cent in the upper income group of Rs. 901 and above. In East Godavari, the income and the dependence did not follow any pattern.

* This may partly explain why they continue to be non-benficiaries.

However, in the lower income groups of Rs. 101 – Rs. 200 and Rs. 201 – Rs. 300 there has been greater dependence on the pyraveekar while from Rs. 301 income onwards fluctuations are noticed which do not establish any significant association between the income and the extent of dependence. In the category of non-beneficiaries it is observed that cent per cent from the lowest income group of less than Rs. 100 and high income group of Rs. 901 and above have not approached the middle-man. In East Godavari also no income group from the non-beneficiaries approached a middle-man.

Land holding analysis indicates that from the landless category, 84 per cent took the help of pyraveekars. From the small and marginal farmers more than 78 per cent took their help. The percentage of those who took such help (75%) registered a marginal decline in the case of 5-10 acre group but there is a substantial fall in the case of 10 acres and above as it touched 54 per cent. Although more than half in all the land holding groups depended on the pyraveekar, big farmers appear to have depended less on him.

To another question whether the institution of pyraveekar was necessary at all, 73.6 per cent from Medak and 67.3 per cent from East Godavari replied in the affirmative. From the non-beneficiaries 51.6 per cent from Medak and 32.0 per cent from East Godavari stated that this institution was necessary to get the work done.

The analysis of those who feel the need for the institution (see Appendix-VI. 7, 8, 9, 10, 11 & 12) indicates that a majority of the beneficiaries irrespective of age group in both the districts feel it is necessary. From the non-beneficiaries in the age group of 20-40, more than half from Medak and one-fourth of the respondents from East Godavari expressed opinion in favour of the institution. In the age group of 56 years and above one-fourth from Medak and more than half from East Godavari felt it was necessary.

Caste analysis reveals that among the beneficiaries dependence on the institution of the pyraveekar has been higher among the backward and the scheduled castes. This is true of both the districts. In the case of forward caste non-beneficiaries, 57. 1 per cent from Medak and 25.0 per cent from East Godavari expressed the need for the institution.

The need for the pyraveekar is felt in the district of Medak by all the occupational categories although it is the highest among the marginal farmers. In East Godavari the need for him is not felt by the small and marginal farmers as strongly as the agricultural and non-agricultural labourers. From the non-beneficiaries about 2/3rd from both the districts felt that they could manage without middle-man while 1/3rd felt the need for the institution.

Income data also shows that the need for the institution is felt by all the groups among the beneficiaries. It is slightly lesser in the lower as well as higher income groups. A large number of non-beneficiaries in all the income groups feel that they do not need a pyraveekar. However, in East Godavari a majority of the non-beneficiaries from the higher income group (Rs. 1500 and above) expressed the need for the institution.

The landownership details indicate that from the landless as many as 84 per cent expressed the necessity of the pyraveekar. From the small and marginal farmers about 2/3rd of the respondents expressed the need for them. The data also indicates that even from 5-10 acre group 70 per cent wanted the assistance of pyraveekars. However, from 10 acres and above 45.5 per cent felt the institution helpful. It is interesting to observe that while 78 per cent from small and marginal farmers actually took the help of pyraveekar only 66 per cent expressed the necessity of the institution (Appexdix VI. 13 & 14.)

An attempt is made to find out how far they were responsible for the delay or otherwise in getting the schemes added or reduced by pyraveekar. The data indicates that from those who took the help of the pyraveekar 54 per cent got the schemes in less than three months while 63 per cent of those who did not take the help got their schemes earlier. From those who took the help of pyraveekar 19 per cent stated that it took six months whereas from those who did not take the help it constituted 16 per cent. In the category of one year and more than one year delay from those who depended on pyraveekar it was 27 per cent and from those who did not take the help it was 21 per cent. The data suggests that the delay in the case of those who took the help of pyraveekar has been more.

The analysis largely indicates that the respondents particularly the beneficiaries perceive a need for this institution. They were asked the reasons for it. 170 beneficiaries from Medak and 105 from East Godavari stated that the rules and procedures in the government offices were beyond their comprehension. Sixteen respondents from Medak apprehended that their work would not be attended to, fifteen reported that they were advised by the concerned officers to approach them through a middle-man. Another twelve respondents narrated that the officers did not care for them when they went to the offices. Fear of losing the wages, and the fear that the middle-man would prevent them from getting the benefits were the other reasons for dependence on him. That they are readily available in the village for consultation is yet another cause for such dependence.

In East Godavari the reasons mentioned for dependence are: the middle-man possesses initiative, and villagers can afford to take liberty with him. Fourteen respondents reported that one person pursuing the cases on behalf of a group would be more economical and convenient. Thirteen respondents said that unless there is a person to pursue the matters, the task cannot be accomplished. Eight respondents said that officers declined to talk to them when they visited the offices. Others gave reasons such as: "If we go they (officers) are demanding higher bribes", "middle-man explains to us the positive and negative aspect of the schemes", "bad health" and "fear of being asked to put thumb impression", are the other reasons for dependence on middle-man.

An attempt is made to know why a few respondents did not need the pyraveekar. Twenty four-respondents from Medak and 44 from East Godavari said that they have sufficient experience to deal with the government offices. Twenty respondents from each district complained that the pyraveekars extort huge amount from clients. The other reasons cited are harassing by and undependable nature of the pyraveekars.

To a question about the difficulties in utilising the schemes 79 per cent from those who took the help reported that they faced difficulties in the utilisation of schemes while from those who did not take the help it was 63 per cent. Although both the categories had difficulties relatively more number of respondents who depended on pyraveekar had difficulties.

Further analysis reveals that from those who got the schemes through pyraveekars 88 per cent reported that they utilised the loan for the intended purpose and of those who got the schemes without his help 79 per cent stated that they utilised the loan for the intended purpose. As regards the outcome of the scheme the data show that of pyraveekar-assisted respondents although 88 per cent used the scheme for intended purpose, only 47.4 per cent of them reported that the purpose has been fulfilled, while 63.2 per cent of those who did not seek his help reported that the purpose had been fulfilled in spite of these respondents not getting their assistance (Appendix-VI.15, 16, 17, 18). To the question whether the recipients of the schemes, on the whole feel benefitted from the schemes, 46 per cent from those who took the help of pyraveekar and 57 per cent from the other category stated that they have been benefitted.

When asked to narrate their experiences with the pyraveekar, varied types of responses were given. About sixty respondents from Medak reported that the amount they gave to him ranged between Rs. 50 to Rs. 800. However, a very large number of them reported that it was between Rs. 150 to Rs. 200. Forty six respondents stated that they had to wait for six months for the schemes without any results. On the other hand 24 respondents said that their work was done without any difficulty, although it involved giving of money to pyraveekars. Twenty-three respondents complained that they gave money to pyraveekars but their work was not done. There are other responses which include both positive and negative impressions that the respondents carry of the middle-man. While a few of them stated that the pyraveekar was sympathetic towards them as they were poor and helped them, a few others reported that they were cheated. There are also a few who stated that "since we could not pay the amount demanded by the pyraveekar, he diverted the schemes to others". A few others complained that middle-men appropriated a large part of the subsidy component.

In the case of East Godavari while the broad pattern of responses is the same, the "commission" charged by the pyraveekar appears to be slightly lesser. The respondents in East Godavari had more favourable comments to offer. For instance 24 respondents from the district said that their middle-man was a good man and did the job without involving undue expenditure. Another 21 respondents also said that their pyraveekar took very reasonable amount for doing the job. The 'bondage' between the latter and the beneficiaries appears to be strong; the beneficiaries bought a scooter spending Rs. 5,000 for the pyraveekar for securing the poultry units. Another group of respondents bought a bi-cycle for the middle-man for the 'help' he rendered. The negative responses are; four respondents reported that a middle-man retained milch cattle with himself as he was quite an influential person. And when one of the beneficiaries attempted to secure a second buffalo, he was removed from his work. Instances of delay and harassment by the middle-men are also reported by a few respondents.

From the category of non-beneficiaries about 40 respondents from Medak complained against pyraveekars. They said that all of them paid the amounts to them without receiving any benefit. A few respondents reported that the middle-man did not help them in spite of their repeated requests. There are specific complains which throw light on the working of the institution. Two respondents did not get the sehemes because of misunderstanding between the pyraveekar and the party. The second instance relates to a client who gave Rs. 1,500 to the pyraveekar without any benefit for himself. The third case describes the manipulation of the pyraveekar securing an electric motor.

III

The opinions of the field functionaries, extension officers and village development officers provide further insight into the institution of pyraveekar. This is done to gain an insight into and also an understanding of the phenomenon. These functionaries, being close to the field, have an intimate knowledge of the pyraveekar. In fact, as mentioned earlier, in the absence of strong political institutions, it is the administrative machinery which has to provide the linkages between the people and the governmental agencies. Therefore, views of theses functionaries assume importance.

To the question about role of the pyraveekar two-third of them thought that he has come to play an important role in developmental schemes. About his actual role the field functionaries conceded that it is he who publicised about the schemes and made the rural poor apply for them although the poor neither felt the need for those schemes nor were they equipped for taking up the schemes. In their judgement, therefore, the role of middle-men has been negative. This is evident from the comments such as "they are creating false impression", "they make unnecessary promises", "they adopt means that we cannot approve" and "they are good exploiters".

To another question about the necessity of middle-man, an overwhelming number of the field functionaries thought that there was no need for them. Nevertheless they conceded that the rural poor have a preference for the pyraveekar. When asked about the reasons why people prefer pyraveekars they stated that administrative procedures were so complicated that illiterate people could not but depend on them.

The pyraveekar enjoys confidence of the people partly because he lives with them and partly due to the indifferent attitudes of the officials. The officials agreed that poor people are not cared for. Therefore, people fear that their work would not be attended to if they personally go to the offices. They admit that people are not treated with courtesy and their requests are turned down without assigning any reasons. There are also other reasons such as lack of time and paucity of money with the members of the target groups to invest initially and this is taken care of by the pyraveekar.

To the question why people go to a pyraveekar instead of an extension agency, they gave the following reasons. The most important reason is that middle-men attach more importance to ends than means. They say that middle-men sometimes invest their own money in the initial stages and do not hesitate bribing any agency which an extension agency cannot do. The pyraveekar is readily available and accessible to the villagers. In addition he create hopes in them by indulging in sweet-talk. They go to the extent of saying that the loans would be written off. These are the things which extension agency cannot think of doing.

The field functionaries felt that there was a good rapport between the pyraveekar and the people. People frankly exchange their feelings with the pyraveekar and share their feeling about the actual needs for which the loans would be utilised. There are instances where pyraveekars 'helped' the poor in converting the "benefit" into the form that the recipient of the benefit desired.

The field functionaries feel that most of the pyraveekars

come from the forward castes, landed gentry who are engaged in politics. Of late, however, middle class backward castes are also throwing up pyraveekars.

To the question about the techniques that the pyraveekar uses, they state that in most of the cases the pyraveekars invoke their political linkages. They also have 'perfect understanding' with the concerned officers. They extend hospitality to the officers whenever they visit the villages. The officers depend on them for getting certain schemes implemented in the villages. Some of the pyraveekars have pleasant manners and are very polite and submissive in their behaviour. Such behaviour make them acceptable to the officers. There are also cases where some of the middle-men use aggressive language and manage to get the things done.

On the question of the 'commission' which the middle-men charge, the responses reveal that its range is between 10 per cent to 30 per cent. In most of the cases it is reported to be between 10 per cent to 20 per cent. This indicates that a large chunk of the subsidy is appropriated by the middle-men. It is also stated that the commission depends upon the level of innocence and ignorance of the people on the one hand and the nature of the scheme and quantum of assistance on the other. Asked about the reasonableness of the commission, most of the officers felt that it was unreasonable. They thought that the "commission" was far higher than the expenditure involved.

The above responses indicate that the field officers view that the institution of pyraveekar suffers from a number of shortcomings. They were asked whether there was any alternative to the pyraveekar, an overwhelming majority of the field functionaries thought that this institution was not indispensable. The solutions they offered included: firstly, the official machinery must replace the pyraveekar; secondly, simplification of procedures; thirdly, decentralisation of administrative decision making; fourthly, increase in the staff; and more publicity to the programmes and door delivery of the loan. They thought these measures would eliminate the need for the pyraveekar in an anti-poverty scheme meant for rural poor.

Here an attempt is made to compare the experience of the pyraveekar assisted respondents with those respondents who did not depend on them. This would throw light on the aspects on which the field staff commented. To the question about personal visit to the government offices, 59 per cent pyraveekar assisted respondents and 76 per cent from the other category visited the offices personally. From both the categories more than 80 per cent reported that their work was completed. A further analysis indicate that from those 209 whose work was completed, the pyraveekar assisted respondents constitute 74 per cent whereas 26 per cent belong to the other category. This indicates the growing importance of the pyraveekar.

To another question whether officers adopt a helpful attitude, 27 per cent of the pyraveekar assisted respondents said that they were helpful while 48 per cent of the other category replied in the affirmative. Further a sizeable section stated that they were not aware of the attitudes of officials. Among them the pyraveekar assisted group constitute 34 per cent whereas it is only 18 per cent in the other group.

They were further asked whether officers met them personally on their visit to the villages. From pyraveekar assisted groups 27 per cent stated that officers met them personally whereas from the other group 43 per cent said they met them. This indicates that the gap between bureaucracy and the rural poor relatively is more in the case of pyraveekar assisted groups rather than the self-dependent groups.

IV

The existing administrative structures are found to be inadequate in establishing effective linkages between a development agency like SFDA and the target groups. This has been one of the major limitations of the public policy. This institutional gap in these programmes is filled in by the pyraveekar. The task of this institution is basically to pursue the cases of the members of the target groups by pushing the papers and see that the benefits trickle down to their clients. In fact, it has become the key channel of communication. Thus this institution occupies an important place in the programme and can be considered as an unintended consequence of a public policy.

The institution of pyraveekar originated in a historical phase where the relations between the state and people were indirect. The feudal structure invigorated it and the illiteracy and igno-rance of the people sustained it. The institution stepped into the new roles created by the subsidised target-oriented anti-poverty schemes. For these programmes caused a spurt in the interaction between the people and the administration. Since the rules, regulations and procedures are beyond the comprehension of rural people, dependence on the pyraveekar has become inevitable. Therefore, this institution, as it stands to-day, can be considered as a product of prismatic culture.

The pyraveekar maintains linkages with the politicians in power. He also maintains effective relations with the key decision makers in administration. He looks after them whenever they visit his village. In certain cases he invokes the names of the top leaders or ministers and gets his work done. It is observed that the middle-men are using pyravi as a door to enter political field and then rise in the ladder.

The institution of pyraveekar has come to receive support from the bureaucracy also. The bureaucracy feels "safe" to deal with a few middle-men rather than a large number of members of the target groups. There are instances where the administration discouraged members from directly visiting the government offices. The officers support such a stand on the ground that it is difficult to explain the implication of rules to illiterates and ignorant rural masses. The phenomenon of a few field functionaries turning themselves into pyraveekars is also noticed.

From the point of view of the target groups, dependence on this institution became unavoidable. They feel difficult to deal with complicated cobwebs of administrative machinery. Visits to a number of offices is expensive on the one hand and involve loss of their earnings on the other. Therefore, they think that dependence on a middle man is convenient and economical. They also repose confidence in him as he lives with them in the village.

An analysis of the role of pyraveekar in the SFDA schemes reveals that it is he who publicises the schemes and makes the target groups apply for the schemes. However, on the negative side the 'commission' charged by him cuts into the entire subsidy portion. He transmits distorted information about the loans to the target groups. Further, in the villages he uses subsidy schemes as a leverage to establish his control over the rural poor. He helps only those who are loyal to his group and denies access to the benefits to others who are opposed to this group. Thus pyravee is being used to consolidate the power base of the elite group.

The role of pyraveekar is being played by different types of persons. In Medak district most of them happen to be politicians holding formal positions either in village panchayat or cooperatives. In East Godavari, the role is largely played by the village development officers, karnam, sarpanch and other elite of the village. The VDOs pursue the cases more as pyraveekars than as extension agents. This indicates how the extension agency can acquire certain characteristics rooted in the socio-economic system. In addition there are also professional pyraveekars.

An empirical analysis indicates that those who are recipients of the schemes not only largely depend on the pyraveekars but confide their real necessity in them. The non-beneficiaries are found to be not favourably disposed towards pyraveekars. This partly accounts for their failure to have access to these schemes. Of all the factors that determine the dependence on pyraveekar land holding seem to be the most important factor. It is clear from the data that an overwhelming number of the landless labourers depended on pyraveekars, but the dependence is much less in the case of landowning groups.

The respondents who feel the need for the institution prefer it on the grounds that, firstly, they do not understand the complicated procedures; secondly, the schemes involve contacting multiple agencies; thirdly, officers do not care for them if they go personally; fourthly, the officers themselves direct the poor to go through a middle-man; fifthly, the poor lose their wage if they are to go personally to offices; sixthly, depending on middle-man is more economical as he can go on behalf of a group and lastly, the middle-men are accessible and dependable as they live in their own villages.

The extension agency in both the districts admit that this institution has come to play a significant role. They admit that people prefer middle-man to the extension agency. They feel that the institution has a certain degree of built in flexibility and advantages over the extension agency. This includes certain unhealthy practices such as bribing the concerned persons, converting the benefit into the form that the beneficiary wants, advancing money initially for expenditure and so on. Further, they state that the middle-man instigates the target groups to apply for the loan with wrong information. On the whole, in their judgement, the role of the middle-man has been dysfunctional.

The field functionaries think that the institution is not indispensable. As an alternative, they feel that official machinery should take up this role. Increase in the staff, simplification of procedures, decentralisation of decision making, door delivery of the benefit and more publicity to the programmes can help in circumventing the middle-men. Although psychologically this has been the feeling of the field functionaries, operationally the official machinery does not respond to the target group when they visit them nor do they meet them personally during their visit to the villages.

It is evident from the data that the 'commission' that pyraveekars charge cuts into the subsidy component deeply. With regard to the time taken in getting a scheme sanctioned he has been able to expedite the cases, although in implementation the schemes suffered considerably. This indicates that while the pyraveekar can pursue and get the schemes, they cannot sustain them nor are they interested in that aspect of the schemes.

The institution of pyraveekar has come to play a critical role. The pyraveekar has both positive and negative dimensions. On the positive side, he publicises the schemes and makes the target groups apply for them. He pursues the cases on behalf of the target groups. On the negative side, he carries distorted information, introduces unhealthy practices and appropriates a major portion of the subsidy. While the pyraveekar can get the schemes sanctioned, in implementation he is hardly of any use. The pyraveekar assisted members of the target group suffer more than the self-supported members. On the whole, the institution of pyraveekar has had deleterious effects on a vital public policy meant for the rural poor.

7

The SFDA : Target Group Participation

PUBLIC participation has come to be accepted as one of the vital prerequisites for development. Considerable debate has gone into this aspect in development literature. Although there is a wide agreement about the need for participation, there appears to be no consensus on the elements of participation; what constitutes participation is being debated very intensely. It is almost universally accepted that no economic development can take place without the participation of the people; for development is the sum total of the effort of the people in a society. The greater the effort of the people the more will be the production and prosperity. But there appears to be disagreement on the issue of distributive justice. Those who argue for distributive justice maintain that people must assert their rights and demand increasing share in the growing prosperity. This is considered more crucial in the societies where people are unorganised and suffer from wide economic disparities, and low level of civic consciousness.

It has been the general experience of most of the developing societies that the helplessness of the poor, more so the rural poor has been the major cause for increasing state intervention. This is necessitated to provide counter-balancing checks in an unequal society so that the poor would be able to derive benefits of development. A number of research studies revealed that the benefits extended to the poor are cornered by the better-off sections. How to prevent this process is a major challenge the public policies are confronted with. This can be prevented by different means; one, by a political party committed to the people; two, by an administrative system oriented towards the poor, three, enthusiastic voluntary organisation and fourthly, peoples organisations. An analysis of these four instruments which can ensure a better deal for the poor reveals that they have not been very effective in most of the developing countries. In the absence of adequate institutional arrangement and effective linkages between the people and the government, a number of distortions entered the developmental programmes. This was more so, as mentioned earlier, in the case of the societies where people are largely unorganised. In fact, the institution of pyraveekar in the rural areas is one such distortion. Therefore, organising the people is necessary to ensure that benefits reach the poor as envisaged by the policy.

In a way, availing of the benefits extended by the public policy, constitutes positive participation of the people in the development programmes. This, no doubt, is a top down approach to development. Yet, if people are well organised, the distortions would be far lesser than what has happened to most of the public policies intended for rural development. Active participation, on the other hand, would help not only the target groups availing themselves of the benefits that percolate from above but articulate their demands and get what they need. In the process people would develop the capacity to devise development schemes based on their life experiences, understanding of local needs, requirements and resources. There are no better judges of these variables than the people themselves. Further, the people should collectively strive to implement the schemes with mutual understanding and put their best in this effort. It is from this perspective participation should be conceived as a key component in ensuring effectiveness of public policy.

The success of the public policy depends upon peoples' participation for the following reasons. Firstly, increasing participation would rest on increasing awareness. This awareness in turn would be a result of exchange of ideas and information among the people. This increasing consciousness among the people can always be helpful in inculcating scientific attitudes, proper orientation and necessary acceptance of the programmes. Secondly, conscious participation would also result in increasing articulation of demands on the part of the people. This situation would result in a reversal of the top down approach to the problems of the people. People will get not what the policy formulators want them to get but what they themselves want. It is this felt need and awareness that are critical for success of the developmental programmes. Thirdly, public participation through their own organisations would also ensure greater accountability of the system to the people. The administrative instrument today is not directly accountable to the people and increasing participation would make it more responsive and responsible. Fourthly, it is generally observed that the communication between the government and the people is largely distorted. In most of the cases it is a top down communication—from government to people--which is one way. There is no feedback mechanism which is bound to adversely affect the developmental programmes. Increasing participation means more of communication from the people to government. The distortions in information flow can be, to a large extent, avoided through well organised peoples' associations and replace individual professional pyraveekar who for his own reasons acts as channel of communication and provides the missing link between the government and the people. The role played by this institution has already been discussed in an earlier chapter. In their place more responsible intermediaries would emerge on whom people will have control enforcing greater accountability. Thus deviations that entered developmental programmes through pyraveekar can be avoided. Fifthly, organised effort through conscious participation can facilitate effective monitoring of the programmes and continuous evaluation. The learning ability of the society can be raised and the development in all respects can be faster. Lastly, it is capable of ensuring collective effort, which is quite essential for the success of target group oriented anti-poverty schemes.

Organising the people to facilitate their participation has not been a part of the policy framework. For organising the rural poor although it would help in rapid development, it would also lead to unintended consequences. Greater participation would lead to increasing political consciousness resulting in social tensions threatening the power base of the entrenched groups. This would also affect the social hierarchy in the rural social system. And economically it is bound to result in better distribution adversely affecting the privileged groups in the society. Participation also has a cultural and organisational dimension. For it will be a bottom up approach where people would gain increasing control over their own destinies and their dependence on government would get reduced. This calls for strong political will and total commitment to the people. And it has been the general experience that most of the developing countries do not adequately plan for peoples participation nor do they welcome it if such trend is noticed.

II

The SFDA programmes are target oriented anti-poverty programmes. Their focus is basically on the disadvantaged groups in the rural society who have not been able to benefit much from the green revolution and other developmental programmes. As a result the agency is devised to wage a frontal attack on poverty. However, most of the studies indicate that the target groups, particularly the most needy, could not benefit from the schemes as much as the policy envisaged. The inadequate impact of the agency has to be examined from the point of view of participation of target groups in their larger context.

The present study proposes to examine the phenomenon of the target groups participation on the basis of empirical data. Firstly, it is an attempt to examine the dependence of the people on the governmental support. For this purpose the information was elicited from the target groups to find out their dependence on the government and local elite groups. The tendency to leave the matters to government or "elders" would obviously mean lesser conscious participation in the developmental programmes. Further the individualistic orientation is examined to analyse the scope for cooperative approach for development. For participation depends upon the cooperative attitudes among the people. The individualistic orientation works as an impediment to collective participation of the people in development. In addition, the perception of the poverty phenomenon by the target groups is also analysed. This would provide an insight into the participative process in the rural sector. Lastly, the perceptions of the target groups about the future is taken into account to assess the scope for participative development. A positive attitude to the future has a favourable connotation for participation while perception of bleak future breeds apathy reducing the level of participation. These different dimensions of the socio-cultural attitudes of the people are taken into account to assess whether a favourable disposition for participation exists or not.

When the respondents were asked whether the developmental schemes should be taken up only by the government (Table 7.1) 87.9 per cent from Medak district and 96.4 per cent from East Godavari thought that government alone should take up these schemes. 6.9 per cent from Medak and 2.6 per cent from East Godavari could not answer this question. Out of 613 respondents 19 (3.1 per cent) said that the government need not take up all these schemes.

To the question why government should take up these programmes, the following justification was offered. Firstly, they think that it is the responsibility of the government to help the poor people. Secondly, the government should have welfare of the people at its heart. Thirdly, the government should play the role of parents; after all, "we are all children of the government". Fourthly, none else is as competent and powerful as the government to command the resources to undertake these schemes. Fifthly, the people are so poor that they cannot take up anything without help of the government. Sixthly, the people are lazy, poor, quarrelsome and therefore, cannot take up any programme. Seventhly, government alone can advance loans which do not involve exorbitant interest as is the case with the moneylenders who are highly exploitative. Eighthly, the village elite are selfish and corrupt and therefore, the development of the village cannot be left to them. Lastly, the village elite cannot handle the schemes as there are factions and divisions among them.

The above responses throw up three trends; one, that most of the people could not think of any alternative to government and feel that government is resourceful, impartial and objective and think that it is the responsibility of the government to help the poor; two, they think of the elite groups in the village as

TABLE 7.1 : **The need for governments adoption of development schemes—Respondents opinion**

Sl. No.	Name of the village	Govt. alone can take up	Govt. need not take up	Don't know	Total
Medak dist.					
1.	Marpadga	166	7	17	190
		(87.4)	(3.7)	(8.9)	(100)
2.	Sirsingandla	60	4	1	65
		(92.3)	(6.2)	(1.5)	(100)
3.	Peddamasanpally	42	5	3	50
		(84.0)	(10.0)	(6.0)	(100)
	Total	268	16	21	305
		(87.9)	(5.2)	(6.9)	(100)
East Godavari dist.					
4.	Shankavaram	179	3	6	188
		(95.2)	(1.6)	(3.2)	(100)
5.	Vajrakutam	69		1	70
		(98.6)		(1.4)	(100)
6.	Balarampuram	49		1	50
		(98.0)		(2.0)	(100)
	Total	297	3	8	308
		(96.4)	(1.0)	(2.6)	(100)
	Grand Total	565	19	29	613
		(92.2)	(3.1)	(4.7)	(100)

Note : Figures in brackets indicate percentage.

an alternative to the government but discarded the alternative on the grounds that they are corrupt, selfish, faction ridden, inefficient and not interested in the development of the people; three, people at large are also viewed as an alternative to take up the schemes on their own but this was also dropped on the grounds that people are illiterate, poor, inefficient, quarrelsome and cannot discriminate between what is desirable and what is not. In fact poverty as a reason figured very prominently for the inability of the people to take up any developmental scheme on their own. As a result the government emerged as the only organisation to take up the developmental responsibilities. It is significant to note that no reference was made by the respondents to political parties or voluntary organisation or peoples organisations.

Those negligible number of respondents who said that government should not take up these programmes felt that government was indifferent and inefficient. There are leakages and delays in the governmental programmes. A few other respondents maintained that people should develop on their own and the role of the government should be marginal. They added that schemes taken up by people on their own can be implemented efficiently.

To another question very closely related to the above one, the respondents were asked whether they can think of any schemes (Table 7.2) they can undertake on their own without assistance from government. 7.5 per cent from Medak, 12.3 per cent from East Godavari answered in the affirmative. An overwhelming number that is, 86.9 per cent from Medak and 76.6 per cent from East Godavari thought that people cannot take up anything on their own without the aid and help of the government. 5.6 per cent from Medak and 11.4 per cent from East Godavari could not answer the question.

Those respondents who felt that people can take up certain schemes on their own, were asked to list out the type of schemes they can undertake. They said that people can improve agriculture on their own. In fact the loans from the government landed them in the cobwebs of complications. They can also undertake minor irrigation schemes, digging of wells, construction of their own houses, internal road etc.

TABLE 7.2 : **Peoples initiative in the development programmes—respondents opinion**

Sl. No.	Name of the village	Can take up	Cannot take up	Don't know	Total
Medak Dist.					
1.	Marpadga	14 (7.4)	162 (85.3)	14 (7.4)	190 (100)
2.	Sirsingandla	6 (9.2)	58 (89.2)	1 (1.6)	65 (100)
3.	Peddamasanpally	3 (6.0)	45 (90.0)	2 (4.0)	50 (100)
	Total	23 (7.5)	265 (86.9)	17 (5.6)	305 (100)
East Godavari Dist.					
4.	Shankavaram	33 (17.5)	132 (70.3)	23 (12.2)	188 (100)
5.	Vajrakutam		63 (90.0)	7 (1.00)	70 (100)
6.	Balarampuram	5 (10.0)	41 (82.0)	4 (8.0)	50 (100)
	Total	38 (12.3)	236 (76.6)	34 (11.4)	308 (100)
	Grand Total	61 (10.0)	501 (81.7)	51 (8.5)	613 (100)

Note: Figures in brackets indicate percentage.

The other respondents who said that people cannot take up any type of schemes were asked to give the reasons. Even to this question poverty was mentioned as the principal cause for helplessness of the people to take up any scheme. The second widely cited reason has been that people are divided and therefore, cannot take up anything on their own. Thirdly, they blame the political groups, the local elite and dub them as corrupt and dishonest. They think such type of leadership cannot handle any developmental schemes. A few others also said that gap between the rich and the poor is the cause for ineffectiveness of people to work together for development of the village.

The reasons offered by the respondents for inability of the people to take up anything on their own reinforce the earlier conclusion and confirm that there is widespread sense of dependence on the government for anything. They feel that people lack initiative and cannot handle anything on their own. This sense of helplessness renders both active and positive participation difficult. For such an attitude encourages a sense of helplessness where people look for the benefits to trickle down from above.

The participation of people in developmental programmes is partly determined by linkages between the elite groups and the people in the village. Here an attempt is made to find out the attitudes of the people towards different members of the elite groups. This would provide an insight into the elite-mass relations and the role they can play in mobilising support of the people for developmental programmes.

To start with they were asked whether they were in contact with the "elders" in the village (Table 7.3). 91.1 per cent from Medak and 79.9 per cent from East Godavari stated that they were in contact with the village elders.

The next question was whom did they meet usually in the village? The responses show that the village officer (patwari/karnam), the sarpanch, the police patel/munsab are the persons whom the villagers meet frequently. The Samithi President or Ex-Samithi President also figured in the above category. This is signficant in the context that the Ex-Samithi President resides in Marpadga village while the Ex-Samithi President and the Present incumbent hail from the village of

TABLE 7.3 : **The Contacts with the elite in the village**

Sl. No.	Name of the village	Meet	Do not meet	Total
Medak Dist.				
1.	Marpadga	171	19	190
		(90.0)	(10.0)	(100)
2.	Sirsingandla	62	3	65
		(95.4)	(4.6)	(100)
3.	Peddamasanpally	45	5	50
		(90 0)	(10.0)	(100)
	Total	278	27	305
		(91.1)	(8.9)	(100)
East Godavari Dist.				
4.	Shankavaram	135	53	188
		(71.8)	(28.2)	(100)
5.	Vajrakutam	68	2	70
		(97.1)	(2.9)	(100)
6.	Balarampuram	43	7	50
		(86.0)	(14.0)	(100)
	Total	246	62	308
		(79.9)	(20.1)	(100)
	Grand Total	524	89	613
		(85.5)	(14.5)	(100)

Note: Figures in brackets indicate percentage.

Shankavaram. The other members of the elite group are; the heads of castes, landlords, teachers, businessmen and pyraveekars. A few respondents also mentioned friends and relatives.

The respondents were asked to comment on the general behavioural style of the village elders (Table 7.4). 33.8 per cent from Medak and 41.6 per cent from East Godavari held the opinion that leaders take a favourable and helpful attitude towards them. 58.4 per cent from Meadak and 56.8 per cent from East Godavari said that the elite are unhelpful in their attitude towards them. 7.8 per cent from Medak and 1.6 per cent from East Godavari declined to answer the question. This reveals that in the opinion of people village leaders are not helpful to them which strains the elite people relation network. This response is significant because more than 85 per cent of the people go to them for help and assistance.

The respondents were asked the reasons why the elite adopted unhelpful attitude towards them. An overwhelmingly large number of respondents suspected that elite groups work against the development of the poor; the elite are the losers if the poor prosper. Secondly, the elite have become corrupt, selfish and therefore, do not take a helpful attitude towards the poor. The third pattern of responses indicate that these attitudes are determined by the factions and divisions among the elites. The respondents came out with different types of explanations for the unhelpful attitude of the village elite. Their comments include such strong expressions like: the "elite are blood suckers, exploitative, jealous, authoritarian, arrogant" and so on. The running theme throughout the responses has been that the elite are bent upon oppressing the poor. This, according to the poor, explains the hostility of the elite towards them. The very suspicion of the poor about the intentions of the elite would erode the credibility of these groups in the rural areas. This also partly accounts for the increasing dependence of the poor on the government.

The following are the responses of those few respondents who said that elite groups were helpful. Most of the respondents said that elders in the villages helped them in securing government loans. The second major response has been that elders provide them moral support in the case of any

TABLE 7.4 : **Attitudes of the village elite towards the poor : Respondents' opinion**

Sl. No	Name of the village	Helpful	Not helpful	Don't know	Total
Medak Dist.					
1.	Marpadga	68	102	20	190
		(35.8)	(53.7)	(10.5)	(100)
2.	Sirsingandla	23	40	2	65
		(35.4)	(61.6)	(3.0)	(100)
3.	Peddamasanpally	12	36	2	50
		(24.0)	(72.0)	(4.0)	(100)
	Total	103	178	24	305
		(33.8)	(58.4)	(7.8)	(100)
East Godavari Dist.					
4.	Shankavaram	55	130	3	188
		(29.3)	(69.1)	(1.6)	(100)
5.	Vajrakutam	54	16	—	70
		(77.1)	(22.9)		(100)
6.	Balarampuram	19	29	2	50
		(38.0)	(58.0)	(4.0)	(100)
	Total	128	175	5	308
		(41.6)	(56.8)	(1.6)	(100)
	Grand Total	231	353	29	613
		(37.7)	(57.6)	(4.7)	(100)

Note : Figures in brackets indicate percentage.

crisis. The third pattern of response has been that although they take "commission" for doing their work, the elders pursue the schemes and get them sanctioned from government. A few also said that they look after the welfare of the village. The schemes for which they received the help include a large number of SFDA schemes. This pattern indicates that people perceive the village elite only as channel through which the governmental schemes flow to the village. As a result the elite lost their autonomous entity and are being replaced by the government.

Next we tried to find out how people assess their representatives (Appendix VII.1) including members of panchayat, sarpanch, samithi president, M.L.A., and M.P. Most people said that the attitude of the sarpanch and the members of the panchayat is negative towards them. With regard to the samithi president, the M.L.A. and the M.P. a majority of them could not answer the question as they did not come in direct contact with these functionaries. It is interesting to observe that while in Medak 53.8 per cent did not come in contact with Samithi President in East Godavari 83.4 per cent had contacts. But they held that the attitude of the Samithi President was negative. 71.1 per cent from Medak and 59.1 per cent from East Godavari had no contacts with the M.L.A. And with the M.P. it was as high as 78.7 per cent from Medak and 88.3 per cent from East Godavari. It reveals that the public representatives occupying the key positions in Samithi, Legislature and Parliament do not seem to have mueh rapport with the people while those who have contacts are reported to be negative in their attitude. Thus public representatives who have to act as effective links between government and the people are considered unhelpful. This lack of confidence renders them ineffective as public representatives who are to articulate the needs and demands of the people on the one hand and mobilise their support for developmental schemes on the other.

The emerging trends accentuate increasing dependence of the people on the governmental machinery. The elite in a developing society have a crucial role to play. The representatives, in fact, are considered to be the substitute for public participation in a democratic context. But the pattern of responses indicate the gradual and growing erosion of legitimacy of these representatives. A majority of the respondents have come to believe that their representatives are selfish, corrupt and hostile. In short the elite groups and public representatives do not enjoy public confidence. And the leaders of higher ranks have no contacts with the people. The elite who in the past had an autonomous entity vis-a-vis the people are being relegated into the background. People have come to see through and look beyond the elite groups. This creates a vacuum between the government and the people rendering mass mobilising instruments at the local level ineffective. This in turn takes away the initiative from the people and in its place widespread parasitic tendencies would thrive rendering participation in the real sense extremely difficult.

The participative dimension is also dependent upon cooperative disposition of the people. Therefore, a few questions were asked to elicit opinions on the basis of which it is attempted to assess the individualistic and cooperative traits among the people. To start with they were asked a question about who should decide the schemes to be taken up for the benefit of the entire village (Appendix VII.2). 35.1 per cent from Medak and 45.8 per cent from East Godavari thought that all the villagers should decide together about the schemes to be taken up for benefit of the people. It is interesting to observe that in Medak district this response was by and large the same in all the three villages. But in East Godavari 42 per cent from Shankavaram village, which received maximum attention, and 71.4 per cent from Vajrakutam—an average village—said that all the villagers should decide. From Balarampuram—a neglected village—only 24 per cent subscribed to this view. 24.3 per cent in Medak district and 13.3 per cent in East Godavari thought that it was the poor people in the villages who should decide about the developmental schemes. Thirdly, 20.6 per cent in Medak and 18.8 per cent in East Godavari expressed that the elite in the village should decide about the schemes. While the responses are identical from most of the village, the data indicates that about 30 per cent from the village of Sirsingandla and 34 per cent from Balarampuram opined that elite should decide about the schemes. It is significant that 20 per cent from Medak and 18.8 per cent from East Godavari felt that the schemes to be taken up for the village should be left to the choice of the government itself.

The respondents were asked another question which was slightly different from the above question. Here they were asked who should decide (Appendix VII.3) about the schemes if the government is giving them to the families of the target groups. 3.0 per cent from Medak and 1.0 per cent from East Godavari said that all the villagers should decide about it. 7.9 per cent from Medak and 1.6 per cent from East Godavari felt that the poor people in the villages should decide. 16.4 per cent from Medak and 7.1 per cent from East Godavari thought that village elite should decide. 59.3 per cent from Medak and 75.3 per cent from East Godavari thought that it should be left to the individual families to decide what scheme they would like to have. 12.1 per cent from Medak and 12.3 per cent from East Godavari thought that government should decide about the schemes.

Another question they were asked was about the basis for allotment of schemes (Table 7.5). 61.3 per cent from Medak and 69.8 per cent from East Godavari maintained that family should be the basis for allotment of schemes. 25.9 per cent and 26.3 per cent thought that the scheme should be given to a group or a cluster of families. 10.2 per cent from Medak and 1 per cent from East Godavari said that caste should be the basis for allotment of schemes. This convincingly indicates the family centred nature of rural social system. For they think that development schemes should revolve around the family unit. The support for community and even caste as a basis for allotment of schemes is very weak.

The respondents were asked questions about the individualistic and cooperative tendencies. As has been pointed out earlier the cooperative culture would be more favourable for participation than individualistic culture. Therefore, an attempt was made to find out the dominant tendency among the rural people by asking a few questions related to land, one of the most important variables in the rural sector. For purposes of development they were asked, whether they welcomed the idea of all the land in the village being brought together for cooperative farming (Table 7.6). While 37.4 per cent from Medak and 29.6

TABLE 7.5 : **The unit for allotment of the schemes**

Sl. No.	Name of the village	Individual	Some families	Caste	Others	Total
	Medak Dist.					
1.	Marpadga	116 (61.1)	52 (27.4)	14 (7.4)	8 (4.2)	190 (100)
2.	Sirsingandla	43 (66.2)	20 (30.8)	2 (3.0)	—	65 (100)
3.	Peddamasanpally	28 (56.0)	7 (14.0)	15 (30.0)	—	50 (100)
	Total	187 (61.3)	79 (25.9)	31 (10.2)	8 (2.6)	305 (100)
	East Godavari Dist.					
4.	Shankavaram	110 (58.5)	73 (38.8)	1 (0.5)	4 (2.1)	188 (100)
5.	Vajrakutam	65 (92.9)	1 (1.4)	1 (1.4)	3 (4.3)	70 (100)
6.	Balarampuram	40 (80.0)	7 (14.0)	1 (2.0)	2 (4.0)	50 (100)
	Total	215 (69.8)	81 (26.3)	3 (1.0)	9 (2.9)	308 (100)
	Grand Total	402 (65.6)	160 (26.1)	34 (5.5)	17 (2.8)	613 (100)

Note : Figures in brackets indicate percentage.

per cent from East Godavari supported the proposition, 49.5 per cent from Medak and 59.1 per cent from East Godavari opposed the idea of cooperative farming. 13.1 per cent from Medak and 11.4 per cent from East Godavari could not answer the question. This means that while about 1/3rd of the respondents supported the idea of cooperative farming more than half opposed it.

People were asked a direct question about their willingness to put their land in the common pool for the purpose of cooperative farming (Table 7.7). About 58.5 per cent from Medak and 59.2 per cent from East Godavari refused to put their land in the common pool. From those who own land 41.5 per cent from Medak and 40.2 per cent from East Godavari expressed their willingness for cooperative farming.

The respondents who did not favour cooperative farming were asked the reasons for their opposition to this proposition. They came out with following explanations. Firstly, people cannot work together. Secondly, combining property would only encourage laziness among the people. Thirdly, bringing together the strong and weak would result in greater exploitation. Fourthly, a few fear that it would result in bloodshed and in the killing of the people. Some others asked the question "how can you club unequals together"? They mentioned other reasons such as differences in the nature of soil, personal assets, capacity for investment, personal commitment to the agriculture etc. The major reasons appear to be absence of cooperative attitudes among the people and the feeling that it would result in tensions among the people in the rural areas is also haunting them. There is also the fear that it would adversely affect the production. They argued that people would shift their burden of work to others and escape their work. In other words they think cooperative ventures would encourage laziness, escapism and tensions in the villages.

Another question "if the government was distributing surplus land what should be the basis for such a distribution?" was put to the respondents (Appendix VII.4). 56.4 per cent from Medak and 89.9 per cent from East Godavari expressed that the basis for distribution of surplus land should be the family and not any other criterion. However, 31.9 per cent from Medak and 9.1 per cent from East Godavari thought that a cluster of families should be the basis for distribution of land. 8.2 per cent from Medak and 0.3 per cent from East Godavari thought that caste can also be the basis for allotment of the surplus land. This indicates that people are not in favour of cooperative type of farming even in the wake of any distribution of surplus land.

Those respondents who felt that the surplus land should be redistributed to a cluster of families, were asked the reasons for such an approach. A large number of them said that this would bring most of the poor and landless families together. This can also result in improvement in the living conditions of the people. They added that farming would be economical and efficient. However, they insisted that when the families are clustered the economic basis of the families should be identical.

Those respondents who thought that land should be distributed on the basis of family were asked the reasons for such an approach. The responses were similar to the responses evoked by the cooperative farming. Most of the respondents supported family as an ideal unit on the grounds that, firstly, they would work hard with commitment to the land and put their best in cultivation; secondly, they would be free to plan their cultivation; thirdly, they argued that clustering of families together would result in a number of differences and tensions in the group relations causing dead-locks in the group effort; and lastly, they thought that it would encourage individual laziness, buck passing and escapistic tendencies among members of the group. A few responses smack of pessimism about the cooperative effort in cultivation. All these causes indicate that people are individualistic and cooperative culture is largely absent. Such a culture may be conducive for competitive growth but not a cooperative venture. Since participation pre-supposes cooperative disposition, the existing attitude is largely unfavourable to such a process.

The fourth dimension of participation deals with peoples' understanding of the causes of and solutions to poverty. For this purpose we attempted to analyse their perceptions of poverty, economic inequalities on the one hand and the solutions they had in their mind for these problems on the other. It was thought that this would provide an insight into the

TABLE 7.6 : **Support of the respondents of the cooperative farming**

Sl. No.	Name of the village	Support	Strongly support	No answer	Oppose	Strongly oppose	Total
	Medak Dist.						
1.	Marpadga	44	14	30	98	4	190
		(23.2)	(7.4)	(15.8)	(51.6)	(2.1)	(100)
2.	Sirsingandla	25	8	3	25	4	65
		(38.5)	(12.3)	(4.6)	(38.5)	(6.2)	(100)
3.	Peddamasanpally	20	3	7	16	4	50
		(40.0)	(6.0)	(14.0)	(32.0)	(8.0)	(100)
	Total	89	25	40	139	12	305
		(29.2)	(8.2)	(13.1)	(45.6)	(3.9)	(100)
	East Godavari Dist.						
4.	Shankavaram	36	35	26	76	15	188
		(19.1)	(18.6)	(13.8)	(40.4)	(8.0)	(100)
5.	Vajrakutam	10	5	4	49	2	70
		(14.3)	(7.1)	(5.7)	(70.0)	(2.9)	(100)
6.	Balarampuram	2	3	5	27	13	50
		(4.0)	(6.0)	(10.0)	(54.0)	(26.0)	(100)
	Total	48	43	35	152	30	308
		(15.6)	(14.0)	(11.4)	(49.4)	(9.7)	(100)
	Grand Total	137	68	75	291	42	613
		(22.3)	(11.1)	(12.2)	(47.5)	(6.9)	(200)

Note : Figures in brackets indicate percentage.

TABLE 7.7 : **Willingness to pool the land for co-operative farming**

Sl. No.	Name of the village	Willing	Not willing	Total
	Medak Dist.			
1.	Marpadga	60 (34.1)	116 (65.9)	176 (100)
2.	Sirsingandla	35 (57.3)	26 (42.7)	61 (100)
3.	Peddamasanpally	23 (34.1)	24 (65.9)	47 (100)
	Total	118 (41.5)	166 (58.5)	284 (100)
	East Godavari Dist.			
4.	Shankavaram	54 (50.5)	53 (49.5)	107 (100)
5.	Vajrakutam	10 (17.5)	47 (82.5)	57 (100)
6.	Balarampuram	18 (45.0)	22 (55.0)	40 (100)
	Total	82 (40.2)	122 (59.8)	204 (100)
	Grand Total	200 (41.0)	288 (59.0)	488* (100)

*Landless respondents are not posed this question.

Note : Figures in brackets indicate percentage.

attitudinal pattern which is crucial to an understanding of the participative phenomenon.

The respondents were asked to give the causes for existence of poverty in villages. The responses revolved round certain major causes. Firstly, an overwhelming majority think that since land is central to economic life; poverty is the result of landlessness. The second type of causes traced poverty to the failure of monsoon frequently. This response has to be understood in the physical context of the respondents as they are drawn from drought prone areas. The third cause pointed out was "laziness and foolishness" of the poor people. Fourth category of responses blamed their ancestors for not earning property for them. The fifth type think that poverty exists because of the gap between the rich and the poor and exploitation of the latter by the former. Sixth category consists of those who think that God and Karma account for the existence of poverty. Lastly, there were also responses which include population explosion and bad habtis of the poor people such as extravagance, unnecessary expenditure on social and religious items, drinking habits and so on.

To probe further they were asked certain questions relating to their consciousness of poverty. For this purpose they were asked whom did they consider to be rich? The responses broadly revolved round three factors namely money, land and gold. The imagination of the poor people about riches ranged between three thousand rupees to a crore of rupees of income per year. With regard to the land it ranged between five acres of land to hundreds of acres. With regard to the livestock it ranged from five to six pair of bullocks and 200 sheep to five buffalos coupled with a few acres of land with electric motor or oil engine. There are also responses which include items like tractors, lorries, taxies, buildings and so on. Some of them also said that men who have two square meals, no outstanding loan, not dependent on others, capable of lending money to others are also considered rich. This indicates that the term rich includes a wide spectrum. Therefore, their estmation of distance from the rich presents a wide variation.

They were also asked to describe the poor. The responses broadly indicate that poor are those who do not have land, are deprived of the basic necessities of life such as food and clothes, are dependent on their physical labour, and live on loans and borrowed money. The beggars and destitutes are included in this category. A few respondents include the small and marginal farmers in it. This indicates that the spectrum with regard to the categorisation of the poor is not as wide as that of the rich.

Another aspect of this analysis covered perceptions of respondents of their own conditions. For this purpose they were asked whether they categorised themselves as poor (Table 7.8). To this question 86.2 per cent from Medak and 79.2 per cent from East Godavari put themselves in the category of poor, while 12.8 per cent from Medak and 20.8 per cent from East Godavari did not think so. Those who categorised themselves as poor were asked the reasons for their poverty. They said that they did not have adequate food and clothes to protect themselves. Others said that they were solely dependent on their physical labour. Quite a large number of them said that they did not have land to depend upon. Those persons who have some land said that their lands were not fertile nor are they provided with any sources of irrigation. They added that frequent failure of monsoon rendered them poor. A few others complained that they did not have money for investment. There were also complaints that the cost of inputs has gone up rendering economics of cultivation prohibitive.

Those persons who did not consider themselves poor said that they had enough to eat and were not dependent on others for financial help. They also said that they were relatively better off than many others in the village. However, they were not prepared to be categorised as rich but thought that their conditions were not as bad as those who were entirely dependent on their physical labour and were denied basic necessities.

The respondents were asked about the measures for eradication of poverty of their individual families. Most of the respondents asked for increasing assistance in the form of governmental programmes. In fact most of the solutions they suggested revolved round SFDA schemes.* The first

* This could be partly because the study was on SFDA, and accentuation on those schemes, probably they thought would be of some help.

TABLE 7.8 : **The respondents categorisation as poor**

Sl. No.	Name of the village	We are poor	We are not poor	Don't know	Total
	Medak Dist.				
1.	Marpadga	160	27	3	190
		(84.2)	(24.2)	(1.6)	(100)
2.	Sirsingandla	61	4	—	65
		(93.8)	(6.2)		(100)
3.	Peddamasanpally	42	8	—	50
		(84.0)	(16.0)		(100)
	Total	263	39	3	305
		(86.2)	(12.8)	(1.0)	(100)
	East Godavari Dist.				
4.	Shankavaram	154	34	—	188
		(81.9)	(18.1)		(100)
5.	Vajrakutam	46	22	2	70
		(65.7)	(31.4)	(2.9)	(100)
6.	Balarampuram	44	6	—	50
		(88.0)	(12.0)		(100)
	Total	244	62	2	308
		(79.2)	(20.1)	(0.6)	(100)
	Grand Total	507	101	5	613
		(82.7)	(16.5)	(0.8)	(100)

Note : Figures in brackets indicate percentage.

priority of those who had land fell upon new wells. This is indicative of the poor nature of their lands and inadequate sources of irrigation. However, the first priority of the landless people has been land. Other measures suggested have been plough bullocks, carts and bullocks, goat and sheep and so on. A few of them also pleaded for an increase in agricultural wages. The responses indicate that an overwhelmingly large number sought developmental programmes such as land, loans and improvement in the agricultural potential through the governmental help and support. Thus they think that their poverty can be eradicated only through governmental support.

To the question whether poverty in the villages could be removed at all, (Table 7.9) 70.5 per cent from Medak and 72.4 per cent from East Godavari thought that it could be done. However, quite a large number of them qualified their answer with a comment that the developmental schemes should be implemented seriously. 17.4 per cent from Medak and 16.8 per cent from East Godavari thought that it could not be eradicated. 12.1 per cent from Medak and 10.7 per cent from East Godavari could not reply to this question. This further indicates that their hopes are pinned on governmental schemes and assistance whether at the individual level or village level.

Further they were asked about the measures to remove poverty. They said that poverty could be removed if proper policies are formulated and government comes forward with more number of programmes and extend generous assistance to the poor. They pleaded that poor people should be given land. This they think can be an effective solution. They suggested that the existing land in the villages should be redistributed. A few others thought that irrigation potential in the rural areas should be strengthened by constructing tanks and digging new wells. A few others thought that opening new industries would solve the problem of poverty. A few other added that it was linked with people's industry and reduction in the dominance of the local leaders.

Those who felt that poverty could not be removed observed that the existing conditions in the villages were not conducive for removal of poverty. Most of the respondents in this category blamed the poor for their bad habits, particularly

TABLE 7.9 : **Respondents opinion about removal of poverty**

Sl. No.	Name of the village	Poverty will be removed	Poverty will not be removed	Don't know	Total
	Medak Dist				
1.	Marpadga	130	30	30	190
		(68.4)	(15.8)	(15.8)	(100)
2.	Sirsingandla	50	11	4	65
		(76.9)	(16.9)	(6.2)	(100)
3.	Peddamasanpally	35	12	3	50
		(70.0)	(24.0)	(6.0)	(100)
	Total	215	53	37	305
		(70.5)	(17.4)	(12.1)	(100)
	East Godavari Dist				
4.	Shankavaram	133	40	15	188
		(70.7)	(21.2)	(8.0)	(100)
5.	Vajrakutam	54	4	12	70
		(77.1)	(5.7)	(17.2)	(100)
6.	Balarampuram	36	8	6	50
		(72.0)	(16.0)	(12.0)	(100)
	Total	223	52	33	308
		(72.4)	(16.8)	(10.7)	(100)
	Grand Total	438	105	70	613
		(71.5)	(71.1)	(11.4)	(100)

Note : Figures in brackets indicate percentage.

addiction to alcohol. A few thought that frequent failure of monsoon accounted for existence of poverty. Some others believed that poverty was caused by God and Karma and therefore could not be removed by man. A few thought that population expansion and laziness of the people accounted for the poverty of the villages.

The respondents traced poverty to the landlessness. They largely categorised themselves as poor. Increasing help from the government and redistribution of land are some of the solutions suggested by them. As the emphasis appeared to be on land, incremental policies such as SFDA may not evoke deep interest of the people preventing their active participation.

The fifth dimension that is examined to analyse the participative phenomenon in the rural areas has been an examination of the perception of the people of their future. This was done by enquiring into their assessment of the past, present and future. It was thought that it would provide an insight into time dimension which partly shaped their attitudes towards life and development. It was assumed that positive view of future leads to more of participation while the negative view results in increasing withdrawal.

The respondents were asked to compare the existing conditions with the conditions prevailing in the days of their parents (Appendix VII.5). To this question 30.2 per cent from Medak and 16.6 per cent from East Godavari thought that there was an improvement in the conditions when compared with the olden days. 24.3 per cent from Medak and 26.6 per cent from East Godavari felt that there was no change in the situation. 44.9 per cent in Medak and 54.5 per cent from East Godavari thought that there was a deterioration in the conditions of the people compared to the days of their parents. And 0.7 per cent from Medak and 2.3 per cent from East Godavari could not reply to this question. This means a very large number of rural people feel that either there has been a stagnation or deterioration in their living conditions.

Those who thought that there was improvement in conditions stated that they have more property. The second category of responses revolved round the feeling that today the government was more helpful than in the past. A few of them also felt that because of the developmental programmes there has been more work and therefore more income. Quite a few of them observed that people had more food and modern facilities such as electricity, oil engines etc. There were also a few who said that practices like bonded labour disappeared.

Those who felt that they did not find any difference in the conditions said that there has not been any addition either to their property or income. They maintained that the property earned by their parents was only the asset they continued to possess. The frequent failure of the monsoon stagnated the living conditions. Quite a large number of them held that increase in their wages had been neutralised by increase in the prices. A considerable number of people said that they were solely dependent on their physical labour right from ancestral times and found no difference in the conditions.

Those who said that they perceived deterioration in the conditions were asked the reasons for such a trend. The responses revolved round four major causes. Firstly, a majority of them said that there was fragmentation of land because of the distribution among sons which affected the income of families adversely. Secondly, inflation and increasing prices account for stagnation and deterioration. Thirdly, they drew the attention to the degeneration in the ethical values in the society. There were also a few responses which included failure of the monsoon, increase in the cost of inputs, expenditure on social functions such as marriages, education, etc. A few others thought that old occupational pattern was upset rendering a section of the society unemployed. These causes, they thought resulted in the deterioration in the living conditions of the people.

To assess the perception of the respondents of their future, they were asked the way they foresaw the future of their children (Appendix-VII.6). This question would throw light on the optimism that people have of the future. To this question 24.9 per cent from Medak and 16.6 per cent from East Godavari thought that their children would lead a better life. 6.9 per cent from Medak and 7.8 per cent from East Godavari thought that there would not be any difference in the conditions. 16.4 per cent from Medak and 15.3 per cent from East Godavari felt that there would be further deterioration in the conditions of their children. However, 51.8 per cent from Medak and 60.4 per cent from East Gadavari could not predict the future of their children. This clearly indicates that while people could compare their conditions with that of their parents they were not sure of the conditions in the future.

Those respondents who thought that the conditions of their children would be better than their own came out with the following reasons; firstly, increasing assistance from the government; secondly, the children would earn more as they were getting education; thirdly, the children were more intelligent and wise. A few fathers complimented their children and stated that they were hard working and capable of improving their conditions.

Those respondents who did not foresee any change in the living conditions of their children thought; firstly, there was no scope for the children to acquire additional land and hence there would not be any improvement in their conditions; secondly, they were dependent on physical labour and their children also would do the same. Some respondents hoped that hard work on the part of their children and assistance from government might prevent further deterioration in the conditions.

The 16 per cent respondents who foresaw degeneration in the conditions also emphasised the importance of land. They did not hope that their children would acquire land; on the other hand, they thought that the children would be subjected to more hardships. The second category of responses traced it to unhealthy habits. Thirdly, the increasing prices and degeneration in moral values would make things worse in future. A few others thought that increase in the population would result in the worsening of conditions in the future.

The above analysis reveals that, by and large, majority of the people feel that there has been degeneration in their living conditions; they are not clear about their future. The perceptions are woven around the question of land in rural areas. The existing attitude is not an encouraging indicator for participation. The people who do not view the present optimistically and are unsure about the future may not take much interest in the developmental process.

III

Public participation in development is crucial for development. In anti-poverty schemes such as small farmers development, the participation of the target groups can ensure effectiveness of the policy. Participation is of two types; one, positive participation where the target groups take advantage of the benefits extended to them; two, active participation which involves not only that the target groups avail themselves of the benefits but articulate their needs and demands. Total participation is possible only when the people are organised and possess higher level of political consciousness. In most of the developing societies the policy framework does not adequately plan organisation of the people for participation.

In the absence of such a thrust, the policies suffer a good deal in implementation and this is more so in the case of target group oriented anti-poverty schemes. This aspect is neglected mainly because it is feared that peoples organisations would throw up a number of unintended consequences affecting the power base of the entrenched elite groups in the rural areas. In tune with this approach the policy for the small farmers development paid no attention to the organisation of the target groups. Since peoples participation is not likely to be initiated by the policy, it must come from the target groups themselves. The scope for this process was also examined.

For the purpose of this analysis the following factors were examined. One, the dependence of target groups on governmental support; two, the dependence of target groups on elite in the rural areas; three, the cooperative approach towards developmental schemes; four, the perceptions of target groups about poverty and lastly, the perception of the target groups about the future.

About the dependence on government, the data reveal that an overwhelming number of respondents thought that government alone should undertake the developmental schemes. The people felt that government was resourceful, impartial and objective and maintained that it was the responsibility of the government to help the poor. They considered the elite groups as an alternative to the government but ruled out the possibility on the grounds that they were corrupt, selfish, faction ridden, inefficient and not interested in the development of the poor. The peoples organisations were also viewed as an alternative to undertake the schemes on their own but this alternative was also ruled out on the grounds that people were illiterate, poor, inefficient, and quarrelsome. Added to it they felt that the poverty ridden people were helpless to do anything on their own. Logically the government was looked upon as the sole benefactor of the poor. The respondents could not think of even a single scheme that people can initiate on their own. This indicates the total dependence on government. This total surrender of initiative leads to the psychosis of helplessness. Thus the scope for participation is reduced to a minimum.

The opinion about the elite groups and peoples linkages with them constitute another important dimension of participation. A very large number of the respondents have contacts with the elite which includes the elected representatives. The respondents feel that the elite are unhelpful and suspect that they are opposed to the development of the poor. They described them as selfish, corrupt, faction ridden, partisan and exploitative. In a developing society where the elites are considered to be crucial and treated as an effective link between government and the people, this pattern of responses indicates a gradual and growing erosion of legitimacy of these groups and weakening of linkages between people and the government, The people have come to see through and look beyond the elite groups. This created a vacuum between the government and the people rendering mass mobilising instruments at the local level ineffective. This in turn takes away the initiative from the levels closer to the people causing leadership crisis rendering mass mobilisation extremely difficult.

The third dimension examined is the cooperative disposition of the people. For this purpose the individualistic and cooperative attitudes are analysed. It is assumed that cooperative attitude is more conducive for participation than individualistic culture. To the question about cooperative farming there was hardly any support from the respondents. The respondents wanted distribution of surplus land on an individual basis and opposed pooling the land for any purpose. The cooperative effort in agriculture was opposed on the grounds that people are lazy, quarrelsome and cannot work together. Secondly, they apprehended that production will fall as people would have no commitment to work. Thirdly, there was the fear that this would result in tensions and greater exploitation. On the other hand they thought individualistic approach leads to personal involvement and provides freedom to individual to plan at his own level. This would make him put forth his best efforts in agriculture. Thus there is a strong propensity towards individualistic orientation. This disposition is a barrier for any group effort and participative process.

The fourth dimension deals with the understanding of the target groups about the phenomenon of poverty. These groups traced the causes for poverty and economic inequalities to the landlessness, failure of monsoon and laziness of the people. A few of them blamed their ancestors for not earning the property and a few others thought that the exploitation in the society accounted for poverty. Their description of the riches and the poverty indicates that while about the riches they are vague, about poverty they are clear. Most of them categorised themselves as poor on the grounds that they were deprived of the basic necessities of life—this included food and clothing. Thus the target groups have an understanding and consciousness of poverty.

The respondents were asked to suggest measures for eradication of poverty. Most of the respondents suggested more schemes in the form of governmental assistance. They asked for more land and those who have land asked for a new well or strengthening of irrigation sources. They also sought for livestock and agricultural schemes. They also pleaded for an increase in the agricultural wages. They suggested increasing assistance from the government, and greater seriousness and commitment in implementation of the public policies. They also suggested redistribution of land, strengthening of irrigation potential and increase in industrialisation. This pattern of responses conclusively establish that the poor look only to the government for removal of poverty and expect the government to initiate several measures. There has not been even a single solution indicating the preparedness of the poor to undertake something on their own.

The last dimension that is examined to analyse the participative phenomenon is the perception of the people of their future. They were asked to make a comparative assessment of the past, present and future. It is assumed that positive view of future leads to more of participation while the negative view results in withdrawal. When they were asked to compare their present living conditions with the past, most of them felt that either there was stagnation or deterioration in the conditions. About the future they either foresaw deterioration or were not clear about it. This temporal perspective indicates the growing pessimism among the poor. This attitude is more likely to cause withdrawal than participation in development.

Thus all the five factors examined indicate that there is helpless dependence on the state. They hope that their problems can be solved only by the government. The local elite and public representatives are rapidly losing their credibility. The respondents have no confidence in the capacity of the people to undertake any developmental schemes which is indicative of surrender of initiative. Added to it their disposition is conditioned by individualistic orientation and pessimistic perspective. Such an outlook has greater propensity to engender apathy which would be a major impediment to any public policy and more so to antipoverty oriented public policies like Small Farmers Development Agency.

8

Conclusion

PUBLIC policies have assumed considerable importance in modern times. The modern state uses public policy as an important source of legitimation and justification for its existence. For the state to-day adopts the stick and carrot approach. In fact the welfare state has had its origins in the transformation of the state from its totally coercive character to assumption of developmental role. The appalling poverty and deep rooted inequalities in the society call for increasing intervention of the state in the process of social change. Since independence, the main thrust of plans and programmes in India has been the removal of poverty. But most of the strategies adopted in fifties and sixties proved to be counter productive. The investigations both by the Government and independent researchers reveal that poverty instead of declining registered further rise; those below the poverty line increased both in relative and absolute numbers. As a result, in the seventies the policy laid stress on frontal attack on poverty. It is in the wake of this shift in the policies, that the small farmers development agency was conceived.

It has been pointed out by a number of studies that poverty in India is concentrated among certain specific groups such as small and marginal farmers and agricultural labourers in the rural areas. These sections could not derive benefit from the green revolution. It was the better off sections who appropriated the fruits of the green revolution. Therefore, the small farmers development agency strategy was expected to provide relief to these categories by offering subsidy of 25 per cent to the small farmers and 33 per cent to the marginal farmers and agricultural labourers. The subsidy was given partly to stimulate commercial and cooperative banks to extend their umbrella to cover these neglected sections, who had no access to these financial institutions and partly to provide relief in the loan burden. The policy, in the ultimate analysis, is expected to help a large majority of those below the poverty line to cross the abyss.

The SFDA has been in operation for a decade. Recently, the policy has undergone a change; in the place of SFDA now we have District Rural Development Agency. The SFDA approach raised academic curiosity and government itself sponsored a number of evaluation studies. The research studies conducted on the performance of the SFDA pointed out that the coverage of the target groups has been low leaving a yawning gap between promise and performance. Most of the studies held that the benefits extended by the agency did not 'percolate' to the target groups. Lack of awareness about the agency, mis-utilisation of the loans and non-cooperation from the elite groups are pointed out as important causes for the ineffectiveness of the agency. With regard to the viability of the schemes and their impact on target groups, the uneconomic nature of the land holdings, insensitivity to the micro local problems, inadequacy of the schemes, geo-climatic unsuitability and frail infrastructure are pointed out as causes which rendered the schemes unviable. Obviously such schemes cannot make the intended impact on the target groups. The third type of problems relate to administrative structure and its behavioural style. Almost all the studies reported that the existing administrative system did not possess the 'commitment' nor was its structure adequate and vigorous to implement the programmes. A couple of studies highlighted that imaginative administrative leadership, careful planning and programming could produce a positive impact.

The studies on the whole left a few important gaps; they did not examine the impact in terms of the number of members crossing the poverty line, the inherent weaknesses of the administrative machinery and the role of middleman. Further hardly any study touched the target group participation—an important aspect. Therefore, the present study probed into:

(a) viability of the schemes and their impact on the target groups;
(b) suitability of administrative structures;
(c) role of middle-man; and
(d) target group participation in the programme.

An examination of socio-economic setting under which the SFDA scheme has been operating is done. For this purpose the conditions of six villages selected for the study and the socio-economic profile of 613 respondents are presented and discussed. The general socio-economic conditions in all the six villages are dismal. These villages do not have most of the basic necessities. The priorities do not appear to be rational as some villages have telephone facilities but not drinking water. The wages are low and the land is unevenly distributed. The dominance of the forward castes in the landownership is quite striking. Most of the backward and scheduled caste members are found in the category of small and marginal farmers and agricultural labourers. The land in general is not of high quality, nor is it provided with irrigation facilities. Relatively the villages which are endowed with better facilities and resources received greater attention of the SFDA than those which are backward and handicapped by the paucity of resources.

The socio-economic profile of the respondents is yet another factor which can throw light on the general environment. The respondents are young or middle-aged but illiterate. A large number of them including the small and marginal farmers depend on their physical labour to eke out their livelihood. The dependence of small and marginal farmers on physical labour indicates non-viable nature of their holdings. In spite of engaging themselves both in primary and secondary occupations, the income levels reveal that 83.1 per cent in Medak and 76.6 per cent in East Godavari are below the poverty line. A sizeable number of them do not own any livestock nor agricultural implements. An overwhelming number of them have one or two pair of clothes and only about 1.5 per cent of them have dependable shelter over their heads. These conditions indicate the appalling nature of poverty which poses a formidable challenge to an anti-poverty policy like the SFDA.

An examination of the work of SFDA in this area and its impact on these poverty ridden people reveals that it failed to make the intended impact on the living conditions of the target groups. The coverage itself was low. The sixteen agencies put together in Andhra Pradesh ought to have helped ten lakh households to cross the poverty line, but they could cover only 48 per cent of the target. Among those covered, the agricultural labourers constitute only 17 per cent. At the micro level the data indicate that about one-third of the members of the target group did not know about the agency. And those who knew about it knew it only as a subsidy providing agency. This indicates that the target groups were not sufficiently educated about the agency and its objectives.

The impact of the agency on those members of the target group who are covered under its schemes depends on the way the schemes are formulated, implemented and subsequently sustained. The data indicates that two-thirds of the respondents faced difficulties in getting the schemes and three-fourths faced difficulties in implementation. The difficulties relate to pilferages of subsidy, delay in processing the schemes and undue expenditure involved. In the case of implementation absence of appropriate technology, inadequacy of the existing infrastructure and pressing economic problems of the households largely account for poor implementation and distorted results.

As the schemes could not be effectively implemented, its negligible impact on the target groups can be noticed. The target groups neither had substantial employment nor rise in the income. The members of lower strata of the target groups suffered even loss of income owing to these schemes. It is further noticed that those who have land and slightly better income could, to some extent, avail themselves of the schemes. Interestingly the programme generated a bit of additional employment but not income to the landless category. The impact on poverty line indicates that hardly any small and marginal farmer below the poverty line could cross the line. On the contrary, from the agricultural labourers a few, who were above the poverty line, slipped below the poverty line.

Obviously, the schemes had adverse and counter productive impact on the category of agricultural labourers.

The SFDA sponsored a number of schemes, viz., minor irrigation, animal husbandry and agricultural development for benefit of the target groups. An assessment of the viability of these schemes reveals that almost all types of the schemes are fraught with difficulties in securing the schemes and their implementation. Such a pattern renders most of the schemes non-viable.

Under minor irrigation, a majority of the recipients reported that the schemes did not generate additional employment although half of the small farmers and one-third of the marginal farmers reported additional income. When judged from the impact the schemes made on the poverty line, no scheme is qualified to be categorised as viable. For although there was a slight rise in the income, it was not adequate to cross the poverty line. Of all the minor irrigation schemes, well-development scheme proved to be slightly beneficial to the small farmers and oil engine to the marginal farmers. On the darker side, the new well scheme proved to be a flop in most of the cases. The minor irrigation schemes could not make substantial impact mainly on account of absence of appropriate technology and geo-climatic unsuitability of the schemes.

The second major programme, namely, animal husbandry proved to be more injurious than the minor irrigation schemes. For it generated additional employment but not income. Of the three livestock schemes—milch cattle, sheep rearing and poultry—the milch cattle and poultry schemes proved to be counter productive. Under milch cattle scheme half of the recipients and all the poultry beneficiaries reported a fall in their income. The agricultural labourers on an-aggregate suffered 13.6 per cent of decline in their income due to the schemes. The recipients of the sheep units reported additional income. Yet it was not substantial enough to enable the beneficiaries to cross the poverty line. The livestock schemes largely suffered on account of inadequacy of infrastructure and unsuitability of geo-climatic conditions.

With regard to the agricultural schemes—the cart and bullock, plough bullock, land development—there has been rise in the income of the recipients of the schemes. Yet the rise has not been adequate to quality the schemes to be categorised as viable. For most of the beneficiaries could not cross the poverty line.

Among the other schemes the nylon net schemes, compared to most of the other schemes, proved to be viable. For the schemes generated 40.2 per cent additional per capita income and a few could even cross the poverty line. The scheme has inherent potentiality to become viable. The other schemes like mango tree, cashew nut tree schemes proved to be non-viable. The recipients of the mango tree scheme suffered a considerable decline in their income.

An analysis of viability of the schemes reveals that some of the schemes could indeed generate additional income but it was not enough to enable the members of the target groups to cross the poverty line. Therefore, generation of additional income by itself does not make a scheme viable. It also indicates that some of the recipients are so poor that even a substantial rise in the income could not help them in crossing the poverty line. The data further indicates that schemes had relatively better impact on those who had land. Secondly, physical assets like cart, plough, house sites have given a 'psychological gain' to the target groups. Thirdly, target groups with traditional skills like shepherds, fishermen derived greater benefit from the schemes than the other groups. Of all the categories, therefore, the agricultural labourers who neither have a piece of land nor any skill suffered most under the schemes.

The overall unimpressive performance of small farmers development agency has to be traced to a number of factors which include the role of bureaucracy and middle-man and non-participation of the target groups in the developmental process.

The small farmers development agency is an autonomous administrative institution devised for purposes of covering specific target groups under anti-poverty schemes. The agency is given a fixed amount and a target to be achieved within a stipulated time. The agency seeks to implement the schemes through the existing bureaucratic machinery at the district level. The functionaries of SFDA including the Project Director are drawn from the regular bureaucratic machinery. Thus we find that a new agency is called upon 'to operate through old structures and their functionaries'. An autonomous agency of this type does not seem to enjoy any advantages. On the contrary, the functionaries at the district and block level are not happy with the creation of the agency. This resulted in non-cooperative attitudes calling for greater degree of coordination—which has been one of the casualties of development administration. The rural administrative system suffers from two maladies: one, it is devoid of multiple coordinating points and two, while differentiation has been occurring fast, integration of the system has been lagging far behind.

That the SFDA is not properly conceived is evident from: one, absence of field staff of its own and helpless dependence on the existing grass-root bureaucracy; two, ineffective linkages with the other structures; and three, absence of monitoring and evaluation.

The grass-root bureaucracy on which SFDA solely depended suffers from innumerable infirmities. The growing centralisation of decision-making, proliferation of the agencies, criss-cross and non-formal linkages characterise the structure of the organisation. Absence of reward and punishment system, undue expansion at mid points, low level of technical and managerial competence and wastage of time further incapacitate the structure. The behavioural orientation of the bureaucrats is not conducive for healthy implementation of anti-poverty programmes. Lack of concern for the poor, pessimistic disposition, elitistic and authoritarian culture, depersonalised approach are deleterious to developmental process. Growing localism, obsession with self-development, superficial understanding of the root causes for the problems lead to negative orientation producing counter productive results. Added to it the rural environment is changing qualitatively. The increasing consciousness of the people call for greater response from bureaucracy. The bureaucracy of the type that continues to exist in rural areas is bound to get increasingly paralysed in a rapidly changing environment.

The rural poor obviously cannot be happy with such a type of bureaucracy. They are bitter in their comments. The landless labourers think that they are not cared for by the bureaucrats as they are poor, ill dressed and live in bad physical conditions. In contrast the landed gentry offered a few favourable comments on the bureaucracy. As a result the poor do not risk personal visits to government offices nor can take advantage of the schemes offered by the SFDA. As the bureaucracy is largely alienated from the poor, the poor are increasingly depending on middle-men who operate outside the bureaucratic framework.

The middle-man—popularly known as pyraveekar in Telangana region of Andhra Pradesh—is an institution which seeks to fill in the existing gaps in the rural organisation. The task of the institution is basically to pursue the cases, chase the files, push up the papers and see that the schemes trickle down to the members of the target groups. In fact it has become the main channel of communication between the bureaucratic set-up and the rural poor. Although the institution originated in the feudal set-up, it gained additional momentum in the wake of subsidy based anti-poverty schemes.

The middle-man maintains effective linkages with the politicians in power and key decision makers in the administration. Pyravee has become a stepping stone for those who wish to enter politics. And for those who are in it, it is a source of political sustenance. The bureaucracy feels 'safe' to deal with a few middle-men instead of a large number of members of the target group. The members of the target groups feel at home with the pyraveekar as they can confide their needs and take his assistance in tailoring the SFDA benefit to suit their personal needs and priorities. They see in him a skilled person who can steer through the cobwebs of complicated bureaucratic procedures. It is empirically found that most of those who depended on pyraveekar got the schemes while a large number of those who were reluctant to take his assistance did not get the schemes.

An analysis of the role of pyraveekar in SFDA schemes reveals that it is he who publicised the schemes and 'goaded' the terget groups to apply for them. Those who depended on pyraveekar are mostly the landless labourers. On the darker side his 'commission' cuts deep into the subsidy component of the scheme. He transmitted distorted information about the loans and used it as a leverage to establish and consolidate his hegemony over the rural poor.

The extension agency conceded that pyraveekar has come to occupy a dominant place in the developmental programmes in general and anti-poverty schemes in particular. Although they think that the institution has had an unhealthy effect on the schemes, they admit that the members of the target group repose greater confidence in him than in the extension agency. They, as a remedial measure, suggested increase in the staff, simplification of procedures, decentralisation of decision making and door delivery of the benefit. Although conceptually the extension agency is opposed to the institution, operationally they respond favourably to the machinations of the institution of pyraveekar.

The failure of bureaucracy has given rise to this new phenomenon in the rural sector. This can be considered as an unintended consequence of an ill-conceived public policy. The institution, on the whole, has had a deleterious effect on the SFDA schemes.

The best way to fill in the organisational gaps in the rural sector is to create peoples organisations and ensure their active participation in the developmental process. Participation of the people can ensure effective implementation of SFDA schemes and can have far-reaching effects on the rural socio-economic set-up. Peoples' participation can be of two types: one, positive participation where the target groups take full advantage of the schemes extended to them; two, active participation which involves not only availing themselves of the benefits but articulating their needs and demands. For these purposes people require to be organised.

In most of the developing countries the policy framework does not adequately plan organisation of the people. In the absence of such a thrust, the policies suffer a good deal in formulation and implementation. The people in power, although they are aware of the potentialities of peoples' organisations, do not risk such steps as they fear that it would erode their power base.

For the purpose of assessing the potential for participation the following aspects are examined: one, the dependence of target groups on governmental assistance; two, the dependence of target groups on elite; three, cooperative approach to developmental process; four, perceptions of poverty and five, perception of their future.

About the dependence of the target groups on the government the data strongly suggests how it is increasing. They feel that the role of a resourceful and impartial government should be that of a benefactor. They rule out a role to the local elite and peoples organisations on the ground that people are illiterate, poor, inefficient and quarrelsome. They wondered how poverty ridden people can help themselves. Such attitudes lead to psychosis of helplessness and surrender of initiative reducing the scope for any meaningful participation of the people in the developmental process.

About the linkages with the local elite, the data reveals large area of interaction. However, most of the respondents consider the elite as unhelpful and expressed the feeling that the rural elite are opposed to the development of the poor. They described them as selfish, corrupt, faction ridden, partisan and exploitative. This indicates the erosion of legitimacy and credibility of the rural elite. The poor have come to see through and look beyond the local elite groups. This attitudinal pattern also knocks away the local initiative causing leadership crisis. Mass organisations and mass mobilisation become difficult until new leadership emerges with greater credibility from the poor themselves.

An analysis of the third dimension relating to attitudes towards cooperative effort reveals a heavy individualistic bias among the target groups. Cooperative approach is opposed on the grounds that men by nature are lazy, quarrelsome and cannot work together. They fear that production would fall under cooperative effort as there would not be individual commitment which in turn, according to them, would result in greater tensions and exploitation. Such attitude towards cooperation would work as a formidable impediment in building participative culture.

About the phenomenon of poverty, the target groups traced the causes to landlessness, failure of monsoon and laziness of the people. While a few blamed the ancestors for not earning the property, a few others thought exploitation in the society accounted for existence of poverty. Interestingly karma has not figured prominently as a cause for their misery. About measures for eradication of poverty they suggested increasing governmental assistance and effective implementation of anti-poverty schemes. They also suggested redistribution of land and strengthening of irrigation potential. Landless labourers pleaded for higher wages. There was also a suggestion for greater industrialisation. The pattern of responses conclusively establish that poor look to the government and government alone for eradication of poverty.

The last dimension examined has been the perception of target groups of the future. It is assumed that positive view of future leads to more participation and negative view to withdrawal. About the present conditions they feel that there is either stagnation or deterioration. About the future they foresee further deterioration in condition. A considerable number of them are also vague about it. Such temporal perspective indicates pessimistic tendency resulting in withdrawal rather than participation.

Thus all the five factors examined indicate the widespread psychosis of helplessness. They look to the government to solve all their problems. The local elite have come to be viewed as anti-people and anti-development. Added to it, they are conditioned by individualistic philosophy. Their temporal perspective smacks of pessimism. Such an outlook would cause apathy towards developmental process and result in increasing withdrawal instead of active participation in developmental process. The net impact of such attitudinal pattern on an anti-poverty programme like SFDA is bound to be negative.

The policy for small farmers development, it is obvious, could not create a significant impact on the target groups. The schemes proved to be too ill-organised to be viable infact. Some of the schemes proved to be counter productive. The agricultural labourers are not only bypassed but are put to greater misery. The administrative machinery is not properly oriented nor is it vigorous to help the poor. The middlemen, as a result, have been appropriating the benefits. The poor as a class are yet to develop participative culture to overcome the serious limitations of a public policy and an inegalitarian socio-economic system. Thus the Small Farmers Development Agency—another important public policy—like green revolution failed to make a positive impact on the rural poor.

APPENDICES

APPENDIX II. 1

EDUCATIONAL PARTICULARS OF RESPONDENTS

Sl. No.	Name of the village	EDUCATION				Total Educated
		Illiterates	Primary	Secondary	College	
1.	Marpadga	130 (68.4)	43 (22.6)	11 (5.8)	6 (3.2)	60 (31.6)
2.	Sirsingandla	52 (80.0)	12 (18.5)	1 (1.5)		13 (20.0)
3.	Peddamasanpally	40 (80.0)	8 (16.0)	2 (4.0)		10 (20.0)
	Total	222 (72.8)	63 (20.7)	14 (4.6)	6 (1.9)	83 (27.3)
4.	Shankavaram	99 (52-7)	68 (36.2)	19 (10.1)	2 (1.0)	89 (47.3)
5.	Vajrakutam	43 (61.4)	25 (35.7)	2 (2.9)		27 (38.6)
6.	Balarampuram	43 (86.0)	5 (10.0)	2 (4.0)		7 (14.0)
	Total	185 (60.1)	98 (31.8)	23 (7.5)	2 (0.6)	123 (39.9)
	Grand Total	407 (66.4)	161 (26.3)	37 (6.0)	8 (1.3)	206 (33.6)

Note : Figures in brackets indicate percentage.

APPENDIX II. 2

AGE PARTICULARS OF RESPONDENTS

Sl. No.	Age Group	MEDAK				EAST GODAVARI				Total of two districts
		Marpadga	Sirsingandla	Peddamasan-pally	Total	Shanka-varam	Vajra-kutam	Bala-ram-puram	Total	
1.	20-40 years	107	27	27	161	119	43	30	192	353
		(56.3)	(41.5)	(54.0)	(52.8)	(63.3)	(61.4)	(60.0)	(62.4)	(57.6)
2.	41-55 years	55	26	13	94	43	17	15	75	169
		(28.9)	(40.1)	(26.0)	(30.8)	(22.9)	(24.3)	(30.0)	(24.3)	(27.6)
3.	56 and above	28	12	10	50	26	10	5	41	91
		(14.8)	(18.4)	(20.0)	(16.4)	(13.8)	(14.3)	(10.0)	(13.3)	(14.8)
	Total	190	65	50	305	188	70	50	308	613

Note : Figures in brackets indicate percentage.

APPENDIX II. 3

OCCUPATIONAL PARTICULARS OF RESPONDENTS

Sl. No.	Name of the village	PRIMARY OCCUPATION				SECONDARY OCCUPATION			
		Agriculture	Business	A.L.	Others	Agriculture	Business	A.L.	Others
1.	Marpadga	143 (75.3)	—	27 (14.2)	20 (10.5)	34 (17.9)	—	69 (36.3)	40 (21.1)
2.	Sirsingandla	43 (66.2)	1 (1.5)	11 (16.9)	10 (15.4)	15 (23.1)	—	13 (20.0)	19 (29.0)
3.	Peddamasanpally	29 (58.0)	—	11 (22.0)	10 (20.0)	19 (38.0)	—	18 (36.0)	8 (16.0)
	Total	215 (70.5)	1 (0.3)	49 (16.1)	40 (13.1)	68 (22.3)	—	100 (32.8)	67 (22.0)
4.	Shankavaram	83 (44.2)	1 (0.5)	70 (37.2)	34 (18.1)	23 (12.2)	—	13 (6.9)	13 (6.9)
5.	Vajrakutam	51 (72.9)	—	14 (20.0)	5 (7.1)	11 (15.7)	4 (5.7)	25 (35.7)	26 (8.6)
6.	Balarampuram	24 (48.0)	—	25 (50.0)	1 (2.0)	11 (22.0)	—	17 (34.0)	5 (10.0)
	Total	158 (51.3)	1 (0.3)	109 (35.4)	40 (13.0)	45 (14.6)	4 (1.3)	55 (17.9)	44 (14.3)
	Grand Total	373 (60.8)	2 (0.3)	158 (25.8)	80 (13.1)	113 (18.4)	4 (0.7)	155 (25.3)	111 (18.1)

Note : Figures in brackets indicate percentage.

APPENDIX-II. 4

FAMILY PARTICULARS OF THE RESPONDENTS

Sl. No.	Name of the village	Family Type			Family size				
		Joint	Single	Total	Upto 5	6—10	11—15	16—20	Total
	Medak Dist.								
1.	Marpadga	76	114	190	109	73	7	1	190
		(40.0)	(60.0)		(57.4)	(38.4)	(3.7)	(0.5)	
2.	Sirsingandla	25	40	65	37	26	2	—	65
		(38.5)	(61.5)		(56.9)	(40.0)	(3.1)		
3.	Peddamasanpally	18	32	50	31	18	1	—	50
		(36.0)	(64.0)		(62.0)	(36.0)	(2.0)		
	Total	119	186	305	177	117	10	1	305
		(39.0)	(61.0)		(58.0)	(38.4)	(3.3)	(0.3)	
	East Godavari Dist.								
4.	Shankavaram	39	149	188	109	77	2	—	188
		(20.7)	(79.3)		(58.0)	(41.0)	(1.0)		
5.	Vajrakutam	15	55	70	43	25	—	2	70
		(21.4)	(78.6)		(61.4)	(35.7)		(2.9)	
6.	Balarampuram	10	40	50	32	16	2	—	50
		(20.0)	(80.0)		(64.0)	(32.0)	(4.0)		
	Total	64	244	308	184	118	4	2	308
		(20.8)	(79.2)		(59.7)	(38.3)	(1.3)	(0.6)	
	Grand total	183	430	613	361	235	14	3	613
		(29.9)	(70.1)		(58.9)	(38.3)	(2.3)	(0.5)	

Note : Figures in brackets indicate percentages

APPENDIX—II. 5

EMPLOYMENT PARTICULARS OF HOUSEHOLDERS

Sl. No.	Work Combiration	WORKING DAYS 1—60	61-120	121-180	181-240	241-300	301-365	Total
1	2	3	4	5	6	7	8	9
1.	Own Cultivation	17 (1.1)	22 (1.4)	37 (2.3)	99 (6.3)	29 (1.8)	44 (2.8)	248 (15.7)
2.	Attached labour						55 (3.5)	55 (3.5)
3.	Contract labour	3 (0.2)	3 (0.2)	1 (0.1)		2 (0.1)	18 (1.1)	27 (1.7)
4.	Daily wage labour	13 (0.8)	51 (3.2)	105 (6.6)	28 (1.8)	55 (3.5)	16 (1.0)	268 (16.9)
5.	Others	2 (0.1)	6 (0.4)	16 (1.0)	8 (0.5)	29 (1.8)	119 (7.5)	180 (11.4)
6.	Own cultivation + Attached labour						5 (0.3)	5 (0,3)
7.	Own cultivation + Daily wage labour	40 (2.5)	100 (6.3)	135 (8.5)	94 (5.9)	115 (7.3)	96 (6.1)	580 (36.7)
8.	Own cultivation + others	4 (0.3)	4 (0.3)	10 (0.6)	7 (0.4)	25 (1.6)	101 (6.4)	151 (9.6)

1	2	3	4	5	6	7	8	9
9.	Own cultivation + daily wage + others		1 (0.1)			4 (0.3)	11 (0.7)	16 (1.0)
10.	Own cultivation + Contract labour + daily wage labour		23 (1.5)	2 (0.1)		5 (0.3)		30 (1.9)
11.	Contract labour + Others		1 (0.1)		1 (0.1)		1 (0.1)	3 (0.2)
12.	Contract labour + daily wage labour + others		2 (0.1)	4 (0.3)	3 (0.2)	8 (0.5)		17 (1.1)
	Total	79 (5.0)	213 (13.5)	310 (19.6)	240 (15.2)	272 (17.2)	466 (29.5)	1580 (100)

Note : Figures in brackets indicate percentage.

APPENDIX—II. 6

EMPLOYMENT PARTICULARS OF HOUSEHOLDS

Sl. No.	Employ= ment	Work combination									
		MEDAK					EAST GODAVARI				
		O.A.	D.L.	O.A. + D.L.	Others	Total	O.A.	D.L.	O.A. + D.L	Others	Total
1.	0—60	12 (7.7)	4 (4.5)	29 (7.1)	8 (2.4)	53 (5.4)	5 (5.4)	9 (5.0)	11 (6.4)	1 (0.7)	26 (4.4)
2.	61—120	18 (11.6)	14 (15.7)	58 (14.3)	15 (4.5)	105 (10.6)	4 (4.3)	37 (20.7)	42 (24.3)	25 (16.8)	108 (18.2)
3.	121—180	22 (14.2)	29 (32.6)	96 (23.6)	21 (6.3)	168 (17.0)	15 (16.1)	76 (42.5)	39 (22.5)	12 (8.1)	142 (23.9)
4.	181—240	68 (43.9)	17 (19.1)	86 (21.1)	16 (4.8)	187 (19.0)	31 (33.3)	11 (6.1)	8 (4.6)	3 (2.0)	53 (8.9)
5.	241—300	8 (5.2)	18 (20.2)	57 (14.0)	39 (11.6)	122 (12.4)	21 (22.6)	37 (20.7)	58 (33.5)	34 (22.8)	150 (25.3)
6.	301—365	27 (17.4)	7 (7.9)	81 (19.9)	236 (70.4)	351 (35.6)	17 (18.3)	9 (5.0.)	15 (8.7)	74 (49.7)	115 (19.4)
	Total	155 (9.8)	89 (5.6)	407 (25.8)	335 (21.2)	986 (62.4)	93 (5.9)	179 (11.3)	173 (10 9)	149 (9.4)	594 (37.6)

N.B. : O.A. = Own Agriculture; D.L. = Daily labour

Note : Figures in brackets indicate percentage.

APPENDIX— II. 7

LIVESTOCK PARTICULARS RESPONDENTS

Sl. No.	Name of the village	No. of Non-Possessers	No. of possessers of poultry unit	No. of possessers of sheep unit	No. of possessers of milch cattle, bullocks etc.	No. of possessors of all kinds of livestock	Total no.
1.	Marpadga	30 (15.8)	3 (1.6)	8 (4.2)	120 (63.2)	29 (15.2)	190
2.	Sirsingandla	5 (7.7)	—	3 (4.6)	46 (70.8)	11 (16.9)	65
3.	Peddamasanpally	12 (24.0)	—	4 (8.0)	30 (60.0)	4 (8.0)	50
	Total	47 (15.3)	3 (0.9)	15 (4.9)	196 (64.3)	44 (14.4)	305
4.	Shankavaram	80 (42.6)	17 (9.1)	8 (4.2)	82 (43.6)	1 (0.53)	188
5.	Vajrakutam	2 (2.8)	13 (18.5)	3 (4.6)	44 (62.6)	8 (11.5)	170
6.	Balarampuram	21 (42.0)	—	—	27 (54.0)	2 (4.0)	50
	Total	103 (33.4)	30 (9.7)	11 (3.6)	153 (49.7)	11 (3.6)	308
	Grand Total	150 (24.5)	33 (5.4)	26 (4.2)	349 (57.0)	55 (8.9)	613

Note : Figures in brackets indicate percentage.

APPENDIX - II. 8

AGRICULTURAL IMPLEMENTS PARTICULARS OF RESPONDENTS

Sl. No.	Name of the village	Implements not possessed	Ploughs (one item)	Ploughs & others (two items)	Possession of all items
1.	Marpadga	36 (18.9)	10 (5.3)	94 (49.5)	50 (26.3)
2.	Sirsingandla	14 (21.5)	2 (3.1)	36 (55.4)	13 (20.0)
3.	Peddamasanpally	18 (36.0)	9 (18.0)	13 (26.0)	10 (20,0)
	Total	68 (22.3)	21 (6.9)	143 (46.9)	73 (23.9)
4.	Shankavaram	129 (68.6)	52 (27.7)	5 (2.7)	2 (1.0)
5.	Vajrakutam	12 (17.1)	5 (7.1)	14 (20.1)	39 (55.7)
6.	Balarampurm	34 (68.0)	13 (26.0)	2 (4.0)	1 (2.0)
	Total	175 (56.8)	70 (22.8)	21 (6.8)	42 (13.7)
	Grand Total	243 (39.6)	91 (14.8)	164 (26.8)	115 (18.8)

Note : Figures in brackets indicate perecentage.

APPENDIX-II. 9

VEHICLE PARTICULARS OF RESPONDENTS

Sl. No.	Name of the village	No vehicle	Cart	Bi-cycle	Bi-cycle and cart	Total
1.	Marpadga	152 (80.0)	26 (13.7)	7 (3.7)	5 (2.6)	190 (100)
2.	Sirsingandla	51 (78.5)	7 (10.8)	4 (6.2)	3 (4.5)	65 (100)
3.	Peddamasanpally	34 (68.0)	10 (20.0)	3 (6.0)	3 (6.0)	50 (100)
	Total	237 (77.8)	43 (14.1)	14 (4.6)	11 (3.5)	305 (100)
4.	Shankavaram	131 (69.7)	20 (10.6)	30 (15.9)	7 (3.8)	188 (100)
5.	Vajrakutam	31 (44.3)	22 (31.4)	11 (15.7)	6 (8.6)	70 (100)
6.	Balarampuram	43 (86.0)	3 (6.0)	3 (6.0)	1 (2.0)	50 (100)
	Total	205 (66.6)	45 (14.6)	44 (14.3)	14 (4.5)	308 (100)
	Grand Total	442 (72.0)	88 (14.4)	58 (9.5)	25 (4.1)	613 (100)

Note : Figures in brackets indicate percentage.

APPENDIX-III. 1

STATEMENT SHOWING THE NUMBER OF BENEFICIARIES BENEFITED (S. Cs. & S. Is) (S.F., M.F., & A.L.) UNDER SFDA SINCE INCEPTION TO 1979-80

Sl. No.	Years	Small Farmers			Marginal Farmers			Agri Labourers			Total		
		All	S.Cs	S.Ts	All	S.Cs	S.Ts	All	S.Cs	S.Ts	All	S.Cs	S.Ts
1.	IV Plan	11266	824	440	15201	2195	927	9627	2172	204	36094	5191	1571
		(6.7)	(7.3)	(3.9)	(6.5)	(14.4)	(6.1)	(11.8)	(22.6)	(2.1)	(7.5)	(14.5)	(4.4)
2.	1974-75	11342	443	143	14466	1745	1631	5783	845	132	31591	3043	1906
		(6.8)	(4.0)	(1.3)	(6.2)	(12.7)	(11.3)	(7.1)	(14.6)	(2.2)	(6.6)	(9.6)	(6.0)
3.	1975-76	51375	13218	334	65287	23352	1431	10169	3097	28	126831	39667	1798
		(30.6)	(25.7)	(0.7)	(28.5)	(35.8)	(2.2)	(12.5)	(38.5)	(0.3)	(26.3)	(34.3)	(1.4)
4.	1976-77	17957	3681	733	32963	10774	2643	9903	2619	378	60823	17074	3754
		(10.7)	(20.5)	(4.1)	(14.2)	(32.7)	(2.0)	(12.1)	(26.1)	(3.78)	(12.5)	(28.1)	(6.2)
5.	1977-78	34639	8988	1489	40285	13254	2641	11746	3977	909	86670	26219	5099
		(20.7)	(25.9)	(4.3)	(17.3)	(32.9)	(6.6)	(14.6)	(33.9)	(7.3)	(18.0)	(31.3)	(5.6)
6.	1978-79	25603	6504	2189	41602	14497	2593	19713	9344	929	86918	30381	5711
		(15.3)	(25.9)	(8.5)	(17.9)	(34.9)	(6.2)	(24.2)	(47.4)	(4.7)	(18.1)	(35.0)	(6.6)
7.	1979-80	15450	2863	1896	22452	5968	1237	14586	7766	648	52488	16597	3781
		(9.29)	(11.5)	(12.5)	(9.8)	(26.6)	(5.5)	(17.9)	(53.2)	(4.47)	(10.9)	(31.67)	(7.3)
	Total	167,632	36.567	7224	232,256	71785	13103	81527	29820	3228	481,415	138,172	23,555
		(100)	(21.8)	(4.3)	100)	(30.9)	(5.6)	(100)	(36.7)	(3.9)	(100)	(28.7)	(4.9)

Note : Figures in brackets indicate percentage.

APPENDIX-III. 2

THE NUMBER OF BENEFICIARIES BENEFITED UNDER SFDA UP TO 1978-79

Sl. No.	Name of the village	Small farmers	Marginal farmers	Agriculture labourer
1970-1971				
1.	Srikakulam	26365	47104	14262
2.	Vishakhapatnam	3463	25206	26438
3.	Nalgonda	38708	44973	2202
4.	Cuddapah	12659	6657	6218
1974-1975				
5.	Adilabad	4990	3063	1010
6.	Khammam	17161	4348	1948
7.	Medak	6027	4689	140
8.	Hyderabad	3778	4562	1909
9.	East Godavari	14116	13025	6254
10.	Nellore	4975	19478	815
1975-76				
11.	Karimnagar	4347	9404	227
12.	Nizamabad	4716	5661	613
13.	Warangal	3424	3465	1787
14.	Prakasam	5020	8165	2699
1976-77				
15.	Krishna	1518	3628	682
16.	Guntur	1825	4326	707

APPENDIX — III. 3

THE AMOUNT RELEASED BY THE CENTRAL AND STATE GOVERNMENTS UNDER SFDA SINCE INCEPTION

(*Rs. in lakhs*)

Sl. No.	Name of the Agency	IV Plan	'74-'75	'75-'76	'76-'77	'77-'78	'78-'79	'79-'80	Total
	IV Plan Series								
1.	Srikakulam	109.72	56.40	118.70	40.23	41.85	34.09	69.27	470.26
2.	Vishakhapatnam	45.67	0.32	54.72	15.04	26.21	51.00	18.99	211.95
3.	Nalgonda	100.63	32.16	116.52	16.75	52.65	40.05	43.79	402.55
4.	Cuddapah	45.31	22.88	83.71	4.61	3.40	2.64	3.23	165.78
	1974-75 Series								
5.	Adilabad			7.63	10.86	28.34	40.52	25.22	112.57
6.	Khammam			8.15	29.32	98.41	50.37	32.84	219.09
7.	Medak			5.35	27.07	40.13	33.70	15.91	122.16
8.	Hyderabad			17.80	45.31	45.00	42.20	28.40	178.71
9.	East Godavari			12.09	46.06	57.73	48.65	48.53	213.06
10.	Nellore			17.00	39.44	68.53	45.20	21.22	191.39
	1975-76 Series								
11.	Karimnagar				5.09	45.16	44.00	13.54	107.79
12.	Nizamabad				18.26	44.02	56.04	19.80	138.12
13.	Warangal			1.05	21.70	37.68	22.76	26.36	109.55
14.	Prakasam				25.00	32.63	46.58	23.75	127.96
	1976-77 Series								
15.	Krishna				5.04	24.72	4.53	35.27	69.56
16.	Guntur				5.20	33.19		17.60	55.99
	Total	301.33	111.76	442.76	354.98	679.65	562.33	443.72	2896.29

APPENDIX-III. 4

AMOUNT UTILISED BY SFDA AGENCIES SINCE INCEPTION

(*Rs. in Lakhs*)

Sl. No.	Name of the Agency	IV Plans	'74-'75	'75-'76	'76-'77	'77-'78	'78-'79	'79-'80	Total
	IV Plan Series								
1.	Srikakulam	64.55	56.40	84.88	32.33	39.30	24.77	53.16	355.39
2.	Vishakhapatnam	31.69	8.23	54.57	9.07	26.38	51.88	18.93	200.75
3.	Nalgonda	46.47	19.58	115.48	15.28	49.05	40.34	48.36	334.76
4.	Cuddapah	41.90	15.81	90.18	2.71	3.54	3.38	2.52	160.04
	1974-75 Series								
5.	Adilabad			2.03	9.70	18.00	38.89	23.70	92.32
6.	Khammam			27.55	42.25	33.70	42.45	27.18	173.13
7.	Medak			4.38	26.91	21.92	32.12	11.90	97.23
8.	Hyderabad			7.25	24.83	69.88	41.21	19.51	162.68
9.	East Godavari			10.02	41.96	42.92	41.40	42.69	178.99
10.	Nellore		0.44	15.98	37.71	51.77	35.53	18.72	160.15
	1975-76 Series								
11.	Karimnagar				6.59	28.31	43.54	23.50	101.94
12.	Nizamabad				15.59	24.70	41.05	20.02	101.36
13.	Warangal			0.86	20.04	30.71	18.83	23.77	94-21
14.	Prakasam				24.59	29.57	46.24	19.66	120.06
	1976-77 Series								
15.	Krishna				1.95	22.46	28.93	12.46	65.80
16.	Guntur				3.20	11.74	28.93	12.46	56.33
	Total	184.81	100.46	413.18	314.71	503.95	553.21	377.60	2447.92

APPENDIX-III. 5

THE AMOUNT RELEASED AND UTILISED UNDER SFDA UP TO 1979-1980

Sl.	Name of the Agency	The amount released by central & state governments under SFDA.	The amount utilised by SFDA.
IV Plan Series			
		Rs. in Lakhs	Rs. in Lakhs
1.	Srikakulam	470.26	355.39
2.	Vishakhapatnam	211.95	200.75
3.	Nalgonda	402.55	334.76
4.	Cuddapah	165.78	160.04
1974-74 Series			
5.	Adilabad	112.57	92.32
6.	Khammam	219.09	173.13
7.	Medak	122.16	97.23
8.	Hyderabad	178.71	152,68
9.	East Godavari	223.06	178.99
10.	Nellore	191.39	160.15
1975-76 Series			
11.	Karimnagar	107.79	101.94
12.	Nizamabad	138.12	101.36
13.	Warangal	109.55	94.21
14.	Prakasam	127.96	120.06
1976-77 Series			
15.	Krishna	69.56	65.80
16.	Guntur	55.99	49.11
	Total	2906.49	2447.92

APPENDIX-III. 6

STATEMENT SHOWING THE AMOUNT OF LOAN DISBURSED BY COOPERATIVE INSTITUTIONS AND COMMERCIAL BANKS FOR IV PLAN

(Rs. in lakhs)

S.F.D.A.	Cooperative institutions				Commercial banks				Total			
	STL	MTL	LTL	TOTAL	STL	MTL	LTL	TOTAL	STL	MTL	LTL	TOTAL
IV Plan Series												
1. Srikakulam	10.00	9.6	8.98	28.58	18.54	7.31		25.85				74.45
2. Vishakhapatnam		4.02	6.40	10.42		13.82	2.68	16.50				26.92
3. Nalgonda												
4. Cuddapah	72.00	10.00	66.00	148.00	30.00	14.00		44.00				192.00
1974-75 Series												
5. Adilabad												
6. Hyderabad												
7. Medak												
8. Khammam												
9. East Godavari												
10. Nellore												
1975-76 Series												
11. Karimnagar												
12. Nizamabad												
13. Warangal												
14. Prakasam												
1976-77 Series												
15- Krishna												
16. Guntur												
Total	82.00	23.62	81.38	187.00	48.54	35.13	2.68	86.35				293.37

APPENDIX-III. 7

STATEMENT SHOWING AMOUNT OF LOAN DISBURSED BY COOPERATIVE INSTITUTIONS AND COMMERCIAL BANKS FOR 1974-1975

(Rs. in lakhs)

Sl. No.	S.F.D.A.	Cooperative institutions				Commercial banks				Total			
		STL	MTL	LTL	Total	STL	MTL	LTL	Total	STL	MTL	LTL	Total
	IV Plan Series												
1.	Srikakulam	15.61	4.33	12.00	31.94	15.41	8.16		23.56				83.70
2.	Vishakhapatnam		4.17	4.26	8.43		7.30		7.30				15.73
3.	Nalgonda												
4.	Cuddapah	20.00	4.88	30.00	54.88	14.00	8.00		22.00				76.88
	1974-75 Series												
5.	Adilabad												
6.	Hyderabad												
7.	Medak												
8.	Khammam												
9.	East Godavari												
10.	Nellore												
	1975-76 Series												
11.	Karimnagar												
12.	Nizamabad												
13.	Warangal												
14.	Prakasam												
	1976-77 Series												
15.	Krishna												
16.	Guntur												
	Total	35.61	13.38	46.26	95.25	29.41	23.46		52.86				176.31

APPENDIX-III. 8

STATEMENT SHOWING THE AMOUNT OF LOAN DISBURSED BY COOPERATIVE INSTITUTIONS AND COMMERCIAL BANKS FOR 1975-76

(*Rs. in lakhs*)

Sl.	S.F.D.A	Cooperative institutions				Commercial banks				Total			
No.		STL	MTL	LTL	TOTAL	STL	MTL	LTL	TOTAL	STL	MTL	LTL	TOTAL
	IV Plan Series												
1.	Srikakulam	19.00	4.20	21.15	44.33	12.00	9.00		41.00				65.33
2.	Vishakhapatnam		41.58	53 29	94.87		14.05	9.19	23.24				118.11
3.	Nalgonda	154.71	66.66	134.01	355.38	2.22	219.99		222.21				577.54
4.	Cuddapah	7.00	10.00	58.00	75.00	28.00	14.00	1.54	43.54				118.54
	1974-75 Series												
5.	Adilabad			1.75	1.75								1.75
6.	Khammam	44.52	2.00	6.08	52.60								52.60
7.	Medak			1.20	1.20		2.17		2.17				3.37
8.	Hyderabad	0.52	16.40	5.53	22.45		38.87		38.87				61.76
9.	East Godavari	0.69	6.78	9.05	16.52		1.22		1.22				17.32
10.	Nellore			9.87	9.87		8.27		8.27				18.14
	1975-76 Series												
11.	Karimnagar												
12.	Nizamabad												
13.	Warangal												
14.	Prakasam												
	1976-77 Series												
15.	Krishna												
16.	Guntur												
	Total	226.44	147.62	299.93	673.97	42.22	307.57	10.73	380.52				1034.46

APPENDIX-III. 9

STATEMENT SHOWING THE AMOUNT OF LOAN DISBURSED BY COOPERATIVE INSTITUTIONS AND COMMERCIAL BANKS FOR 1976-77

(*Rs. in lakhs*)

Sl. No.	S.F.D.A.	Cooperative institutions				Commercial banks				Total			
		STL	MTL	LTL	TOTAL	STL	MTL	LTL	TOTAL	STL	MTL	LTL	TOTAL
	IV Plan Series												
1.	Srikakulam	32.06	7.15	22.43	61.64	8.08	28.92		37.00				98.64
2.	Vishakhapatnam		2.92	10.45	13.37		9.28		9.28				22.65
3.	Nalgonda	0.43	3.66	13.40	17.49		17.36		17.36				34.85
4.	Cuddapah			7.83	7.83								7.83
	1974-75 Series												
5.	Adilabad		8.51	8.77	17.28		7.43		7.43				24.71
6.	Khammam		2.24	37.49	39.73		23.50	6.61	30.11				69.84
7.	Medak		14.54	6.49	21.03		15.60		15.60				36.63
8.	Hyderabad		10.16	6.50	16.66		39.92		39.92				56.58
9.	East Godavari	58.09	7.75	12.17	78.01		55.92	6.43	62.35				140.36
10.	Nellore	0.15	5.37	35.96	41.48	0.43	2.11	0.02	2.56				44.04
	1975-76 Series												
11.	Karimnagar		0.38		0.38		4.08		4.08				4.46
12.	Nizamabad		19.12	9.02	28.14		8.68		8.69				36.83
13.	Warangal			0.32	0.32		34.29		34.29				34.61
14.	Prakasam		10.45	19.66	30.11		34.93	0.96	35.81				65.92
	1976-77 Series												
15.	Krishna						4.06		4.06				4.06
16.	Guntur		0.67		0.67		0.78		0.78				1.45
	Total	90.73	92.92	190.49	374.14	8.51	286.87	14.02	309.40				683.46

APPENDIX-III. 10

STATEMENT SHOWING THE AMOUNT OF LOAN DISBURSED BY COOPERATIVE INSTITUTIONS AND COMMERCIAL BANKS FOR 1977-78

(Rs. in lakhs)

Sl. No.	S.F.D.A.	Cooperative institutions				Commercial banks				Total			
		STL	MTL	LTL	TOTAL	STL	MTL	LTL	TOTAL	STL	MTL	LTL	TOTAL
IV Plan Series													
1.	Srikakulam	5.00	1.25	21.25	27.50	5.00	36.33	23.85	65.18				92.68
2.	Vishakhapatnam		11.59	34.85	46.44		31.54	3.46	35.00				81.44
3.	Nalgonda		10.71	12.47	23.18		66.77		66.77				89.95
4.	Cuddapah			10.62	10.62								10.62
1974-75 Series													
5.	Adilabad		3.98	13.99	17.97		18.22		18.22				36.19
6.	Khammam		2.57	31.66	34.23		48.38	1148.87	1197.25				1231.48
7.	Medak		8.45	21.18	29.63		14.98		15.98				45.61
8.	Hyderabad		22.86	16.24	39.10		22.38		22.38				61.48
9.	East Godavari	58.36	12.39	15.93	86.58	5.00	55.33	0.73	61.06				147.64
10.	Nellore		4.92	76.85	72.77		1.28		1.28				74.05
1975-76 Series													
11.	Karimnagar	9.68	23.53	23.97	57.18		13.77		13.77				70.95
12.	Nizamabad		10.12	26,75	36.87		15.48		15.48				52.35
13.	Warangal			14.68	14.68		36.61		36.61				51.29
14.	Prakasam	16.18	17.98	19.09	53.28		2.29	11.38	13.67				66.92
1976-77 Series													
15.	Krishna		4.35	5.10	9.45		33.11		33.11				42.56
16.	Guntur		9.26	3.02	12.28		9.99		9.99				22.27
	Total	89.12	143.96	338.65	571.73	10.00	407.46	1188.29	1606.75				2177.44

APPENDIX-III. 11

STATEMENT SHOWING THE AMOUNT OF LOAN DISBURSED BY COOPERATIVE INSTITUTIONS AND COMMERCIAL BANKS FOR 1978-79

(*Rs. in lakhs*)

Sl. No.	S.F.D.A.	Cooperative institutions				Commercial banks				Total			
		STL	MTL	LTL	TOTAL	STL	MTL	LTL	TOTAL	STL	MTL	LTL	TOTAL
	IV Plan Series												
1.	Srikakulam		1.11	0.55	1.66		36.57		36.57				38.23
2.	Vishakhapatnam		26.89	26.00	52.89	8.41	41.14	9.45	59.00				111.89
3	Nalgonda		6.63	27.01	33.64		107.71		107.71				141.35
4.	Cuddapah			9.54	9.54								9.54
	1974-75 Series												
5.	Adilabad		2.18	37.70	39.88		28.37		28.37				68,25
6.	Khammam	124.42	0.44	20.26	145.12		29.15	63.26	92.41				237.53
7.	Medak		5.52	25.98	31.50		29.25		29.25				60.75
8.	Hyderabad	1.90	17.77	14.29	33.96		42.86		42.86				78.79
9.	East Godavari	165.70	13.09	13.15	191.94		60.69		60.69				252.63
10.	Nellore	0.27	6.19	30.53	36.99	4.74			4.74				41.73
	1975-76 Series												
11.	Karimnagar	0.14	49.84	21.02	72.00		22.80		22.80				94.80
12.	Nizamabad		10.98	52.00	62.98		27.66	6.16	33.82				96.80
13.	Warangal			8.05	8.05		12.56		12.56				20.61
14.	Prakasam	4.98	18.04	33.63	56.55	5.99	17.86	33.71	57.56				114.21
	1976-77 Series												
15.	Krishna		8.76	10.15	18.91		39.27		39.27				58.18
16.	Guntur		17.72	2.52	20.24		39.40		39.40				59.64
	Total	298.41	185.16	332.38	815.95	19.14	535.29	112.58	667.01				1482.96

APPENDIX-III. 12

STATEMENT SHOWING THE AMOUNT OF LOAN DISBURSED BY COOPERATIVE INSTITUTIONS AND COMMERCIAL BANKS FOR 1979-80

(*Rs. in lakhs*)

Sl. No.	S.F.D.A.	Cooperative institutions				Commercial banks				Total			
		STL	MTL	LTL	Total	STL	MTL	LTL	Total	STL	MTL	LTL	Total
	IV Plan Series												
1.	Srikakulam		20.98		20.98		180.16		180.16				201.14
2.	Vishakhapatnam		1.73	0.15	1.88		11 78		11.78				13.66
3.	Nalgonda		4.42	20.01	24.43		95.55		95.55				199.98
4.	Cuddapah		0.39		0.39								0.39
	1974-75 Series												
5.	Adilabad		1.13	12.53	13.66		17.30		17.30				30.96
6.	Khammam		14.87	1.04	15.91		33.84		33.94				49.75
7.	Medak		12.34	3.56	15.90		0.63		0.63				16 53
8.	Hyderabad	11.91	5.31	5.32	22.54		29.63		39.63				52.17
9.	East Godavari	56.95	18.72	34.41	110.08		47.18		47.18				157.26
10.	Nellore	0.02	2.17	14.62	16.81	0.55	1.76	5.32	7.63				24.44
	1975-76 Series												
11.	Karimnagar		14.30	20.89	35.19		3.48	0.04	3.52				38.71
12.	Nizamabad		5.12	24.20	29.32		11.44	1.46	12.90				42.22
13.	Warangal			21.54	21.54		30.54		30.54				52.08
14.	Prakasam	9.40	5.63	6.32	21.35	10.23	12.86	4.19	27.28				48.63
	1976-77 Series												
15.	Krishna		5.59	0.34	5.93		19.61	0.61	19.62				25.55
16.	Guntur		2.44	0.03	2.47		10.54		10.54				13.01
	Total	78.28	115.14	164.96	358.38	10.78	506.30	11.02	528.10				886.48

APPENDIX-III. 13

NUMBER OF PARTICIPANTS ENROLLED AS MEMBERS OF COOPERATIVES UNDER SFDA SINCE INCEPTION

Sl.	S.F.D.A.	IV Plan	1974-75	1975-76	1976-77	1977-78	1978-79	Total
	IV Plan Series							
1.	Srikakulam	13239	7944	9456	4141	974		35754
2.	Vishakhapatnam	9949	3630	4325	1696	16946	2855	39401
3.	Nalgonda			24756	892	715	1005	27368
4.	Cuddapah	2605	1565	1659	797	802	810	8248
	1974-75 Series							
5.	Adilabad				2556	571	1011	4138
6.	Khammam				1661	1075	482	3218
7.	Medak			36	1263	1641	1135	4075
8.	Hyderabad			4743	5335	3148	919	14145
9.	East Godavari			734	12880	1389	856	15859
10.	Nellore			2671	9410	9145	9314	30540
	1975-76 Series							
11.	Karimnagar				672	2472	1579	4723
12.	Nizamabad				1293	1378	1350	4021
13.	Warangal				1098	594	643	2335
14.	Prakasam				4764	5730	9334	19828
	1976-77 Series							
15.	Krishna				252	1101	1823	3176
16.	Guntur				580	840	207	1627
	Total	25793	13939	48390	49290	33221	33223	203856

APPENDIX-III. 14

NUMBER OF PARTICIPANTS ENROLLED AS MEMBERS OF COOPERATIVES UNDER SMALL FARMERS SINCE INCEPTION

Sl. No.	Name of the Agency	IV Plan	1974-75	1975-76	1976-77	1977-78	1978-79	Total
1.	Srikakulam	7744	4504	2455	686	119		15508
2.	Vishakhapatnam	89	461	582	142	369	369	2301
3.	Nalgonda			12220	432	403	790	13845
4.	Cuddapah	1253	701	689	729	731	732	4835
5.	Adilabad				1893	403	625	2921
6.	Khammam				972	706	378	2056
7.	Medak			15	332	529	634	1510
8.	Hyderabad			2532	3370	1755	440	8097
9.	East Godavari			676	4460	238	232	5606
10.	Nellore			498	288	2774	4103	7663
11.	Karimnagar				361	1436	814	2611
12.	Nizamabad				711	608	569	1888
13.	Warangal				529	319	267	1115
14.	Prakasam				1790	1897	2691	6378
15.	Krishna				124	231	513	868
16.	Guntur				251	309	50	610
	Total	9086	5666	19667	17070	12827	13496	77812

APPENDIX-III.15

NUMBER OF PARTICIPANTS ENROLLED AS MEMBERS OF COOPERATIVES UNDER MARGINAL FARMERS SINCE INCEPTION

Sl. No.	Name of the Agency	IV Plan	1974-75	1975-76	1976-77	1977-78	1978-79	Total
1.	Srikakulam	3503	1680	3820	2127	517		11647
2.	Vishakhapatnam	6026	2053	3026	976	703	1300	14084
3.	Nalgonda			11015	407	294	204	11920
4.	Cuddapah	686	479	502	40	42	47	1796
5.	Adilabad				663	168	296	1127
6.	Khammam				543	350	76	969
7.	Medak			9	902	711	307	1629
8.	Hyderabad			2038	1717	1345	179	5309
9.	East Godavari			58	7530	490	497	8575
10.	Nellore			2173	9043	6371	5211	22798
11.	Karimnagar				311	1034	762	2107
12.	Nizamabad				491	760	763	2014
13.	Warangal				526	258	307	1091
14.	Prakasam				2625	3120	5767	11512
15.	Krishna				88	628	736	1452
16.	Guntur				302	345	157	804
	Total	10215	4212	22671	28291	17136	16609	98854

APPENDIX-III. 16

NUMBER OF PARTICIPANTS ENROLLED AS MEMBERS OF COOPERATIVES UNDER AGRICULTURAL LABOURERS

Sl. No.	Name of the Agency	IV Plan	1974-75	1975-76	1976-77	1977-78	1978-79	Total
1.	Srikakulam	1992	1760	3181	1328	338		8599
2.	Vishakhapatnam	3834	1116	717	578	574	897	7716
3.	Nalgonda			1521	53	18	11	1603
4.	Cuddapah	666	385	478	28	29	31	1617
5.	Adilabad						90	90
6.	Khammam				146	19	28	193
7.	Medak				9		28	37
8.	Hyderabad			143	248	48	300	739
9.	East Godavari				890	661	127	1678
10.	Nellore				79			79
11.	Karimnagar					2	3	5
12.	Nizamabad				91	10	18	119
13.	Warangal				43	17	69	129
14.	Prakasam				349	713	876	1938
15.	Krishna				40	242	574	856
16.	Guntur				27	186		213
	Total	6492	3261	6040	3909	2857	3052	25611

APPENDIX-III.17

ADDITIONAL EMPLOYMENT GENERATED BY THE SCHEMES

	Generated	Not generated	Total
Landless	21 (46.7)	24 (53.3)	45
0.1 to 2.5	51 (43.2)	67 (56.8)	118
2.6 to 5.0	39 (42.9)	52 (57.1)	91
5.1 to 10	10 (71.4)	4 (28.6)	14
10.1 & above	1 (14.3)	6 (85.7)	7
Total	122 (44.4)	153 (55.6)	275

APPENDIX-III.18

ADDITIONAL INCOME GENERATED BY THE SCHEMES

	Increased	Not increased	Decreased	Total
Landless	16 (35.6)	11 (24.4)	18 (40.0)	45
0.1 to 2.5	46 (39.0)	43 (36.4)	29 (24.6)	118
2.6 to 5.0	29 (31.9)	41 (45.0)	21 (23.1)	91
5.1 to 10	6 (42.9)	6 (42.9)	2 (14.2)	14
10.1 & above	4 (57.1)	3 (42.9)	0	7
Total	101 (36.7)	104 (37.8)	70 (25.5)	275

Note : Figures in brackets indicate percentage.

	APPENDIX-III. 19 ADDITIONAL EMPLOYMENT GENERATED			*APPENDIX-III. 20* ADDITIONAL INCOME GENERATED				*APPENDIX-III. 21* DIFFICULTIES FACED IN GETTING THE SCHEME		
Income	Generated	Not generated	Total	Increased	Not increased	Decreased	Total	Faced	Not faced	Total
0—300	34 (51.5)	32 (48.5)	66	21 (31.8)	23 (34.8)	22 (33.3)	66	35 (53.0)	31 (47.0)	66
301—900	67 (48.9)	70 (51.1)	137	56 (40.9)	49 (35.8)	32 (23.3)	137	80 (58.4)	57 (41.6)	137
901—1500	14 (27.5)	37 (72.5)	51	15 (29.4)	27 (52.9)	9 (17.6)	51	34 (66.7)	17 (33.3)	51
1501 & above	7 (33.3)	14 (66.7)	21	9 (42.9)	5 (23.8)	7 (33.3)	21	12 (57.1)	9 (42.9)	21
Total	122 (44.4)	153 (55.6)	275	101 (36.7)	104 (37.8)	70 (25.5)	275	161 (58.5)	114 (41.5)	275

Note : Figures in brackets indicate percentages.

APPENDIX-III. 22 — **ADDITIONAL EMPLOYMENT GENERATED**

APPENDIX-III. 23 — **ADDITIONAL INCOME GENERATED**

APPENDIX-III. 24 — **DIFFICULTIES FACED IN GETTING THE SCHEME**

Caste	Generated	Not generated	Total	Incereased	Not incereased	Decreased	Total	Faced	Not faced	Total
S.C.	43	45	88	25	34	29	88	49	39	88
	(48.9)	(51.1)		(28.4)	(38.6)	(32.3)		(55.7)	(44.3)	
B.C.	41	46	87	46	33	8	87	50	37	87
	(47·1)	(52.9)		(52.9)	(37.9)	(9.2)		(57.5)	(42.5)	
O.C.	38	62	100	30	37	33	100	62	38	100
	(38.0)	(62.0)		(30.0)	(37.0)	(33.0)		(62.0)	(38.0)	
Total	122	153	275	101	104	70	275	161	114	275
	(44.4)	(65.6)		(36.7)	(37.8)	(25.5)		(58.5)	(41.5)	

Note : Figures in brackets indicate percentages.

APPENDIX-III. 25

ADDITIONAL EMPLOYMENT GENERATED

Family type	Generated	Not generated	Total
Joint	44 (54.3)	37 (45.7)	81
Single	78 (40.2)	116 (59.8)	194
Total	122 (44.4)	153 (65.6)	275

APPENDIX-III. 26

ADDITIONAL INCOME GENERATED

Family type	Increased	Not increased	Decreased	Total
Joint	36 (44.4)	34 (42.0)	11 (13.6)	81
Single	65 (33.5)	70 (36.1)	59 (30.4)	194
Total	101 (36.7)	104 (37.8)	70 (25.5)	275

APPENDIX-III. 27

DIFFICULTIES FACED IN GETTING THE SCHEME

Family type	Faced	Not faced	Total
Joint	44 (54.3)	37 (45.7)	81
Single	117 (60.3)	77 (39.7)	194
Total	161 (58.5)	114 (41.5)	275

Note : Figures in brackets indicate percentages.

APPENDIX-III. 28

DIFFICULTIES FACED IN USING THE SCHEME

Caste	Faced	Not faced	Total
S.C.	76 (85.4)	13 (14.6)	89
B.C.	70 (76.9)	21 (23.1)	91
O.C.	65 (68.4)	30 (31.6)	95
Total	211 (76.7)	64 (23.3)	275

Note : Figures in brackets indicate percentages.

APPENDIX-III. 29

DIFFICULTIES FACED IN USING THE SCHEME

Income	Faced	Not faced	Total
0—300	60 (80.6)	7 (10.4)	67
301—900	100 (73.5)	36 (26.5)	136
901—1500	37 (74.0)	13 (26.0)	50
1501 & above	14 (63.6)	8 (36.4)	22
Total	211 (76.7)	64 (23.3)	275

APPENDIX-III. 30

DIFFICULTIES IN GETTING THE SCHEME

	Faced	Not faced	Total
Landless	15 (33.3)	30 (66.7)	45
0—2.5	77 (65.3)	41 (34.7)	118
2.6—5.0	59 (64.8)	32 (35.2)	91
5.1—10.0	5 (35.7)	9 (64.3)	14
10.1 & above	5 (71.5)	2 (28.6)	7
Total	161 (58.5)	114 (41.5)	275

APPENDIX-III. 31

DIFFICULTIES IN IMPLEMENTING THE SCHEME

	Faced	Not faced	Total
Landless	45 (100.0)	0	45
0—2.5	91 (77.1)	27 (22.9)	118
2.6—5.0	62 (68.1)	29 (31.9)	91
5.1—10.0	10 (71.4)	4 (28.6)	14
10.1 & above	3 (42.9)	4 (57.1)	7
Total	211 (76.7)	64 (23.3)	275

Note : Figures in brackets indicate percentages.

APPENDIX-III. 32

TIME TAKEN IN GETTING THE SCHEME

Caste	Below 3 months	Six months	Above six months	Total
S.C.	58 (65.1)	16 (18.0)	15 (16.9)	89
B.C.	29 (31.9)	22 (24.1)	40 (44.0)	91
O.C.	69 (72.6)	12 (12.6)	14 (14.8)	95
Total	156 (56.7)	50 (18.2)	69 (25.1)	275

Note : Figures in brackets indicate percentages.

APPENDIX-III 33

TIME TAKEN IN GETTING THE SCHEME

Income	Below 3 months	Six months	Above six months	Total
0—300	37 (56.1)	10 (15.2)	19 (28.8)	66
301—900	72 (52.6)	29 (21.2)	36 (26.3)	137
901—1500	32 (64.0)	7 (14.0)	11 (22.0)	50
1501 & above	15 (68.2)	4 (18.2)	3 (13.6)	22
Total	156 (56.7)	50 (18.2)	69 (25.1)	275

APPENDIX-III. 34

TIME TAKEN IN GETTING THE SCHEME

LAND	Below 3 months	Six months	Above six months	Total
Landless	36 (80.0)	6 (13.3)	3 (6.7)	45
0.1—2.5	63 (53.4)	17 (14.4)	38 (32.2)	118
2.6—5.0	48 (52.7)	21 (23.1)	22 (24.1)	91
5.1—10.0	6 (42.8)	4 (28.6)	4 (28.6)	14
10.1 & above	3 (42.8)	2 (28.6)	2 (28.6)	7
Total	156 (56.7)	50 (18.2)	69 (25.1)	275

APPENDIX-III. 35

BENEFITED BY THE SCHEME

LAND	Benefited	Not benefited	Total
Landless	19 (42.2)	26 (57.8)	45
0.1—2.5	52 (44.1)	66 (55.9)	118
2.6—5.0	47 (51.6)	44 (48.4)	91
5.1—10.0	7 (50.0)	7 (50.0)	14
10.1 & above	4 (57.1)	3 (42.9)	7
Total	129 (46.9)	146 (53.1)	275

Note : Figures in brackets indicate percentages.

APPENDIX-III. 36

BENEFITED BY THE SCHEMES

Caste	Benefited	Not benefited	Total
S.C.	33 (37.1)	56 (62.9)	89
B.C.	54 (59.3)	37 (40.7)	91
O.C.	42 (44.2)	53 (55.8)	95
Total	129 (46.9)	146 (53.1)	275

Note : Figures in brackets indicate percentages.

APPENDIX-III. 37

BENEFITED BY THE SCHEMES

Income Rs.	Benefited	Not benefited	Total
0—300	23 (34.8)	43 (65.2)	66
301—900	72 (52.2)	66 (47.8)	138
901—1500	20 (40.8)	29 (59.2)	49
1501 & above	14 (63.6)	8 (36.4)	22
Total	129 (46.9)	146 (53.1)	275

APPENDIX-III 38

THE RESPONDENTS APPLIED FOR THE SCHEMES

Land	Applied	Not applied	Total
Landless	2 (4.9)	39 (95.1)	41
0.1—2.5	39 (50.0)	39 (50.0)	78
2.6—5.0	37 (51.4)	35 (48.6)	72
5.1—10.0	3 (60.0)	2 (40.0)	5
10.1 & above	0	0	0
Total	81 (41.3)	115 (58.7)	196

APPENDIX-III- 39

THE RESPONDENTS APPLIED FOR THE SCHEMES

Income Rs.	Applied	Not applied	Total
41			
0—300	22 (38.6)	35 (61.4)	57
301—900	48 (43.6)	62 (56.4)	110
901—1500	8 (42.1)	11 (57.9)	19
1500 & above	3 (30.0)	7 (70.0)	10
Total	81 (41.3)	115 (58.7)	196

APPENDIX-III. 40

THE RESPONDENTS APPLIED FOR THE SCHEMES

Caste	Applied	Not applied	Total
S.C.	21 (40.4)	31 (59.6)	52
B.C.	37 (45.7)	44 (54.3)	81
O.C.	23 (36.5)	40 (63.5)	63
Total	81 (41.3)	115 (58.7)	196

Note : Figures in brackets indicate percentages.

APPENDIX-IV. 1

MINOR IRRIGATION—NATURE OF DIFFICULTIES FACED BY BENEFICIAREIS

Sl. No.	Nature of difficulties	Medak				East Godavari				Two districts			
		SF	MF	AL	Total	SF	MF	AL	Total	SF	MF	AL	Total
1.	Economical	4 (5.8)	—	—	4 (5.8)	—	—	—	—	4 (5.8)	—	—	4 (5.8)
2.	Technical	9 (13.0)	12 (17.4)	—	21 (30.4)	—	—	—	—	9 (13.0)	12 (17.4)	—	21 (30,4)
3.	Personal	3 (4.3)	3 (4·3)	—	6 (8,7)	—	—	—	—	3 (4.3)	3 (4.3)	—	6 (8.7)
4.	Geo-climatical	4 (5.8)	1 (1.4)	—	5 (7.2)	1 (1 4)	2 (2.9)	—	3 (4.3)	5 (7.2)	3 (4.3)	—	8 (11.6)
5.	Infrastructural	3 (4.3)	2 (2.9)	—	5 (7.2)	1 (1.4)	2 (2.9)	—	3 (4.3)	4 (5.8)	4 (5.8)	—	8 (11.6)
6.	Others	1 (1.4)	—	—	1 (1.4)	1 (1.4)	—	—	2 (2.1)	1 (1.4)	—	—	2 (2.9)
7.	Multiple problems	9 (13.0)	12 (17.4)	1 (1.5)	22 (31.9)	2 (2.9)	1 (1.4)	—	3 (4.3)	11 (15.9)	13 (18.8)	1 (1.4)	25 (36.2)
	Total	33 (47.8)	30 (43.5)	1 (1.4)	64 (92.8)	5 (7.2)	5 (7.2)	—	10 (14.5)	38 (55.0)	35 (50.7)	1 (1.4)	74 (107.0)

Note : Figures in brackets indicate percentages.

APPENDIX-IV. 2

ANIMAL HUSBANDRY—NATURE OF DIFFICULTIES FACED BY BENEFICIARIES

Sl. No.	Nature of difficulties	Medak				East Godavari				Total			
		SF	MF	AL	Total	SF	MF	AL	Total	SF	MF	AL	Total
1.	Economical	1 (1.2)	3 (3.6)		4 (4.8)	2 (2.4)	4 (4.8)	3 (3.6)	9 (10.8)	3 (3.6)	7 (8.4)	3 (3.6)	13 (15.7)
2.	Technical	1 (1.2)	1 (1.2)		2 (2.4)			1 (1.2)	1 (1.2)	1 (1.2)	1 (1.2)	1 (1.2)	3 (1.2)
3.	Personal	2 (2,4)	1 (1.2)		3 (3.6)		2 (2.4)		2 (2.4)	2 (2.4)	3 (3.6)		5 (6.0)
4.	Geo-climatical	5 (6.0)			5 (6.0)	3 (3.6)	4 (4.8)	1 (1.2)	8 (9.6)	8 (9.6)	4 (4.8)	1 (1.2)	13 (15.7)
5.	Infrastructural	1 (1.2)	1 (1.2)		2 (2.4)	3 (3.6)	16 (19.3)	13 (15.7)	32 (38.6)	4 (4.8)	17 (20.5)	13 (15.7)	34 (41.0)
6.	Others	5 (6.0)			5 (6.0)	2 (2.4)	2 (2.4)		4 (4.8)	7 (8.4)	2 (2.4)		9 (10.8)
7.	Multiple Problems		1 (1.2)		1 (1.2)	7 (8.4)	10 (12.0)	11 (13.3)	28 (33.7)	7 (8.4)	11 (13.3)	11 (13.3)	29 (34.9)
	Total	15 (18.1)	7 (8.4)		22 (26.5)	17 (20.5)	38 (45.8)	29 (34.9)	84 (101.2)	32 (38.6)	45 (54.2)	29 (34.9)	106 (127.7)

Note : Figures in brackets indicate percentages.

APPENDIX-IV. 3

AGRICULTURAL SCHEMES—NATURE OF DIFFICULTIES FACED BY BENEFICIARIES

Sl. No.	Nature of difficulties	Medak				East Godavari				Total			
		SF	MF	AL	Total	SF	MF	AL	Total	SF	MF	AL	Total
1.	Economical		2 (11.1)		2 (11.1)						2 (11.1)		2 (11.1)
2.	Personal					2 (11.1)			2 (11.1)	2 (11.1)			2 (11.1)
3.	Geo-climatic	1 (5.6)			1 (5.6)					1 (5.6)			1 (5.6)
4,	Infrastructural	2 (11.1)			2 (11.1)	2 (11.1)	1 (5.6)		3 (16.7)	4 (22.2)	1 (5.6)		5 (27.8)
5.	Others	1 (5.6)			1 (5.6)		1 (5.6)		1 (5.6)	1 (5.6)	1 (5.6)		2 (11.1)
6.	Multiple Problems	2 (11.1)	2 (11.1)		4 (22.2)		2 (11.1)		2 (11.1)	2 (11.1)	4 (22.2)		6 (33.3)
	Total	6 (33.3)	4 (11.1)		10 (55.5)	4 (22.2)	4 (22.2)		8 (44.4)	10 (55.6)	6 (33.3)		18 (7.8)

Note : Figures in brackets indicate percentages.

APPENDIX-IV. 4

OTHER SCHEMES—NATURE OF DIFFICULTIES FACED BY BENEFICIARIES

Sl. No.	Nature of difficulties	Medak SF	Medak MF	Medak AL	Medak Total	East Godavari SF	East Godavari MF	East Godavari AL	East Godavari Total	Two Districts SF	Two Districts MF	Two Districts AL	Two Districts Total
1.	Geo-climatical					1 (7.1)		4 (28.6)	5 (35.7)	1 (7.1)		4 (28.6)	5 (35.7)
2.	Infrastructural					3 (21.4)	1 (7.1)	3 (21.4)	7 (50.0)	3 (21.4)	1 (7.1)	3 (21.4)	7 (50.0)
3.	Others							1 (7.1)	1 (7.1)			1 (7.1)	1 (7.1)
4.	Multiple Problems					1 (7.1)			1 (7.1)	1 (7.1)			1 (7.1)
	Total					5 (35.7)	1 (7.1)	8 (57.1)	14	5 (35.7)	1 (7.1)	8 (57.1)	14

Note : Figures in brackets indicate percentages.

APPENDIX-IV. 5

RELATED PROGRAMMES—DIFFICULTIES IN GETTING THE SCHEMES

Sl. No.	Name of the village	Faced SF	Faced MF	Faced AL	Did not face SF	Did not face MF	Did not face AL	Total
Medak Dist.								
1.	Marpadga	15	10	3	2	12		42
		(35.7)	(23.8)	(7.1)	(4.8)	(28.6)		(100)
2.	Sirsingandla	5	7	1	2	1		16
		(31.3)	(43.8)	(6.2)	(12.5)	(6.2)		(100)
3.	Peddamasanpally	4	6	1	1			12
		(33.3)	(50.0)	(8.4)	(8.4)			(100)
	Total	24	23	5	5	13		70
		(34.1)	(32.8)	(7.1)	(7.2)	(18.8)		(100)
East Godavari Dist.								
4.	Shankavaram	3	4	13		4	3	27
		(11.1)	(14.8)	(48.1)		(14.8)	(11.1)	(100)
5.	Vajrakutam	5	2		3			10
		(50.0)	(20.0)		(30.0)			(100)
6.	Balarampuram		5	4	1	1	3	14
			(35.7)	(28.6)	(7.1)	(7.1)	(21.4)	(100)
	Total	8	11	17	4	5	6	51
		(15.7)	(21.6)	(33.3)	(7.8)	(9.8)	(11.8)	(100)
	Grand Total	32	34	22	9	18	6	121
		(26.4)	(28.1)	(18.2)	(7.4)	(14.9)	(4.9)	(100)

Note : Figures in brackets indicate percentages.

APPENDIX IV. 6

RELATED PROGRAMMES—DIFFICULTIES IN IMPLEMENTING THE SCHEMES

Sl No.	Name of the village	Faced			Did not face			Total
		SF	MF	AL	SF	MF	AL	
	Medak Dist.							
1.	Marpadga	13 (31.0)	14 (33.3)	2 (4.8)	4 (9.5)	8 (19.0)	1 (2.8)	42 (100)
2.	Sirsingandla	2 (12.5)	3 (18.9)	1 (6.2)	5 (31.3)	5 (31.3)		16 (100)
3.	Peddamasanpally	4 (33.3)	6 (50.0)	1 (8.4)	1 (8.4)			12 (100)
	Total	19 (27.1)	23 (32.8)	4 (5.7)	10 (14.3)	13 (18.6)	1 (1.4)	70 (100)
	East Godavari Dist.							
4.	Shankavaram	3 (11.1)	5 (18.5)	9 (33.3)		3 (11.1)	7 (25.9)	27 (100)
5.	Vajrakutam	8 (80.0)	2 (20.0)					10 (100)
6.	Balarampuram		3 (21.4)	4 (28.6)	1 (7.1)	3 (21.4)	3 (21.4)	14 (100)
	Total	11 (21.6)	10 (19.6)	13 (25.5)	1 (2.0)	6 (11.8)	10 (19.6)	51 (100)
	Grand Total	30 (24.8)	33 (27.3)	17 (14,0)	11 (9.0)	19 (15.7)	11 (9.0)	121 (100)

Note : Figures in brackets indicate percentages.

APPENDIX-IV. 7

RESULTS OF THE RELATED PROGRAMMES—BENEFICIARIES OPINION

Sl. No.	Name of the village	Benefited SF	Benefited MF	Benefited AL	Not benefited SF	Not benefited MF	Not benefited AL	Total
Medak Dist.								
1.	Marpadga	9 (21.4)	14 (33.3)	2 (4.8)	8 (19.0)	8 (19.0)	1 (2.0)	42 (100)
2.	Sirsingandla	5 (31.3)	8 (50.0)		2 (12.5)		1 (6.2)	16 (100)
3.	Peddamasanpally	1 (8.4)	2 (16.6)		4 (33.3)	4 (33.3)	1 (8.4)	12 (100)
	Total	15 (21.4)	24 (34.3)	2 (2.9)	14 (20.4)	12 (17.1)	3 (4.3)	70 (100)
East Godavari Dist.								
4.	Shankavaram	3 (11.3)	6 (22.2)	9 (33.3)		2 (7.4)	7 (25.9)	27 (100)
5.	Vajrakutam	8 (80.0)	2 (20.0)					10 (100)
6.	Balarampuram	1 (7.1)	5 (5.7)	5 (35.7)		1 (7.1)	2 (14.3)	14 (100)
	Total	12 (23.5)	13 (25.5)	14 (27.4)		3 (5.9)	9 (17.6)	51 (100)
	Grand Total	27 (22.3)	37 (30.6)	16 (13.2)	14 (11.6)	15 (12.4)	12 (9.9)	221 (100)

Note : Figures in brackets indicate percentages.

APPENDIX-IV 8

ADDITIONAL EMPLOYMENT GENERATED

Sl. No.	Schemes	Generated	%	Not generated	%	Total
1.	New Well	11	30.6	25	69.4	36
2.	Well deepening	2	33.3	4	66.7	6
3.	Oil engine	5	50.0	5	50.0	10
4.	Electric motor	22	52.4	20	47.6	42
5.	Milch cattle	49	46.2	57	53.8	106
6.	Sheep	13	65.0	7	35.0	20
7.	Poultry	3	100.0	0		3
8.	Plough bullock	2	8.3	22	91.7	24
9.	Cart and bullock	2	25.0	6	75.0	8
10.	Land development	2	100.0	0		2
11.	Mango	1	33.3	2	66.7	3
12.	Cashew	0		4	100.0	4
13.	Sprayer	0		1	100.0	1
14.	Nylon nets	7	70.0	3	30.3	10
	Total	119	43.3	156	56.7	275

APPENDIX-IV. 9

ADDITIONAL INCOME GENERATED

Sl. No.	Schemes	Increased	%	Not increased	%	Dec-reased	%	Total
1.	New Well	15	41.7	17	47.2	4	11.1	36
2.	Well deepening	2	33.3	2	33.3	2	33.4	6
3.	Oil engine	4	40.0	2	20.0	4	40.0	10
4.	Electric motor	17	40.5	20	47.6	5	11.9	42
5.	Milch cattle	23	21.7	35	33.0	48	45.3	106
6.	Sheep	10	50.0	9	45.0	1	5.0	20
7.	Poultry	0		3	100.0	0		3
8.	Plough bullock	14	58.3	9	37.5	1	4.2	24
9.	Cart and bullock	5	62.5	2	25.0	1	12.5	8
10.	Land development	0		0		2	100.0	2
11.	Mango	0		2	66.7	1	33.3	3
12.	Cashew	0		3	75.0	1	25.0	4
13.	Sprayer	0		1	100.0	0		1
14.	Nylon Nets	10	100.0	0		0		10
	Total	100	36.4	105	38.1	70	25,5	275

APPENDIX-IV. 10

DIFFICULTIES IN GETTING THE SCHEME

Sl. No.	Schemes	Faced	%	Not faced	%	Total
1.	New Well	21	58.3	15	41.7	36
2.	Well deepening	3	50.0	3	50.0	6
3.	Oil engine	6	60.0	4	40.0	10
4.	Electric motor	28	66.7	14	33.3	42
5.	Milch cattle	55	51.9	51	48.1	106
6.	Sheep	16	80.0	4	20.0	20
7.	Poultry	2	66.7	1	33.3	3
8.	Plough bullock	18	75.0	6	25.0	24
9.	Cart and Bullock	5	62.5	3	37.5	8
10.	Land development	0		2	100.0	2
11.	Mango	2	66.7	1	33.3	3
12.	Cashew	4	100.0	0		4
13.	Sprayer	1	100.0	0		1
14.	Nylon Nets	0		10	100 0	10
	Total	161	58.5	114	41.5	275

APPENDIX-IV. 11

TIME TAKEN IN GETTING THE SCHEME

Sl. No.	Schemes	Below 3 months	%	Six months	%	Above 6 months	%	Total
1.	New Well	15	41.7	10	27.8	11	30.6	36
2.	Well deepening	5	83.3	1	16.7	0		6
3.	Oil engine	4	50.0	3	30.0	3	30.0	10
4.	Electric motor	13	31.0	11	26.2	18	42.9	42
5.	Milch cattle	96	90.6	6	5.7	4	3.8	106
6.	Sheep	3	15.0	4	20.0	13	65.0	20
7.	Poultry	1	33.3	0		2	66.7	3
8.	Plough bullock	7	29.2	7	29.2	10	41.7	24
9.	Cart and bullock	6	75.0	0		2	25.0	8
10.	Land development	2	100.0	0		0		2
11.	Mango	1	33.3	1	33.4	1	33.3	3
12.	Cashew	1	25.0	0		3	75.0	4
13.	Sprayer	1	100.0	0		0		1
14.	Nylon Nets	1	10.0	7	70.0	2	20.0	10
	Total	156	56.7	50	18.2	69	25.1	275

APPENDIX-IV. 12

DIFFICULTIES IN USING THE SCHEMES

Sl. No.	Schemes	Faced	%	Not faced	%	Total
1.	New well	30	83.3	6	16.7	36
2.	Well deepening	2	33.3	4	66.7	6
3.	Oil engine	7	70.0	3	30.0	10
4.	Electric motor	30	71.4	12	28.6	42
5.	Milch cattle	87	82.1	19	17.9	106
6.	Sheep	15	75.0	5	25.0	20
7.	Poultry	3	100.0	0		3
8.	Plough bullock	11	45.8	13	54.2	24
9.	Cart and bullock	5	62.5	3	37.5	8
10.	Land development	2	100.0	0		2
11.	Mango	2	66.7	1	33.3	3
12.	Cashew	4	100.0	0		4
13.	Sprayer	0		1	100.0	1
14.	Nylon nets	8	80.0	2	20.0	10
	Total	206	74.9	69	25.1	275

APPENDIX-IV. 13

BENEFITED BY THE SCHEMES

Sl. No.	Schemes	Benefited	%	Not benefited	%	Total
1.	New Well	20	55.6	16	44.4	36
2.	Well deepening	4	66.7	2	33.2	6
3.	Oil engine	6	60.0	4	40.0	10
4.	Electric motor	20	47.6	22	52.4	42
5.	Milch cattle	31	29.2	75	70.8	106
6.	Sheep	15	75.0	5	25.0	20
7.	Poultry	0		3	100.0	3
8.	Plough bullock	14	58.3	10	41.7	24
9.	Cart and bullock	5	62.5	3	37.5	8
10.	Land development	1	50.0	1	50.0	2
11.	Mango	1	66.7	2	33.3	3
12.	Cashew	1	25.0	3	75.0	4
13.	Sprayer	1	100.0	0		1
14.	Nylon nets	10	100.0	0		10
	Total	129	46.9	146	53.1	275

APPENDIX-V. 1

OFFICES VISITED BY THE RESPONDENTS

Multiple responses

Sl. No.	Name of the office	No. of offices visited in Medak district	(%)	No. of offices visited in East Godavari district	(%)	Total
1.	Block office	97	46.2	113	53.8	210
2.	Tehsil office	111	73.5	40	26.5	151
3.	R.D.O. office	21	67.7	10	32.3	31
4.	Collectorate	10	32.3	21	67.7	31
5.	Revenue Board	3	100.0			3
6.	Registration office	15	43.9	20	57.1	35
7.	Banks	49	72.1	19	28.9	68
8.	Electricity office	19	95.0	1	5.0	20
9.	S.F.D.A.	2	22.2	7	77.8	9
10.	Others	22	30.0	18	70.0	40
	Total	349	58.4	249	41.6	598

APPENDIX-V. 2

OFFICERS VISITED—CASTE—INCOME—LANDWISE

	Caste			Income				Land				
	SC	BC	OC	0-300	301-900	901-1500	1501-above	Land-less	0.1-2.5	2.6-5.0	5.1-10.0	10.1-above
Visited	113	106	111	79	174	54	23	40	144	119	19	8
	(54.1)	(49.8)	(58.1)	(50.0)	(52.7)	(62.8)	(59.0)	(34.8)	(56.6)	(56.9)	(79.2)	(72.7)
Not visited	96	107	80	79	156	32	16	75	110	90	5	3
	(45.9)	(50.2)	(41.9)	(50.0)	(47.3)	(37.2)	(41.0)	(65.2)	(43.4)	(43.1)	(20.8)	(27.3)
Total	209	213	191	158	330	86	39	115	254	209	24	11
	(100.0)	(100.0)	(100.0)	(100.0)	(100.0)	(100.0)	(100.0)	(100.0)	(100.0)	(100.0)	(100.0)	(100.0)

Note : Figures in brackets indicate percentages.

APPENDIX-V. 3

ATTITUDES OF OFFICERS—CASTE—INCOME—LANDWISE

	Caste			Income				Land				
	SC	BC	OC	0-300	301-900	901-1500	1501-above	Land-less	0.1-2.5	2.6-5.0	5.1-10 0	Above
Helpful	49 (23.4)	54 (25.0)	57 (29.8)	38 (24.1)	92 (27.9)	23 (26.7)	8 (20.5)	19 (16.5)	67 (26.3)	62 (30.1)	8 (32.0)	4 (36.4)
Not helpful	73 (35.1)	75 (35.2)	67 (35.1)	45 (28.5)	110 (33.3)	38 (44.2)	19 (48.7)	26 (22.6)	95 (37.6)	79 (36.9)	11 (48.0)	4 (36.4)
Don't know	87 (41.6)	84 (39.4)	67 (35.1)	75 (47.5)	128 (38.8)	25 (29.1)	12 (30.8)	70 (60.9)	92 (36.1)	68 (33.1)	5 (20.0)	3 (27.2)
Total	209 (100.0)	213 (100.0)	191 (100.0)	158 (100.0)	330 (100.0)	86 (100.0)	39 (100.0)	115 (100.0)	254 (100.0)	209 (100.0)	24 (100.0)	11 (100.0)

Note : Figures in brackets indicate percentages.

APPENDIX-V. 4

OFFICERS PERSONALLY CONTACTED VILLAGERS—CASTE, INCOME, AND LANDWISE

	Caste			Income				Land				
	SC	AC	OF	0-300	301-900	901-1500	1501-above	Land-less	0.1-2.5	2.6-5.0	5.1-10	Above
Yes	61	42	50	36	82	21	14	17	72	48	10	6
	(29.2)	(19.7)	(26.2)	(22.8)	(24.8)	(24.4)	(35.9)	(14.8)	(28.3)	(23.0)	(41.7)	(54.5)
No	148	171	141	122	248	65	25	98	182	161	14	5
	(70.8)	(80.3)	(73.8)	(77.2)	(75.2)	(75.6)	(64.1)	(85.2)	(71.7)	(77.0)	(58.3)	(45.5)
Total	209	213	191	158	330	86	39	115	254	209	24	11
	(100.0)	(100.0)	(100.0)	(100.0)	(100.0)	(100.0)	(100.0)	(100.0)	(100.0)	(100.0)	(100.0)	(100.0)

Note : Figures in brackets indicate percentages.

APPENDIX-VI. 1

ASSISTANCE FROM MIDDLEMAN—AGE

Sl. No.	District and age group	SFDA & Related Beneficiaries			Non-Beneficiares		
		Yes	No	Total	Yes	No	Total
	Medak						
1.	20-40 years	95 (85.5)	16 (14.5)	111 (100)	33 (66.0)	17 (34.0)	50 (100)
2.	41-55 years	60 (91.0)	6 (9.1)	66 (100)	17 (60.7)	11 (39.3)	28 (100)
3.	56 & above	33 (94.2)	2 (5.8)	35 (100)	9 (60.0)	6 (40.0)	15 (100)
	Total	188 (88.6)	24 (11.4)	212 (100)	59 (63.4)	34 (36.6)	93 (109)
	East Godavari						
4.	20-40 years	89 (68.4)	41 (31.6)	130 (100)	10 (16.2)	52 (83.8)	62 (100)
5.	41-55 years	38 (82.6)	8 (17.4)	46 (100)	9 (31.0)	20 (69.0)	29 (100)
6.	56 & above	21 (72.4)	8 (27.6)	29 (100)	5 (41.7)	7 (58.3)	12 (100)
	Total	148 (72.1)	57 (27.9)	205 (100)	24 (23.3)	79 (76.7)	103 (100)

Note : Figures in brackets indicate percentages.

APPENDIX-VI. 2

ASSISTANCE FROM MIDDLEMAN—CASTE

Sl. No.	District	SFDA & Related beneficiaries			Non Beneficiaries		
		Yes	No	Total	Yes	No	Total
	Medak						
1.	Scheduled Caste	84 (91.3)	8 (8.7)	92 (100)	15 (42.8)	20 (57.2)	35 (100)
2.	Backward Caste	93 (93.0)	7 (7.0)	100 (100)	30 (57.7)	22 (42.3)	52 (100)
3.	Other Caste	12 (60.0)	8 (40.0)	20 (100)	3 (50.0)	3 (50.0)	6 (100)
	Total	189 (89.1)	23 (10.9)	212 (100)	48 (51.6)	45 (48.4)	93 (100)
	East Godavari						
4.	Scheduled Caste	58 (86.5)	9 (13.5)	67 (100)	10 (62.5)	6 (37.5)	16 (100)
5.	Backward Caste	19 (76.0)	6 (24.0)	25 (100)	5 (14.3)	30 (85.7)	35 (100)
6.	Other Caste	71 (62.8)	42 (37.2)	113 (100)	20 (38.4)	32 (61.6)	52 (100)
	Total	148 (72.1)	57 (27.9)	205 (100)	35 (34.0)	68 (66.0)	103 (100)

Note : Figures in brackets indicate percentages.

APPENDIX-VI. 3
ASSTISTANCE FROM MIDDLEMAN—EDUCATION

Sl. No.	District	SFDA & Related benefldiaries			Non Beneficiaries		
		Yes	No	Total	Yes	No	Total
	Medak						
1.	Illiterate	135	11	146	43	33	76
		(93.4)	(7.6)	(100)	(56.5)	(43.5)	(100)
2.	Primary	47	3	50	11	2	13
		(94.0)	(6.0)	(100)	(84.6)	(15.4)	(100)
3.	Secondary	4	6	10	2	2	4
		(40.0)	(60.0)	(100)	(50.0)	(50.0)	(100)
4.	Higher Secondary & above	2	4	6	—	—	—
		(33.3)	(66.7)	(100)			
	Total	188	24	212	56	37	93
		(88.7)	(11.3)	(100)	(60.2)	(39.8)	(100)
	East Godavari						
5.	Illiterate	96	29	125	13	47	60
		(76.8)	(23.2)	(100)	(21.7)	(78.3)	(100)
6.	Primary	33	27	60	7	31	38
		(55.0)	(45.0)	(100)	(18.4)	(81.6)	(100)
7.	Secondary	13	4	17	5	—	5
		(76.4)	(23.6)	(100)	(100)		(100)
8.	Higher Secondary & above	2	1	3	—	—	—
		(66.7)	(33.3)	(100)			
	Total	144	61	205	25	78	103
		(70.2)	(29.8)	(100)	(32.0)	(68.0)	(100)

Note : Figures in brackets indicate percentages.

APPENDIX-VI. 4
ASSISTANCE FROM MIDDLEMAN—OCCUPATION

Sl. No.	District	SFDA & Related beneficiaries			Non Beneficiaries		
		Yes	No	Total	Yes	No	Total
	Medak						
1.	Small Farmers	91	10	101	30	15	45
		(90.1)	(9.9)	(100)	(66.7)	(33.3)	(100)
2.	Marginal Farmers	84	8	92	24	16	40
		(91.3)	(8.7)	(100)	(60.0)	(40.0)	(100)
3.	Agricultural Labourers	11	8	19	4	4	8
		(57.9)	(42.1)	(100)	(50.0)	(50.0)	(100)
	Total	186	26	212	58	35	93
		(87.7)	(12.3)	(100)	(62.4)	(37.6)	(100)
	East Godavari						
4.	Small Farmers	37	21	58	6	23	29
		(63.8)	(36.2)	(100)	(20.7)	(79.3)	(100)
5.	Marginal Farmers	46	27	73	10	31	41
		(63.0)	(37.0)	(100)	(24.4)	(75.6)	(100)
6.	Agricultural Labourers	62	12	74	8	25	33
		(83.8)	(16.2)	(100)	(24.2)	(75.8)	(100)
	Total	145	60	205	24	79	103
		(70.7)	(29.3)	(100)	(23.3)	(76.7)	(100)

Note : Figures in brackets indicate percentages.

APPENDIX-IV. 5

ASSISTANCE FROM MIDDLEMAN—INCOME BACKGROUND

Sl. No.	Income group	Medak						East Godavari					
		SFDA & Related Beneficiaries			Non Beneficiaries			SFDA & Related Beneficiaries			Non Beneficiaries		
		Yes	No	Total	Yes	No	Total	Yes	No	Total	Yes	No	Total
1.	0—100	—	—	—	2	1	3	—	—	—	—	1	1
					(66.7)	(33.3)	(100)					(100)	(100)
2.	101—200	14	1	15	6	—	6	16	3	19	1	5	6
		(93.3)	(6.7)	(100)	(100)		(100)	(84.2)	(15.8)	(100)	(16.7)	(83.3)	(100)
3.	201—300	30	4	34	8	7	15	21	5	26	4	8	12
		(88.2)	(11.8)	(100)	(53.3)	(46.7)	(100)	(80.7)	(19.3)	(100)	(33.3)	(66.7)	(100)
4.	301—500	51	5	56	14	19	33	31	21	52	9	18	27
		(91.0)	(9.0)	(100)	(42.4)	(57.6)	(100)	(59.6)	(40.4)	(100)	(33.3)	(66.7)	(100)
5.	501—700	41	4	45	10	3	13	25	9	34	6	16	22
		(91.1)	(8.9)	(100)	(77.0)	(23.0)	(100)	(73.5)	(26.5)	(100)	(27.3)	(72.7)	(100)
6.	702—900	18	5	23	6	2	8	20	8	28	2	10	12
		(78.2)	(21.8)	(100)	(75.0)	(25.0)	(100)	(71.4)	(28.6)	(100)	(16.7)	(83.3)	(100)
7.	901 & above	31	8	39	10	5	15	35	11	46	4	19	23
		(79.5)	(20.5)	(100)	(66.7)	(33.3)	(100)	(76.0)	(24.0)	(100)	(7.4)	(82.6)	(100)
	Total	185	27	212	56	37	93	148	57	205	26	77	103
		(87.3)	(12.7)	(100)	(60.2)	(39.8)	(100)	(72.1)	(27.3)	(100)	(25.4)	(74.6)	(100)

Note : Figures in brackets indicate percentages.

APPENDIX-VI. 6

ASSISTANCE TAKEN BY RESPONDENTS—LANDWISE

	Taken	Not takeh	Total
Landless	63	11	74
	(19.0)	(12.9)	(17.7)
0.1 to 2.5	138	40	178
	(41.6)	(47.1)	(42.7)
2.6 to 5.0	110	24	134
	(33.1)	(28.2)	(32.1)
5.1 to 10.0	15	5	20
	(4.5)	(5.9)	(4.8)
above 10	6	5	11
	(1.8)	(5.9)	(2.6)
Total	332	85	417
	(100.0)	(100.0)	(100.0)

percentages. ındicate brackets in Figures *:Note*

APPENDIX-VI. 7

NECESSITY OF MIDDLEMAN—AGE

Sl. No.	District & age group	SFDA & Related Beneficiaries			Non Bcneficiaries		
		Necessary	Not necessary	Total	Necessary	Not necessary	Total
Medak							
1.	20—40 years	76	37	113	28	20	48
		(67.3)	(32.7)	(100)	(58.3)	(41.7)	(100)
2.	41—50 years	49	16	65	16	13	29
		(75.3)	(24.7)	(100)	(55.2)	(44.8)	(100)
3.	56 and above	31	3	34	4	12	16
		(91.2)	(8.8)	(100)	(25.0)	(75.0)	(100)
	Total	156	56	212	48	45	93
		(73.6)	(26.4)	(100)	(51.6)	(48.4)	(100)
East Godavari							
4.	20—40 years	85	44	129	16	47	63
		(65.9)	(34.1)	(100)	(25.4)	(74.6)	(100)
5.	41—55 years	34	14	48	10	17	27
		(70.8)	(29.2)	(100)	(37.0)	(63.0)	(100)
6.	56 and above	19	9	28	7	6	13
		(67.8)	(32.2)	(100)	(53.8)	(46.2)	(100)
	Total	138	67	205	33	70	103
		(67.3)	(32.7)	(100)	(32.0)	(68.0)	(100)

Note : Figures in brackets indicate percentages.

APPENDIX-VI.8
NECESSITY OF MIDDLEMAN—CASTE

Sl. No.	District & Caste	SFDA & Related Beneficiaries			Non Beneficiaries		
		Necessary	Not necessary	Total	Necessary	Not necessary	Total
	Medak						
1.	Scheduled Caste	69 (75.8)	32 (24.2)	91 (100)	18 (53.0)	16 (47.0)	34 (100)
2.	Backward Caste	80 (80.0)	20 (20.0)	100 (100)	36 (69.2)	16 (30.8)	52 (100)
3.	Other Caste	9 (42.8)	12 (57.2)	21 (100)	4 (57.1)	3 (42.9)	7 (100)
	Total	158 (74.5)	64 (25.5)	212 (100)	58 (62.3)	35 (37.7)	93 (100)
	East Godavari						
4.	Scheduled Caste	59 (88.0)	8 (12.0)	67 (100)	7 (47.7)	9 (52.3)	16 (100)
5.	Backward Caste	21 (84.0)	4 (16.0)	25 (100)	5 (14.2)	30 (85.8)	35 (100)
6.	Other Caste	59 (52.2)	54 (47.8)	113 (100)	13 (25.0)	39 (75.0)	52 (100)
	Total	139 (67.8)	66 (32.2)	205 (100)	25 (32.0)	78 (68.0)	103 (100)

Note : Figures in brackets indicate percentage.

APPENDIX-VI. 9

NECESSITY OF MIDDLEMAN—EDUCATION

Sl. No.	District & group	SFDA & Related Beneficiaries			Non Beneficiaries		
		Necessary	Not necessary	Total	Necessary	Not necessary	Total
	Medak						
1.	Illiterate	121 (82.3)	26 (17.7)	147 (100)	38 (50.7)	37 (49.3)	75 (100)
2.	Primary	32 (66.6)	16 (33.4)	48 (100)	9 (60.0)	6 (40.0)	15 (100)
3.	Secondary	2 (18.1)	9 (81.9)	11 (100)	—	3 (100)	3 (100)
4.	Higher Secondary & above	2 (33.4)	4 (66.6)	6 (100)	—	—	—
	Total	157 (74.0)	55 (20.5)	212 (100)	47 (50.5)	46 (49.5)	93 (100)
	East Godavari						
5.	Illiterate	97 (79.5)	25 (20.5)	122 (100)	21 (33.3)	42 (66.7)	63 (100)
6.	Primary	28 (87.5)	32 (12.5)	60 (100)	7 (18.4)	31 (81.6)	38 (100)
7.	Secandary	10 (47.6)	11 (52.4)	21 (100)	—	—	—
8.	Higher Secondary & above	1 (50.0)	1 (50.0)	2 (100)	1 (50.0)	1 (50.0)	2 (100)
	Total	136 (66.4)	69 (33.6)	205 (100)	29 (28.1)	74 (71.9)	103 (100)

Note : Figures in brackets indicate percentages.

APPENDIX-VI. 10

NECESSITY OF MIDDLEMAN—INCOME BACKGROUND

Sl. No.	Income group	MEDAK						EAST GODAVARI					
		SFDA & Related Beneficiaries			Non Beneficiars			SFDA & Related Beneficiaries			Non Beneficiaries		
		Necessary	Not necessary	Total	Necessary	Not necessary	Total	Necessary	Not necessary	Total	Necessary	Not necessary	Total
1.	0-100	—	—	—	2 (66.7)	1 (33.3)	3 (100)	—	—	—	—	1 (100)	1 (100)
2.	101-200	12 (80.0)	3 (20.0)	15 (100)	3 (50.0)	3 (50.0)	6 (100)	17 (89.5)	2 (10.5)	19 (100)	1 (0.7)	5 (93.3)	6 (100)
3.	201-300	25 (71.4)	10 (28.6)	35 (100)	7 (50.0)	7 (50.0)	14 (100)	18 (66.7)	9 (33.3)	27 (100)	4 (36.3)	7 (63.7)	11 (100)
4.	301-500	42 (77.8)	12 (22.2)	54 (100)	14 (40.0)	21 (60.0)	35 (100)	32 (61.5)	20 (38.6)	52 (100)	12 (44.4)	15 (55.6)	27 (100)
5.	501-700	35 (77.8)	10 (22.2)	45 (100)	10 (71.4)	4 (28.6)	14 (100)	23 (67.6)	11 (32.4)	34 (100)	7 (31.8)	15 (68.2)	22 (100)
6.	701-900	15 (65.2)	8 (34.8)	23 (100)	7 (87.5)	1 (12.5)	8 (100)	17 (60.7)	11 (39.3)	28 (100)	4 (33.3)	8 (66.7)	12 (100)
7.	901 & above	23 (57.5)	17 (42.5)	40 (100)	6 (46.1)	7 (53.9)	13 (100)	32 (71.1)	13 (28.9)	45 (100)	6 (25.0)	18 (75.0)	24 (100)
	Total	152 (71.7)	60 (28.3)	212 (100)	49 (52.6)	44 (47.4)	93 (100)	139 (67.8)	66 (32.2)	205 (100)	34 (33.0)	69 (67.0)	103 (100)

Note : Figures in brackets indicate percentages.

APPENDIX-VI. 11

NECESSITY OF MIDDLEMEN—OCCUPATION

Sl. No.	District & group	SFDA & Related Beneficiaries			Non Beneficiaries		
		Necessary	Not necessary	Total	Necessary	Not necessary	Total
	Medak						
1.	Small Farmers	71	29	100	27	19	46
		(71.0)	(29.0)	(100)	(58.7)	(41.3)	(100)
2.	Marginal Farmers	74	16	90	18	24	42
		(82.2)	(17.8)	(100)	(42.9)	(57.1)	(100)
3.	Agricultural Labourers	13	9	22	5	—	5
		(59.0)	(41.0)	(100)	(100)		(100)
	Total	158	54	212	50	43	93
		(74.5)	(25.5)	(100)	(53.8)	(46.2)	(100)
	East Godavari						
4.	Small Farmers	32	26	58	9	20	29
		(55.1)	(44.9)	(100)	(31.0)	(69.0)	(100)
5.	Marginal Farmers	39	34	73	14	27	41
		(53.4)	(46.6)	(100)	(34.1)	(65.9)	(100)
6.	Agricultural Labourers	63	11	74	10	23	33
		(85.1)	(14.9)	(100)	(30.3)	(69.7)	(100)
	Total	134	71	205	33	70	103
		(65.3)	(34.7)	(100)	(32.0)	(68.0)	(100)

Note : Figures in brackets indicate percentages.

APPENDIX-VI.12

NECESSITY OF PYRAVEEKAR

	Yes	No	Total
Landless	63	11	74
	(21.4)	(8.9)	(17.7)
0.1 to 2.5	126	52	178
	(42.9)	(42.3)	(42.7)
2.6 to 5.0	86	48	134
	(29.3)	(39.0)	(32.1)
5.1 to 10.0	14	6	20
	(4.8)	(4.9)	(4.8)
10.1 and above	5	6	11
	(1.7)	(4.9)	(2.6)
Total	294	123	417
	(100.0)	(100.0)	(100.0)

Note : Figures in brackets indicate percentages.

APPENDIX-VI.13

TIME TAKEN TO GET THE SCHEME SANCTIONED

	Less than 3 months	Above 3 months & less than 6 months	6 months and above	Total
Assisted by Pyraveekar	129 (80.6)	39 (83.0)	58 (85.2)	226 (82.1)
Not assisted by Pyraveekar	31 (19.4)	8 (17.0)	10 (14.8)	49 (17.9)
Total	160 (100.0)	47 (100.0)	68 (100.0)	275 (100.0)

APPENDIX-VI.14

DIFFICULTIES FACED IN UTILISING THE SCHEME

	Faced	Not faced	Total
Assisted by Pyraveekar	180 (85.3)	46 (71.9)	226 (82.1)
Not assisted by Pyraveekar	31 (14·7)	18 (28.1)	49 (17.9)
Total	211 (100.0)	64 (100.0)	275 (100.0)

Note : Figures in brackets indicate percentages.

APPENDIX-VI. 15

UTILISATION OF THE LOAN FOR GIVEN WORK

	Used	Not used	Total
Assisted by Pyraveeker	196 (83.4)	30 (75.0)	226 (82.1)
Not assistec by Pyraveekar	39 (16.6)	10 (25.0)	49 (17.9)
Total	235 (100.0)	40 (100.0)	275 (100.0)

APPENDIX-VI. 16

PURPOSE SERVED BY THE SCHEME

Served	Not served	Total
93 (79.5)	103 (85.8)	196 (82.8)
24 (20.5)	14 (14.2)	38 (17.2)
117 (100.0)	117 (100.0)	234 (100.0)

APPENDIX-VI. 17

WHETHER VISITED GOVT. OFFICE

	Visi-ted	Not visited	Total
Assisted by Pyraveekar	198 (75.9)	138 (88.5)	336 (80.6)
Not assisted by Pyraveekar	63 (24.1)	18 (11.5)	81 (19.4)
Total	261 (100.0)	156 100.0)	417 (100.0)

APPENDIX-VI.18

ATTITUDES OF OFFICIALS

Help-ful	Not helpful	Don't know	Total
92 (70.2)	130 (82.3)	114 (89.1)	336 (80.6)
39 (29.8)	28 (17.7)	14 (10.9)	81 (19.4)
131 (100.0)	158 (100.0)	128 (100.0)	417 (100.0)

Note : Figures in brackets indicate percentages,

APPENDIX-VI.19

BENEFITTED BY THE SCHEME—BENEFICIARIES OPINION

	Benefitted	Not benefited	Total
Assisted by Pyraveekar	191 (75.5)	145 (88.4)	336 (80.6)
Not assisted by Pyraveekar	62 (24.5)	19 (11.3)	81 (19.4)
Total	253 (100.0)	164 (100.0)	417 (100.0)

APPENDIX-VI. 20

OUTCOME OF THE VISIT

	Work done	Work not done	Total
Assisted by Pyraveekar	154 (73.7)	35 (79.5)	189 (74.7)
Not assisted by Pyraveekar	55 (26.3)	9 (20.5)	64 (25.3)
Total	209 (100.0)	44 (100.0)	253 (100.0)

Note : Figures in brackets indicate percentages.

APPENDIX-VII. 1

OPINIONS ON THE ATTITUDES OF THE PUBLIC REPRESENTATIVES TOWARDS THE PEOPLE

Village and District	Sarpanch				Panchayat Members			
	HF	NHF	DK	TOTAL	HF	NHF	DK	TOTAL
Marpadga	70	70	50	190	39	82	69	190
	(36.8)	(36.8)	(26.4)	100	(20.5)	(43.2)	(36.3)	100
Sirsingandla	21	38	6	65	13	39	13	65
	(37.3)	(58.5)	(9.2)	100	(20.0)	(60.0)	(20.0)	100
Peddamasanpally	12	36	2	50	7	33	10	50
	(24.0)	(72.0)	(4.0)	100	(14.0)	(66.0)	(20.0)	100
Medak Total	103	144	68	305	59	154	92	305
	(33.8)	(47.2)	(19.0)	100	(19.3)	(50.5)	(30.2)	100
Shankhavaram	55	125	8	188	55	125	8	188
	(29.3)	(66.5)	(4.3)	100	(29.3)	(66.5)	(4.3)	100
Vajrakutam	55	15	—	70	50	16	4	70
	(78.6)	(21.4)	—	100	(71.4)	(22.9)	(5.7)	100
Balaramapuram	22	24	4	50	21	26	3	50
	(44.0)	(48.0)	(8.0)	100	(42.0)	(52.0)	(6.0)	100
East Godavari Total	132	164	12	308	126	167	15	308
	(42.9)	(53.2)	(3.9)	100	(40.9)	(54.2)	(4.9)	100
Two Districts Total	235	308	70	613	185	321	107	613
	(38.3)	(50.3)	(11.4)	100	(30.2)	(52.4)	(17.5)	100

Note : Figures in brackets indicate percentages.

APPENDIX-VII 1 (Contd.)

Samithi President				M.L.A.				M.P.			
HF	NHF	DK	TOTAL	HF	NHF	DK	TOTAL	HF	NHF	DK	TOTAL
83	38	69	190	31	37	122	190	16	29	145	190
(43.7)	(20.0)	(36.3)	100	(16.3)	(19.5)	(64.2)	100	(8.4)	(15.3)	(76.3)	100
8	7	50	65	3	5	57	65	—	5	60	65
(12.3)	(10.8)	(76.9)	100	(4.6)	(7.7)	(87.7)	100	—	(7.7)	(92.3)	100
3	2	45	50	3	9	38	50	2	3	45	50
(6.0)	(4.0)	(90.0)	100	(6.0)	(18.0)	(76.0)	100	(4.0)	(6.0)	(90.0)	100
94	47	164	305	37	51	217	305	18	37	250	305
(30.8)	(15.4)	(53.8)	100	(12.1)	(16.7)	(71.1)	100	(5.9)	(12.1)	(78.7)	100
55	129	4	188	32	55	101	188	3	18	167	188
(29.3)	(68.6)	(2.1)	100	(17.0)	(29.3)	(53.7)	100	(1.6)	(9.6)	(88.8)	100
20	27	23	70	3	22	45	70	2	10	58	70
(28.6)	(38.6)	(32.9)	100	(4.3)	(31.4)	(64.3)	100	(2.3)	(14.3)	(82.9)	100
4	22	24	50	6	8	36	50	—	3	47	50
(8.0)	(44.0)	(48.0)	100	(12.0)	(16.0)	(72.0)	100	—	(6.0)	(94.0)	100
79	178	51	308	41	85	182	308	5	31	272	308
(25.6)	(57.8)	(16.6)	100	(13.3)	(27.6)	(59.1)	100	(1.6)	(10.4)	(88.3)	100
173	225	215	613	78	136	399	613	23	68	522	613
(28.2)	(36.7)	(35.1)	100	(12.7)	(22.2)	(65.1)	100	(3.8)	(11.1)	(85.2)	100

HF=Helful
NHF=Not Helpful
DK=Don't know

APPENDIX-VII.2

WHO SHOULD DECIDE ABOUT THE VILLAGE DEVELOPMENT PROGRAMMES—RESPONDENTS OPINION

Sl. No.	Name of the village	All Villagers	Poor People	Elite	Govern-ment	Other	Total
Medak Dist.							
1.	Marpadga	69 (36.3)	47 (24.7)	34 (17.9)	36 (18.9)	4 (2.1)	190 (100)
2.	Sirsingandla	20 (30.8)	15 (23.1)	19 (29.2)	11 (16.9)		65 (100)
3.	Peddamasanpally	13 (26.0)	12 (24.0)	10 (20.0)	14 (28.0)	1 (2.0)	50 (100)
	Total	102 (33.4)	74 (24.3)	63 (20.6)	61 (20.0)	5 (1.6)	305 (100)
East Godavari Dist.							
4.	Shankavaram	79 (42.0)	28 (14.9)	31 (16.5)	44 (23.4)	6 (3.2)	188 (100)
5.	Vajrakutam	50 (71.4)	7 (10.0)	10 (14.0)	2 (2.9)	1 (1.4)	70 (100)
6.	Balarampuram	12 (24.0)	6 (12.0)	17 (34.3)	12 (24.0)	3 (6.0)	50 (100)
	Total	141 (45.8)	41 (13.3)	58 (18.8)	58 (18.8)	10 (3.3)	308 (100)
	Grand Total	243 (39.6)	115 (18.8)	121 (19.7)	119 (19.4)	15 (2.4)	613 (100)

Note : Figures in brackets indicate percentages.

APPENDIX-VII. 3

DISCUSSIONS ABOUT THE DEVELOPMENTAL SCHEMES FOR THE POOR: RESPONDENTS OPINION

Sl. No.	Name of the village	All villagers	Poor of the village	Elite of the village	Yourself	Govt. officials	others	Total
	Medak Dist.							
1.	Marpadga	4	16	30	121	18	1	190
		(2.1)	(8.4)	(15.8)	(63.7)	(9.5)	(0.5)	(100)
2.	Sirsingandla		4	11	38	11	1	65
			(6.2)	(16.9)	(58.5)	(16.9)	(1.5)	(100)
3.	Peddamasanpally	5	4	9	22	8	2	50
		(10.0)	(8.0)	(18.0)	(44.0)	(16.0)	(4.0)	(100)
	Total	9	24	50	181	37	4	305
		(3.0)	(7.9)	(16.4)	(59.3)	(12.1)	(1.3)	(100)
	East Godavari Dist.							
4.	Shankavaram		3	8	143	29	5	188
			(0.6)	(4.3)	(76.1)	(15.4)	(2.7)	(100)
5.	Vajrakutam	1	2	2	64		1	70
		(1.4)	(2.9)	(2.9)	(91.4)		(1.4)	(100)
6.	Balarampuram	2		12	25	9	2	50
		(4.0)		(24.0)	(50.0)	(18.0)	(4.0)	(100)
	Total	3	5	22	232	38	8	308
		(1.0)	(1.6)	(7.1)	(75.3)	(12.3)	(2.6)	(100)
	Grand Total	12	29	72	413	75	12	613
		(2.0)	(4.7)	(11.7)	(67.4)	(12.2)	(2.0)	(100)

Note : Figures in brackets indicate percentages.

APPENDIX-VII. 4

THE UNIT FOR THE DISTRIBUTION OF SURPLUS LAND

Sl. No.	Name of the village	Individual	Cluster of families	Caste	Others	Total
	Medak Dist.					
1.	Marpadga	107 (56.3)	61 (32.1)	16 (8.4)	6 (3.2)	190 (100)
2.	Sirsingandla	40 (61.6)	19 (29.2)	3 (4.6)	3 (4.6)	65 (100)
3.	Peddamasanpally	25 (50.0)	17 (34.0)	5 (10.0)	3 (6.0)	50 (100)
	Total	172 (56.4)	97 (31.9)	24 (8.2)	12 (3.9)	305 (100)
	East Godavari Dist.					
4.	Shankavaram	165 (87.8)	22 (11.7)		1 (0.5)	188 (100)
5.	Vajrakutam	67 (95.7)	1 (1.4)	1 (1.4)	1 (1.4)	70 (100)
6.	Balarampuram	45 (90.0)	5 (10.0)			50 (100)
	Total	277 (89.9)	28 (9.1)	1 (0.3)	2 (0.6)	308 (100)
	Grand Total	449 (73.8)	125 (20.4)	25 (4.1)	14 (3.3)	613 (100)

Note : Figures in brackets indicate percentages.

APPENDIX-VII. 5

COMPARISION OF CONDITIONS WITH THE PAST

Sl. No.	Name of the village	Better	Same	Deteriorated	Don't know	Total
Medak Dist.						
1.	Marpadga	58	43	89		190
		(38.5)	(22.6)	(46.8)		(100)
2.	Sirsingandla	17	17	29	2	65
		(26.2)	(26.2)	(44.6)	(3.1)	(100)
3.	Peddamasanpally	17	14	19		50
		(34.0)	(28.0)	(38.0)		(100)
	Total	92	74	137	2	305
		(30.2)	(24.3)	(44.9)	(0.7)	(100)
Eass Godavari Dist.						
4.	Shankavaram	28	43	113	4	188
		(14.9)	(22.9)	(60.1)	(2.1)	(100)
5.	Vajrakutam	18	10	40	2	70
		(25.7)	(14.3)	(57.1)	(2.9)	(100)
6.	Balarampuram	5	29	15	1	50
		(10.0)	(58.0)	(30.0)	(2.0)	(100)
	Total	51	82	168	7	308
		(16.6)	(26.6)	(54.5)	(2.3)	(100)
	Grand Total	143	156	305	9	613
		(23.3)	(25.4)	(49.8)	(1.5)	(100)

Note : Figures in brackets indicate percentages.

APPENDIX-VII. 6
FUTURE OF THEIR CHILDREN

Sl. No.	Name of the village	Will be better	The same	Will deteriorate	Don't know	Total
	Medak Dist.					
1.	Marpadga	44	6	27	113	190
		(23.2)	(3.2)	(14.2)	(59.5)	(100)
2.	Sirsingandla	21	9	14	21	65
		(32.3)	(13.8)	(21.5)	(32.5)	(100)
3.	Peddamasanpally	11	6	9	24	50
		(22.0)	(12.0)	(18.0)	(48.0)	(100)
	Total	76	21	50	158	305
		(24.9)	(6.9)	(16.4)	(51.8)	(100)
	East Godavari Dist.					
4.	Shankavaram	32	12	28	116	188
		(17.0)	(6.4)	(7.5)	(61.7)	(100)
5.	Vajrakutam	13	8	9	40	70
		(18.6)	(11.4)	(12.9)	(57.1)	(100)
6.	Balarampuram	6	4	10	30	50
		(12.0)	(8.0)	(20.0)	(60.0)	(100)
	Total	51	24	47	186	308
		(16.6)	(7.8)	(15.3)	(60.4)	(100)
	Grand Total	127	45	97	344	613
		(20.7)	(7.3)	(15.8)	(56.1)	(100)

Note : Figures in brackets indicate percentages.

Index